ROYAL FAVOURITES
~ of ~
MEDIEVAL ENGLAND
1066–1485

To Graham, always interested in the history, and who left us far, far too soon. Thanks, bro.

To Brenda, a lady in every sense of the word, and the best mother-in-law a girl could have wished for.

ROYAL FAVOURITES
~ of ~
MEDIEVAL ENGLAND
1066–1485

APRIL TAYLOR

PEN & SWORD
HISTORY

AN IMPRINT OF PEN & SWORD BOOKS LTD.
YORKSHIRE – PHILADELPHIA

First published in Great Britain in 2025 by
PEN AND SWORD HISTORY
An imprint of
Pen & Sword Books Ltd
Yorkshire – Philadelphia

ISBN 978 1 39907 935 8

Typeset in Times New Roman 11/13.5 by
SJmagic DESIGN SERVICES, India.
Printed and bound in the UK by CPI Group (UK) Ltd.

The Publisher's authorised representative in the EU for product safety is Authorised Rep Compliance Ltd., Ground Floor, 71 Lower Baggot Street, Dublin D02 P593, Ireland. www.arccompliance.com

For a complete list of Pen & Sword titles please contact
PEN & SWORD BOOKS LIMITED
George House, Units 12 & 13, Beevor Street, Off Pontefract Road, Barnsley, South Yorkshire, S71 1HN, England
E-mail: enquiries@pen-and-sword.co.uk
Website: www.pen-and-sword.co.uk

or

PEN AND SWORD BOOKS
1950 Lawrence Rd, Havertown, PA 19083, USA
E-mail: uspen-and-sword@casematepublishers.com
Website: www.penandswordbooks.com

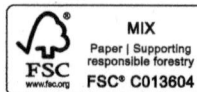

MIX
Paper | Supporting
responsible forestry
FSC
www.fsc.org   FSC® C013604

Contents

Acknowledgements

NO WRITER IS an island or writes a book without help of some kind. First of all, I must thank my editors at Pen and Sword who took a chance that I could write a history book, for their confidence in me, as well as their kindness and patience. Thanks also goes to my husband who is always supportive and encouraging, if sometimes a little bemused as I bombard him with historical facts. I also owe a debt of gratitude to 'Team Taylor' – Nicky Griffiths, Joan Mulqueen and Janet Shell – for providing shoulders and listening ears when the writing life gets tough. And finally, to Hornsea Writers, who started this whole writing gig off in the first place.

Introduction

DOES HISTORY REPEAT itself? And, if so, why?

Why have so many people of influence at the English court from 1066 to 1485 in this volume and 1485 to 1714 in volume two, risen to dizzy heights of power and then been toppled? Was their demise pure arrogance at thinking they were invincible? Was it circumstances over which they actually had no control, but thought they did? Was it because someone wilier than they plotted and schemed and replaced them in the affections of the monarch? Or a combination of all three.

Churchill, an avid historian said, 'Those that fail to learn from history are doomed to repeat it.' Another piece of advice he gave was 'Study history, history, history. In history lies all the secrets of statecraft.'

During the second world war, David Niven, the actor, recounts in *The Moon's a Balloon*, how he defied the Hollywood studio boss, Samuel Goldwyn, and came home to join the army. Niven knew Churchill liked Deanna Durbin and, in 1941, managed to get hold of one of her films, which he offered to play for him. Afterwards, they strolled in the garden. Niven asked Churchill what was going to happen. Churchill replied that he did not know but it was going to be momentous. A few weeks later, the Japanese bombed Pearl Harbour. At a subsequent meeting, Niven asked Churchill how he had known. The great man replied, 'Because, young man, I study history.'

When you do study history, these words make sense. The military blunder of Napoleon invading Russia was repeated by Hitler, although he was not just arrogant but mad. If you mention genocide, people think of the holocaust and the Balkan conflict, but Edward I, after extorting as much money as he could from Jews living in England, then banished them. It was a common view that Jews were a sub-species, and nowhere was this demonstrated more horrendously than in the massacre of Jews in the Clifford Tower in York in 1190. Arrogance or ignorance or both?

The most poignant photo I have ever seen was of 7,000 pairs of children's shoes displayed on the lawn outside the US Capitol in 2018, representing the number of children killed in school shootings since Sandy Hook. Very recent history, but history nonetheless. Repeating itself. And with the usual arrogance of power, the distraught parents and families are offered nothing save 'thoughts and prayers'.

So, when I first came across Edward II and his 'bromances' with first, Piers Gaveston, a Gascon peasant, whose acquisition of power led him to a sticky end, followed by the Despensers – father and son – who did exactly the same thing, and also came to a sticky end; followed by Edward's queen, Isabella of France and her paramour, Roger Mortimer, not only deposing Edward but possibly ordering his murder, and then trying to dominate the young Edward III and – yes, coming to a sticky end – I began to wonder why none of them had taken a backward glance and made a mental note not to be so stupid.

Gaveston and the Despensers were not the only ones. Thomas Becket thought he was powerful enough to defy Henry II, and we all know how that turned out. Moving forwards to the Stuarts, the most famous example is Sarah Churchill, Duchess of Marlborough, who truly believed she could rule England with her husband, through the affection in which she was held by Queen Anne. And so she did for a while, until Anne became less tolerant of Sarah's imperious, arrogant behaviour, at which point, Sarah was dismissed. How she reacted in that situation will be recounted in Volume II.

In this first volume covering the period from the Normans to the beginning of the Tudors, you will read about those who appeared to think they were inviolate – and some had enough sense to know when to bow out gracefully and stay on the right side of the monarch. Or like William Marshal, known as 'the perfect knight', with integrity and unshakeable loyalty to King John, who treated him disgracefully, but William stayed steadfast, even under intense provocation.

This is not an academic tome. Neither is it a book to be read in order unless that floats your boat. It is envisaged as more of a dipping book. Arranged by royal house and monarchs within those houses, I will also endeavour to show the lighter side of outwardly sensible people doing daft things. All monetary comparisons are taken from the Bank of England Inflation Calculator.

Readers will also find a lot of people called Henry, Thomas, Edward, Richard, etc., and sometimes I have called them by their earldom or dukedom, but that, too, can cause confusion. And nowhere is this confusion more ably demonstrated than in the wonderful mock-Shakespeare speech by Jonathan Miller in *Beyond the Fringe*:

> Get thee to Gloucester, Wessex. Do thee to Essex, Exeter.
> Fair Albany to Somerset must eke his route.

And Scroop, do you to Westmoreland, where shall bold York,
Enrouted now for Lancaster, with forces of our Uncle Rutland,
Enjoin his standard with sweet Norfolk's host.
Fair Sussex, get thee to Warwicksbourne,
And there, with frowning purpose, tell our plan
To Bedford's tilted ear, that he shall press
With most insensate speed
And join his warlike effort to bold Dorset's side.
I most royally shall now to bed,
To sleep off all the nonsense I've just said.[1]

Preamble

EDWARD THE CONFESSOR didn't really want to be king. The Anglo-Saxon Chronicle states 'all the people chose Edward for king at London'. He was almost 40 and had spent over half his life in exile in France, to the extent he was probably much happier in a French environment. There are grounds for thinking he was thrust into kingship by his mother, Emma of Normandy, who wanted to safeguard the wealth that had been snatched from her in 1037, but also to guarantee the future. Edward's brother, Harthacnut had been less than popular to say the least, so Emma had more than a vested interest in Edward becoming king.

He was named 'the Confessor' because many people believe him to have been celibate, whereas he was simply childless. According to David Starkey,[1] Edward was everything an eleventh-century king should be. He rode at the head of his troops, commanded his fleet, loved hunting, and, surprisingly, listening to grisly Norse sagas. Edward was also dilatory about attending to affairs of state. However, if put under pressure, he was more than capable of wily and resolute action, most likely because he did not want to go into exile again.

Not at all keen on his mother's domination, Edward allied himself with the family of Godwin, the Earl of Wessex, descended on Emma and, once more, she was deprived of lands and money. By marrying Godwin's daughter, Edith, Edward played into the magnates' hands. In one fell swoop, he exchanged the domination of his mother for domination by the entire Godwin clan.

Relations between them soon fractured and events boiled towards a crisis. This was difficult for the king because the Godwins had a significant power base. By dint of a bit of ducking and diving, Edward managed to delay resolution of the issues, and, by the time it came to a head, the Godwin supremacy had fragmented. The family fled into exile in Flanders. All except Queen Edith. Edward promptly stripped her of lands, money, and power, and banished her to a nunnery. (Now, why didn't Henry VIII think of that with Katherine of Aragon? Oh, hang on, he did. She replied with the Tudor version of 'take a running jump').

Flushed with victory, Edward then invited William, Duke of Normandy, his nephew, to London. It is logical to conclude that this was when Edward nominated William to be his heir. The king's supporters pledged their allegiance to the plan and, just to make sure everything remained on an even keel, Edward sent William back to Normandy with Godwin's son and grandson as hostages to the family's good behaviour.

In effect, by doing this, Edward had decided that the future of England should be French and not Anglo-Saxon. Or had he? In truth, he might still father an heir, especially if he ditched Edith – something Robert of Jumièges, Archbishop of Canterbury, was encouraging him to do. And, of course, he could still change his mind about the succession. In effect, he was playing an astute political game to maintain control of his kingdom. In the meantime, William was a useful ally to have and might even prove to be the best person to take over the throne when the time came. The main problem with Edward's strategy was that most of the country, and certainly the nobility, believed he was handing England over to the French. Slowly but surely, the Godwin faction began to regain their support. They invaded from their base in Flanders and were successful enough to force Edward to come to the negotiating table.

Eventually, an understanding was achieved. Indeed, it held for a long time. Until after Godwin's death, in fact, when his son, Harold Godwinson fell out in a big heap with his brother, Tostig. Tostig was involved with a revolt in Northumbria in October 1065. He was consequently defeated, but refused to accept this, threw his dummy out of the pram, and fled to Flanders, spitting fire, and plotting revenge. Harold had put the interests of England ahead of those of the Godwin family. Tostig became Harold's mortal enemy.

By this time, Edward, having maintained good relations with Harold, had nominated *him* as his heir instead of William. The unrest of late 1065 undermined Edward's health, to the extent that he was too ill to attend the consecration of his greatest project, the building of Westminster Abbey in late December 1065.

Edward the Confessor died on 5 January 1066 and was buried in his new abbey on 6 January. Later that same day, also in Westminster Abbey, Harold Godwinson was crowned King of the English. He immediately went north on a progress. He was back in London by Easter, but on 24 April, Halley's comet was sighted and, still worse, it stayed until 8 June. This was taken as a portent of disaster.

During the spring of 1066, Tostig had carried out a series of coastal raids as far north as Lincolnshire but every attempt to land and foment strife failed. He ended up taking shelter at the Scottish court of his friend, Malcolm III and spent most of the summer in Scotland. That is, until Harald Hardrada decided to chance his arm, and sailed from Norway to the Yorkshire coast, at which point Tostig and Harald joined forces. King Harold Godwinson marched his army roughly 216 miles north and the two forces met at Stamford Bridge, near York on 25 September 1066. Against all the odds, King Harold was victorious. Both Harald Hardrada and Tostig were killed on the battlefield. Some historians believe this was the true ending of the Viking Age.

Then Harold received news that William, Duke of Normandy had landed an invasion fleet at Pevensey on the south coast. He split his forces, leaving some in Yorkshire to mop up any further dissent, before marching the rest of his exhausted army south. It is believed he paused for a few days in London, but the distance between Stamford Bridge in Yorkshire and London is about 216 miles. That meant Harold's troops had marched a total of around 430 miles interrupted by a hard, bloody battle. After a few days' rest, the army then had to march around 76 miles to Battle in Sussex for another fight against fresh, well-trained soldiers. Harold confronted William and his army.

The date was 14 October 1066. The rest is history.

THE NORMANS – 1066–1154

William I – *The Conqueror*

WILLIAM WAS A bastard in more ways than one. He was illegitimate – and regularly referred to as *William the Bastard*. He was also a seriously nasty piece of work. England has had its share of unpleasant monarchs. Most people cite John, but William ran him a close second, or, depending on your point of view, John ran William a close second. Starkey describes William as 'covetous, cruel, puritanical, invincibly convinced of his own rightness and always ready to use terror as a weapon of first, rather than last, resort. He was also deeply pious and sure that God was on his side.'[1]

William was a calculating man who did nothing without malice aforethought and a lot of preparation. Thus, it was with his plans to become the King of England.[2] It may be that William Malet, who acted as Duke William's advisor for the 1066 campaign, lived in Harold Godwinson's household. If so, he would be familiar with Harold as both a courtier and a soldier.[3]

When he landed in Sussex, William contacted Robert fitz Wimarc, one of the Normans he knew who lived in England, asking for local intelligence and advice. Since the duke's plan to succeed Edward the Confessor had been long in the making, it is likely he would have had a covert intelligence system running within the English court for some time.

When William landed, he was told of Harold's victory at Stamford Bridge in Yorkshire. It is unlikely that someone as canny and prepared as William, would not also realise that news of his invasion fleet, had reached Harold and that the latter would immediately have begun to march south with his army. But that would take time. And energy. And Harold had just come through a bloody and brutal battle. By the time he reached London, both he and his army would be weary. So, William sat and waited. He would make Harold come to him and not go to meet him as some other, less astute commander might have done. He had the luxury of time. Time to rest himself and his troops. Time to become familiar with his immediate surroundings and find a good place to make his stand, vanquish Harold and grab the crown of England.

David Crouch maintains that while Hastings was a decisive battle, it was so only because Harold's own claim was based mainly on his personal charisma with no other solid claim, such as heredity to support it.[4] That said, after his victory, it took William some months to make his way to London, partly due to pockets of resistance that were put down very harshly. William himself also became ill on the road, and the clergy spent time debating – or dithering, depending on your point of view – whether or not they should allow the Confessor's nephew, Edgar, to take the throne, or offer it to the Conqueror.

One of William's first actions was the creation of the Domesday book, a public records of towns, villages and individuals in England. It was completed in 1085, two years before his death, and published in 1086. It actually took about five years for William to make the throne truly his. One of the reasons the kingdom was not really settled until 1071 was because William kept going back to Normandy. He returned to put down uprisings in the south-west where Harold's mother, Gytha, lived. Exeter only capitulated when it was made clear to the citizens that King William would 'prosecute the siege to the bitter end'.[5] In other words, all the citizens, to the last child, would be put to the sword. However, this view is not shared by Hugh Thomas.[6]

For several years after Hastings, various crises and rebellions arose, because in victory, the Norman overlords had become arrogant and dismissive of the English (Saxon) population. By 1068, any pretence that Normans and Saxons were on equal terms, was over.

William fitz Osbern and Bishop Odo, William's maternal half-brother, began a campaign of depriving English aristocrats of any kind of meaningful role. Many were excluded from their inheritance and their lands were given to Norman incomers. In short, the Norman rulers were high-handed, superior, and interested only in putting the English in their place. Many English fled abroad. This unrest led to a huge northern rebellion in 1069, which ended with the bulk of West and South Yorkshire starving, dying, or fleeing.[7]

William then moved his army north to the banks of the River Tees. By a policy of savagery, with a dash of mercy and diplomacy, he conquered the North. After which he travelled to Salisbury via Chester. Dispossession and destruction became his watchwords. By 1071, there were no English men holding any kind of high office.

Exactly who accompanied the Conqueror to England has been, and still is, a very hotly debated subject. Despite many lists from such luminaries as Holinshed, Leland, Duchesne et al, there is, even today, no definitive list of those who fought alongside Duke William. Douglas asserts that the *Roll of Battle Abbey*, if it ever existed at all, is a fiction of heraldry.[8]

The list of Norman lords who fought at Hastings was not compiled until over 100 years after the battle. Of the 117 names listed, 74 have only a territory designation with no name to identify a specific person, eg. 'Sire of Soligny' or 'un chevalier de Pirou'. If you also factor in that in the late twelfth century, there would be so many people who avidly wanted their forefathers to have been on the battlefield, and we are left with a completely unreliable list.

In 1071, William tried to capture Hereward the Wake and Morcar, both hiding in the Isle of Ely. Hereward escaped but Morcar was captured, deprived of his earldom, and imprisoned. In 1072, William marched north to defeat the Scottish king, Malcolm, who may well have been forced to surrender his son as a hostage for Malcolm's good behaviour. By 1073, feeling that England was now safe, William was back in Normandy putting down another uprising.

Then in 1075, the Revolt of the Earls blew up. However, William decided his English adherents were well able to sort it out and he remained in Normandy. He spent the next few years moving between Normandy and England mopping up dissent. But in 1078, he fell out bigtime with his eldest son, Robert, probably because the latter felt aggrieved he had no lands to rule. This was too good an opportunity to miss for William's continental enemies. They soon allied themselves with Robert. However, William was more than a match. He took the town of Gerberoi with a surprise attack but was almost killed. After that, father and son came to an agreement whereby Robert was promised Normandy after William's death.

William was a prolific castle builder. He is responsible for the White Tower, a central part of the Tower of London. Early castles would have initially been constructed of earth and timber, but later replaced by stone edifices. He also seized many villages, expelling the population, to create the New Forest. Modern historians declare the effect was overstated by contemporary chronicles, due to the fact that poor soil negated any worthwhile agriculture, and subsequent archaeological digs have revealed the area was sparsely populated.

Towards the end of 1086, William left England. His daughter, Constance, was married to the Duke of Brittany, as part of William's strategy to build an effective opposition to the French monarchs. However, his son, Robert, allied himself with the French king and began to foment trouble for his father. In July 1087, William seized Mantes. He either became ill at this point or he may have been injured by the pommel on his horse's saddle. Whichever, he was taken to the Priory of St Gervase at Rouen and died there in September 1087.

William was buried in the Abbaye-aux-Hommes in Caen.[9]

Fun Fact

When William's father, Robert I of Normandy, saw Herleva washing clothes by a river, it was a *coup de foudre*. He was immediately smitten. William was born soon after. Had Robert done as he should have, and married, William might well never have existed in the history books. But Robert went on pilgrimage to Jerusalem and died on the way home, leaving his illegitimate seven-year-old son as the new Duke of Normandy.

Odo, Bishop of Bayeux

So, basically, William didn't have an easy time of it, trying to bring England to heel and accept him as monarch, while bobbing backward and forward to Normandy to put down unrest there. He needed allies. Bishop Odo, was one. Until, as became a habit in this family, everyone fell out in a big heap. To say they were an argumentative family is something of an understatement.

Odo was born, possibly around 1030. In 1049, William, then Duke of Normandy, made him Bishop of Bayeux. Odo was yet another wily operator. Although an ordained cleric, he is best known as a warrior and statesman. He was an indispensable part of William's inner circle and fought at Hastings, although some historians believe his role in the battle was more that of a cheerleader than an active participant. He commissioned the Bayeux Tapestry to commemorate his half-brother's great triumph.

In 1067, William made Odo, Earl of Kent. When William was not in England, Odo was his trusted royal minister and regent. He also made hay while the sun shone, concentrating on acquiring vast amounts of land in the south-east and East Anglia, and enormous wealth. More worryingly for William, Odo also built a significant personal faction within the new Norman aristocracy. But his ambition wanted more.

Pope Gregory VII attempted to persuade William to make him overlord of England. Fat chance! This was Odo's opportunity. At that time, Pope Gregory was in conflict with Henry IV, the Holy Roman Emperor. William was half-persuaded to support Odo's claim to become the new pontiff.[10] Not at all discouraged, Odo, then commissioned a huge, new palace in Rome. He began using his accumulated wealth to hand out significant bribes among the cardinals, as well as setting up a spy network within the Vatican.

William became aware of these activities and was less than chuffed. He permitted Odo to go as far as the Isle of Wight in preparation for his onward journey to Rome. Imagine his surprise when William himself appeared and arrested him. In 1082, Odo was put on trial for corruption, and here is where it becomes both farce and a contest of wits between the half-brothers. William was, of course, aware that many people were more than happy to see Odo's downfall. However, most people saw his arrest and trial as a sign that there was (more) dissent within the family.

Things did not quite go William's way. The court refused to pass judgement, and Odo refused to recognise it anyway. He maintained that only the Pope – the one whose place he coveted – could judge him. William was not at all worried about that. He, no doubt smiled and retorted that he was not trying the Bishop of Bayeux, but the Earl of Kent. He ordered Odo to be seized and taken to the Tower of London. He stayed there until William died in 1087.

But that is not the end of Odo's story. No doubt missing the excitement of intrigue, he became entangled in the succession crisis of 1087-8. At that time, William Rufus, the middle son of William the Conqueror, had been chosen by his father to have the throne of England, but many people wanted the eldest brother, Robert Curthose, to be king, including, unsurprisingly, Robert, who was already Robert II of Normandy. William Rufus did not have a lot of support and was more than happy to release Odo from the Tower, thinking no doubt that he would support the Conqueror's decision. Not a bit of it. Odo, plus his other brother, Robert of Mortain, supported Robert II's claim.[11]

Unsurprisingly, rebellion ensued. The youngest brother, Henry, who would later become Henry I, played the sides against the middle, but he, too supported Robert. Henry spiked a conspiracy in Normandy that aimed to oust Robert II and replace him with William Rufus. Because of Henry's intervention, the uprising failed. To nobody's surprise, possibly except Henry's, Robert was not in the least grateful for his younger brother's help.[12]

When Odo found he couldn't unseat William Rufus, he settled for Robert in Normandy and William Rufus in England. He joined the first crusade and set out for Palestine, but died on the way in Palermo, in whose cathedral he is buried.

William fitz Osbern

William fitz Osbern's peerage as Earl of Hereford, was one of the first given out by William the Conqueror, but, according to the *Dictionary of National Biography*, the Hereford title was a personal gift and had no territory.[13]

Fitz Osbern was the illegitimate son of Osbert the Seneschal, who became one of the seven-year-old William's legal guardians after the death of Robert, Duke of Normandy in 1035. A number of the Norman barons refused to accept William as his father's heir and conspired to kill him. The plot failed but the Seneschal was killed.[14]

Fitz Osbern was a prime mover in the plan to invade England in 1066, but he is best known for establishing a firm border between England and Wales. He built castles at Wigmore, Monmouth, Chepstow, and Carisbrooke on the Isle of Wight. Carisbrooke became his main base. Although he conquered much of Gwent, his conduct was more geared to peace-making than acting the tyrant. He granted his French tenants liberal laws, which became the model for charters granted by other Norman lords in their boroughs.[15]

Fitz Osbern returned to Flanders in 1070 and was killed at the Battle of Cassel in 1071.

William II (Rufus)

IF WILLIAM THE Conqueror was a WYSIWYG (What You See Is What You Get) sort of chap, William Rufus, his second son was by no means straight-forward. I shall call him Rufus for ease of comprehension. Rufus could be just as determined and vicious as his father, but he also had an inclination towards humour and irony. Not as mindful as the first William, Rufus could act as if he were immortal but we all know people like that, don't we?

He worshipped God when he remembered to, which was very unlike an educated man of the times.[1] As most people will know, his nickname came about because of his red hair, a colour that, even up to relatively modern times, was considered unlucky. Until Henry VIII arrived and then it was conveniently forgotten for 118 years.

Rufus, possibly born around 1061, was brought up in the household of Lanfranc, Archbishop of Canterbury. He became one of William I's primary commanders, and, in 1081, led a campaign against the princes of Gwent. He was very loyal to his father, but despised his elder brother, Robert, who on the conqueror's death became Robert II of Normandy. Robert, having fallen out with his father, gave Rufus free access to William I. On the latter's deathbed in Rouen in 1087, he nominated Rufus to succeed him. By the time William actually died, Rufus was at the French coast on his way to Lanfranc, with sealed letters confirming his accession to the English throne, and giving directions regarding his coronation.

Rufus was in his middle to late twenties when he succeeded his father. Lanfranc was delighted to find someone who, as Crouch says, 'was amenable as any parliamentary candidate to helpful suggestions about his future conduct once he was in power'. Unfortunately, Rufus was about as sincere in his willingness to listen and take counsel as most parliamentary candidates are, until they are actually in power.

To give him his due, he started well. He paid for masses to be said for his father's soul, but he did not release his prisoners, as William had wished. His council of advisors consisted of many churchmen. Lanfranc was, of course, prominent among these, but the bishops of Lincoln and Durham were also very influential on the council. Rufus also appointed a few noblemen, including William de Warenne, Henry de Beaumont, and Robert fitz Hamo, all of whom immediately became the new king's favourites.

Also included in that first flush of goodwill, was Odo of Bayeux. Rufus released him and welcomed him to court, in the logical expectation that Odo would support him. Odo gave Rufus short shrift, however, and almost immediately turned his coat in support of Robert of Normandy. At first, this was of little account, although certainly a reverse. But it became much more serious when the dispute between the two brothers turned into a full-scale rebellion in 1088.

Rufus was in for another shock when Bishop William of Durham, a close friend, decided Robert was the stronger of the two warring brothers, and changed his allegiance. The main centre of the rebellion was Kent and Sussex, but Northumbria also became a hotbed of unrest. Rufus ordered Bishop William's lands to be seized.

Odo and his brother, Robert of Mortain, Duke Robert's uncles, were supporting the elder brother at this point. Their plan was to establish strongholds in Kent and Sussex, whereupon Duke Robert would sail across the Channel emulating his father and then take control of England. Odo made Rochester castle his base, while Mortain went to his castle at Pevensey. Where they both sat and waited for their nephew to come and unseat his younger brother. And waited. Then waited some more but things didn't go to plan.

Rufus promised the English nobles everything if they supported him, from lifting restrictions on the English population, to places on the next rocket ship to Mars. I made that last bit up, but you get the picture.

Everyone, including probably Odo and Mortain, expected Rufus to head full-tilt for the Midlands, which had also risen against him. What he actually did was to march to Rochester and force the castle to submit, which it did in very short order, terrifying Odo in the process. Odo now found himself the meat in the sandwich between Rufus and Lanfranc, who was holding Canterbury for the king. Odo escaped with a very small escort and headed for Mortain at Pevensey.

That suited Rufus perfectly. He had both rats holed up in the same place. He besieged the castle. Six weeks later, Odo surrendered, agreed to ride with Rufus back to Rochester, and then instruct his followers to disperse. Problem sorted. Except…Odo's men refused point blank. In the end, Rufus besieged Rochester as well. This led to disease running rife in the city, and it was *that* which forced the castle to surrender. Rufus permitted his uncles to run back to Normandy. You can imagine the first question when they met up with their nephew, Robert, can't you? Probably along the lines of 'Where the Hell did you get to?'

Meanwhile, back in England, this proved a decisive victory for Rufus. It led to his other rebels, from the south-west right up to Northumbria falling out with each other as to whether it was a good idea to rebel. They eventually submitted. All except Bishop William of Durham, who presumably thought he had nothing to lose. Long story short, he, too, ended up in Normandy in exile, which, all things considered, was fairly generous of Rufus and not at all what his father would have done. Possibly he wanted all the trouble-makers in Normandy where they could be monitored and hopefully cause problems for Duke Robert.

What is interesting about the revolt is that the French who had settled in England mainly supported the rebels, whereas Rufus' English subjects regarded them as betraying the king in much the same way Judas Iscariot betrayed Christ.[2] In character, Rufus appears to have been of a more secular bent than his bishops liked. There are stories of clerical disapproval over 'luxurious fashions and sexual indulgence of courtiers…condemnations of long hair, lavishly cut clothing and pointed shoes'.[3] That just goes to prove the Teddy-boys with their winkle-pickers in 1950s Britain, and the 'permissive society' of the 1960s were nothing new.

Rufus 'feared God but little', according to William of Malmesbury. Questions regarding his sexuality became a kind of 'take your pick' between homosexual, bisexual, or sterile. His sense of humour is demonstrated by an alleged debate he created between his bishops and Jewish scholars. Rufus allegedly stated that if the Jews won, he would convert. This may well be apocryphal, and, of course, from this distance of time, we have no way of confirming or debunking it.

It won't be a surprise to the reader to learn that, once all the tumult was over and the revolts crushed, Rufus forgot all his promises about making life easier for the English. When Lanfranc reminded him of them, Rufus is alleged to have replied 'who can be expected to keep all his promises?'[4]

It is impossible from a distance of 1,000 years to sort wheat from chaff regarding Rufus' character. He did not get on with his clergy, save for Lanfranc who died in 1089. The vast majority of records that do survive are ecclesiastical ones, so they will be biased. It is generally agreed that Rufus was short-tempered and so paranoid that he would react very brutally to anything he felt threatened him.[5]

Since most men at the courts of England and Normandy believed the two kingdoms should be ruled by one man, it wasn't long before Rufus decided it should be him. He used Ranulf of Bayeux – sometimes called Flambard –

to raise monies in secret to fund his enterprise. Long story short, Rouen, Eu, and Aumale became Rufus adherents. Duke Robert had no option but to come to a settlement. So amicable did Rufus and Robert become, the latter exiled their younger brother, Henry. Robert and Rufus then marched up to Scotland to sort out King Malcom.

For the rest of his reign, Rufus travelled around England. In 1093, he fell ill in Gloucester and, being suddenly fearful, appointed Abbot Anselm to be the new Archbishop of Canterbury, much to the latter's horror and dismay. Anselm extracted vows and promises that, should he recover, he would be a better ruler, at which point Anselm gave him the last rites. Rufus recovered and – leopards and spots – reneged on all his promises. You'd sort of guessed that, hadn't you?

By this time, he had also fallen out again with brother Robert, who decided to go and help the Byzantine emperor at that time having trouble with the Turks. Robert died on the way home, so Rufus took over Normandy as well as England.[6] He stayed in Normandy for most of the rest of his life, visiting England when he needed to. And he was in the New Forest on 2 August 1100 when he decided to go hunting.

The demise of Rufus has long been hotly disputed. There are theories about who was and wasn't present, and what actually happened and why. The favoured version is that Rufus and Walter Tirel, a favoured visitor, were pursuing the same stag. Tirel's arrow ricocheted off the stag's back and hit Rufus in the heart. He died instantly.

Contemporary rumours then began to circulate that portents had been visited on Rufus by God. His nephew, Richard, had been killed by a stray arrow the previous year, so great play was made of this. Allegedly, a stream in the village of Hamstead Marshall began to bubble with blood. His courtiers recounted unsettling dreams.

Accounts of what actually happened veer from everybody fleeing the scene, including Tirel, who galloped for the coast and took ship for France to avoid capture; younger brother, Henry standing over the corpse and arranging to gallop to Winchester, seize the treasury, and declare himself king; Henry doing the Winchester bit but taking the body with him and staging the funeral the following day; everybody running away and leaving Rufus' body where it was, to be found by a passing peasant, who loaded it onto a cart and took it to Winchester. Whatever ensued, it probably involved a lot of galloping.

It is true Tirel fled for the coast, but then he would have been worried that Rufus' adherents might well have lynched him without pausing to find out what had happened.[7] Crouch maintains that Henry and the Count of

Meulan stood over the corpse trying to work out how fast Henry could be declared the new king.[8] Starkey believes that Henry left Rufus lying in the forest and rushed to Winchester, leaving the conveniently passing peasant to load Rufus onto his cart and take it to a hasty burial in Winchester.[9]

Christopher Warren Hollister goes a little deeper into what might have happened. Tales of witchcraft and Rufus appearing prior to his death riding a black hairy goat did not emerge until a century after his death. The only circumstantial evidence for murder is Henry's response being so fast, being declared king less than 24 hours after Rufus' demise. This does smack of premeditation. Allied to this theory is that Walter Tirel was connected to the Clare and Gifford families, both of whom supported Henry. Except that it has never been confirmed that anyone from those families was even present, especially when you take into account that 35 years later, when Henry died, Stephen of Blois did exactly the same thing, and rushed to England to declare himself king. Looking back at Rufus' behaviour when William the Conqueror was on his deathbed, so did he.[10]

Most contemporary chronicles state that Rufus and Tirel were alone save for a few servants. Hollister goes with the peasant finding the body theory. There has also been doubt that Tirel fired the arrow at all. Initial accounts do not name the unfortunate archer and Tirel himself, by then back in France, always denied it. Well, he would, wouldn't he? But…by that time, he was safe and had no fear of reprisals. Why would he lie?[11]

So, what was the truth of Rufus' death? The late, great, astronomer, Sir Patrick Moore, frequently asked questions about the cosmos, to which nobody knew the answers. One of his most frequent expressions was 'we just don't know'. The same applies to the death of William Rufus.

Fun Fact

William Rufus was as much a builder as his father. He built the Great Hall at Westminster, still in use today. Rufus is also responsible for repairing London Bridge, using advanced engineering.[12] The bridge was badly damaged in 1091 by a tornado. Rufus raised a special tax specifically for the new bridge's maintenance. This tax was still being raised in the thirteenth century, when it was administered by The Bridge House Estates. Investments made since then mean the fund is still going strong today.

Ranulf Flambard

Ranulf Flambard was the son of a priest of Bayeux in Normandy. His nickname, Flambard, means 'torchbearer' and may have referred to his personality. He began his career under William the Conqueror and on his death, Ranulf chose to serve Rufus. Most historians now accept Ranulf was not so much a favourite of the new king, but he was certainly indispensable.

He supervised the construction of the first stone bridge in London and oversaw the construction of the Great Hall at Westminster. In 1099, he was rewarded with the bishopric of Durham. He was probably born about 1060 and was close to 70 years old when he died in 1128. He acquired the reputation of being a very able financier and administrator and helped to increase the royal revenues. It may be that he played a significant role in the compilation of the Domesday book.

Some sources claim that he was almost illiterate, but this probably means that he was not formally educated. He served as keeper of the Great Seal of the Realm from about 1085, two years before the Conqueror died. At one point he was travelling on the Thames with the Great Seal and was captured by pirates. He threw it into the sea so that they couldn't get hold of it. Flambard is notable for reducing the number of church benefices, for example, at Christchurch, he reduced the number of canons from 25 to 13, simply by not replacing those who died. He kept the revenues that would have gone to those canons and used them to rebuild the church.

As the chief financial administrator, Ranulf bore the brunt of chroniclers' condemnations for extortion in his efforts to increase royal revenues, at which he was very good. He created new methods of raising money. For example, on one occasion when English militia was assembled to fight in Normandy against Duke Robert, instead of sending the soldiers to Normandy, Ranulf dismissed them. But he collected the 10 shillings each man had been given by their district for their maintenance.

He was also a keen litigant. He brought a suit against Anselm on the day of the latter's consecration as Archbishop of Canterbury. Another of his innovations was an attempt to collect what would be called a relief fee due from vassals at the death of an overlord, from the undertenants of church lands when the church office changed hands. He tried this when Wulfstan, Bishop of Worcester died in 1095, but it was not repeated.

Ranulf was also a great builder. He fortified Durham with a wall around the castle and built Norham Castle, to help defend the River Tweed. The first stone bridge at Durham was completed under his aegis. While chroniclers condemn him for his methods of raising money and his morals, the cathedral chapter in Durham held him in very high esteem because of his building activities in defence of the city.

He died on 5 September 1128 and was buried in the chapter house in Durham. His tomb was opened in 1874 and examination of his skeleton revealed that he would have been about 5' 9" (1.75 m) tall. He was fond of clothes and always richly dressed. Known to be generous to his own staff, later in his life, he gave liberally to the poor. His crozier and signet ring were found in his grave, and they were plainer than most people assumed they would be.[13]

Most chroniclers put Ranulf Flambard in the forefront of those responsible for Rufus' behaviour and lay most of the blame on his rapacity for all the misfortunes that befell Rufus. The chief difficulty Rufus had was finding someone capable of 'hardening and sharpening' the feudalism in place in England at that time. Rufus needed somebody single-minded and unscrupulous to sort everything out. For the first time, church benefices were kept vacant, to save money, and the monies that were freed up were allocated to the crown. This exacerbated the disregard and disapproval in which Rufus was held by the clergy. Rufus was not very good at doing anything except making war. His personality was such that he lacked any fixed purpose and had issues focusing on things. Ranulf was generally considered to be the guiding hand behind Rufus' activities.

This supposition does not always hold water. It was Lanfranc who urged, for example, that the Bishop of Durham should be treated as a lay tenant, which meant that the normal ecclesiastical benefices did not apply. Rufus' later struggles with Archbishop Anselm had their parallel in the struggle that was going on all over Europe at that time. The keeping open of benefices was already established and remained common after Rufus' reign. His problem with Anselm was that the cleric was very unworldly and uncompromising, while Rufus was very aggressive and unyielding.

The early chroniclers were adamant that whenever a royal edict went forth taxing England, it was Flambard's custom to double it. He was portrayed as plundering the rich, destroying the poor, and confiscating inheritances: as being mercenary and exceeding all constraints in his actions and violence, by treating supplicants with the same ferocity he treated rebels.

But if we examine that in a critical fashion, it does not hold water.

There is no doubt that Flambard was litigious and many of the criticisms of him majored on this particular aspect of his personality. But this hides an important truth, in that the statements made are very few, and they are often untrustworthy. There is, for example, a thirteenth-century assertion that Flambard wrote a book of laws, but that has never been confirmed. It appears the writer decided it must have been Flambard who wrote them because he was Rufus' chancellor.

A lot has been made of the importance of Flambard during Rufus' reign, and it is true to say that he was very good at raising money when needed. The need for such a man as Ranulf was imperative by the time Rufus was well into his reign and money was tight.

There is evidence that some of the early chroniclers have become confused over Ranulf's designation. Some call him Rufus' treasurer, but there is no actual proof that this is true. There is a possibility that a man called Ranulf was the treasurer of the church of York. He is mentioned by Hugh, the Chanter of York as accompanying the archbishop in 1093. And some chroniclers may have confused that Ranulf, with Ranulf Flambard.[14]

Henry I

WE LAST SAW Henry a few pages ago, on a horse, either with or without his brother's corpse, scurrying to Winchester after his brother, William Rufus, had died. Certainly, he had every intention of seizing the Treasury and declaring himself King of England in the shortest time possible.

William of Malmesbury described Henry I as: 'of middle stature, his hair was black, but scanty near the forehead; his eyes were mildly bright, his chest brawny, his body well fleshed. He was facetious in proper season, nor did multiplicity of business cause him to be less pleasant when he mixed in society. Not prone to personal combat, he verified the saying of Scipio Africanus – 'My mother bore me a commander, not a soldier – wherefore he was inferior in wisdom to no king of modern time; and I may also say, he clearly surpassed all his predecessors in England and preferred contending by counsel, rather than by the sword. If he could he conquered without bloodshed; if it was unavoidable, with as little as possible.' [1]

Most historians agree he was born in Selby, Yorkshire in 1068, the youngest son of William the Conqueror. As a boy, Henry received an excellent education at Abingdon Abbey in Berkshire. He learned Latin and was taught to read and write in English. Because he was the youngest son, and not expected to succeed to his father's throne, he studied English law in preparation for joining the church, a regular route for younger sons. He was also interested in nature and created a zoo at Woodstock. His nickname *Beauclerk* meant 'fine scholar', which he was and very proud of being so. He declared that 'an unlettered King was but a crowned ass'.[2]

David Hume alleges that immediately after Rufus' death, William de Breteuil, keeper of the treasury arrived in Winchester just as Henry was about to grab it and told him that it belonged to the crown and his elder brother, who was now the sovereign. Henry drew his sword and threatened him with instant death if he disobeyed, and, since others loyal to Henry soon arrived, de Breteuil caved in.[3] Henry rushed to London, assembled those loyal to him and, less than three days later, was crowned by Maurice, Bishop of London.

Henry foresaw that being perceived in some quarters to have usurped the crown, he would do well 'to gain the affections of all his subjects'. He took the usual coronation oath, but also passed a charter to remedy many of the 'grievous oppressions which had been complained of during the reigns of his father and brother'. He promised that he would not seize revenues from clerical vacancies, but allow the successor to those sees to inherit the monies. That took care of the ecclesiastical issues.

Regarding civil grievances, he promised that heirs to earls, barons, or military tenants, upon paying the just and lawful tax, would be allowed to succeed to their estates. He ceased owning the monies of wards, had guardians appointed and promised not to dispossess any heiress without guidance from the nobility. Furthermore, should any baron wish to give his female kin in marriage, Henry would not levy a charge upon his consent or refuse permission, unless the nominated groom was his enemy. Should any of the nobility die without leaving a will, he promised heirs would succeed with no hassles.

To give this charter more strength, Henry lodged a copy of it in one abbey in each county. Sounds great, doesn't it? At last, a monarch who is actually thinking about his people. Trouble was, he didn't adhere to any of it throughout the thirty-five years of his reign. Just over a century later, when King John needed to be reminded he was not immortal, the nobles had all on to find one copy of Henry's charter.

Hume's book, for all it was published in 1762, is an enjoyable read. He makes the point that, thus far, the Norman kings of England, by denying the proper order of succession, and burdening the people as well as the nobility with unfair excises and tariffs, acted contrary to the laws of Edward the Confessor. But why let something so trivial as the laws of a king dead some 40 years, revered though he was, stop them getting what they wanted using violence and aggression when it worked so well?

Henry did send Ranulf Flambard, by this time Bishop of Durham, to prison, and then, in direct contravention of the much-vaunted charter, kept the see of Durham vacant for five years and grabbed all its revenues. He asked Anselm to return to the see of Canterbury, but Anselm refused. He sugared the refusal by negotiating Henry's marriage with Matilda, daughter of Malcolm III of Scotland, who had gone into Rumsey nunnery to protect her chastity 'from the brutality of the Normans'. Anselm and the ecclesiastical council assembled for the purpose, agreed that Matilda had never taken monastic vows and was free to marry. Henry married her, an act that was very popular with his subjects and helped establish him on the throne. Quite what Matilda thought about this, we do not know.

At this point, a rather big weed flew into Henry's beautiful garden, in the shape of his eldest brother, Robert, who returned to Normandy from his travels, took possession of his province and began preparing to invade England. This is acquiring stuck record proportions, isn't it? It must have been a shock to Henry to discover that the earls of Shrewsbury, Surrey, and other principal nobles all invited Robert to come and unseat his younger brother, promising to support him if he did.

But Henry had a secret weapon. Anselm, though he had refused the see of Canterbury, became Henry's leading advisor. Henry consulted him and seemed to be governed by his advice. And Anselm was trusted by the people. He reminded soldiers of their oath of allegiance to Henry. Aided by the earls of Warwick and Mellent, Roger Bigod, Richard de Redvers, and Robert fitz Harmon, all powerful barons, Henry marched to Portsmouth where Robert had landed with his army.

It looked as though Robert had landed there to give him easy passage to Winchester, the financial and administrative centre of the realm.[4] However, his sister-in-law was also in Winchester awaiting the birth of her child, so Robert headed for London. At which point, he discovered the nobility who were supporting him had become aware that Henry's forces, including a strong contingent of mercenaries, were on the way. They all believed, probably rightly, that a bloodbath would occur should the two forces meet, and the blood would all be on Robert's side.

As both sides approached Alton in Hampshire, the lords on either side told Henry and Robert they must not fight but negotiate, Anselm being one of the main peacemakers.[5]

Eventually, it was agreed that Robert, on receipt of 3,000 marks annually, would resign all claims upon England; that should either of them die without issue, the other would succeed to their realms; that adherents would not be punished, and that neither Robert, nor Henry, would protect the other's enemies or give them aid.[6]

On advice from Robert de Beaumont, Count de Meulan, Henry waited a while before moving against those earls who had sided with Robert. They were banished from England. Upon hearing this, Robert was so incensed, he came to England to remonstrate with Henry, but became very anxious about his own physical safety, so not only went back to France, but renounced the pension as well. So far, to use a tennis analogy, Henry is two sets up. He was about to win game, set, and match.

Robert's behaviour in scurrying back to Normandy angered many of his own adherents. Normandy fell into chaos, emphasised by how well Henry was governing England. The nobles of Normandy became disillusioned with Robert's governance and, long story short, Henry invaded. After some skirmishes, he took Robert prisoner at the Battle of Tinchebray, fought on 28 September 1106, almost 40 years after the Battle of Hastings.[7] Robert was brought back to England and imprisoned, first in Devizes Castle and then in Cardiff Castle, where he died in 1134, in his early 80s. He is buried in Gloucester Cathedral.

At last, both England and Normandy were under one monarch, and, despite his many deficiencies, Henry was a very able king, so peace broke out for the rest of his reign, apart from a couple of attempts on Normandy, which he quashed by coming to an agreement. He was skilled in what we would call reading the runes, especially when it came to ecclesiastical issues and the barony.

Henry had two children by Matilda. William Adelin and Matilda, sometimes called Maud. He married her to the Emperor Henry V of Germany and began to educate his son as his heir.[8] And then it all fell apart for Henry.

On a frosty November night in 1120, he boarded his ship and set sail for England. Behind him, the *White Ship* cast off from Barfleur after what was described as an 'afternoon and evening in the harbour, drinking hard and encouraging the crew to join in the revelry'.[9] On board was Henry's sole heir, William. As the ship left the harbour, those on shore heard a huge noise, including cries and screams, which they took to be a continuation of the day's merriment. In fact, the ship had collided with a known hazard, the Quilleboeuf rock. It impaled the ship's port side.[10] Attempts to push the ship off the rock only made the size of the hole larger. The *White Ship* tipped over. Those who had not attempted to get off were thrown into the freezing sea. They suffered 'cold water shock', which engenders a gasping reflex. They inhaled freezing water and most were dead within two to three minutes.

At this point, Prince William had escaped in a small rowing boat, but he apparently heard his half-sister, Matilda, screaming for him to rescue her. He turned back but his boat was swamped by people trying to climb aboard. The captain, Thomas FitzStephen, having cast off shouting he would get to England before King Henry, now realised all was lost. He allowed himself to drown, too, his last recorded words being, 'It is vain for me to go on living.'[11] The sole survivor was a local butcher called Berold, who had jumped on board before the ship cast off, determined to have an outstanding bill settled before the flower of Norman aristocracy sailed back to England.

Henry arrived back in England the next morning and travelled to the New Forest to await the arrival of his son. Nobody dared tell him, until his nephew, Theobald of Blois-Chartres plucked up the courage to recount what had happened.[12] In one fell swoop, Henry had lost his only son, a niece, a nephew, and many of his closest loyal advisors. Ironically, the treasury that had been in the hold of the *White Ship* was recovered in its entirety.

After Queen Matilda's death in 1118, Henry married Adelaide of Louvain in 1121, but this union proved childless. On Emperor Henry V's death in 1125, Henry summoned his daughter, the Empress Matilda back to England and forced his barons do homage to her as his heir. In 1128, Matilda married Geoffrey Plantagenet, heir to the county of Anjou, and in 1133 she bore him her first son, the future king Henry II. [13]

When Henry I died at Lyons-la-Forêt in eastern Normandy, his favourite nephew, Stephen of Blois, disregarding Matilda's right of succession, seized the English throne. Matilda's subsequent invasion of England unleashed a bitter civil war that ended with King Stephen's death and Henry II's unopposed accession in 1154.

Henry left behind a peaceful England, one that had, through his efforts, become administratively, very efficient. His justices made regular tours of England, dispensing law and order. His greatest bequest was probably that he turned England from a land ruled by informal and personal whims of the monarch in power, into something approaching a bureaucratic state.

Fun Fact

Sea lampreys are strange fish-like creatures. They have been described as 'swimming noses', moving through the water using odours to guide their way to their food. Their food is generally the blood of other fish species. Henry I, allegedly, loved them so much that, in December 1135, against medical advice, he ate enough of them to kill him. His cause of death has commonly been cited as due to 'a surfeit of lampreys'. The city of Gloucester traditionally sent the monarch a lamprey pie every Christmas, but now only does that on significant royal occasions, the most recent being the Coronation of King Charles III in 2023. [14]

Count Robert of Meulan

The men who prospered and remained prominent during Henry I's reign were those who not only remained loyal to him, but also accepted without reserve his right to the crown. They worked closely with him, using their talents to form a coherent structure of judicial and administrative government.[15] Henry was helped in this by men who had been prominent in the previous two reigns and one of the most prominent of these was Count Robert of Meulan, who will be referred to as Meulan to avoid confusion with Robert, Duke of Normandy. Born c.1040/1050, Meulan was noted as an eloquent speaker, able to mediate in most disputes successfully. He urged Henry to not only maintain existing laws, but also proposed new ones. Henry of Huntingdon, (1088–c.1157), a canon in Lincolnshire, described Meulan as: 'the most sagacious in worldly affairs of all who live between this and Jerusalem'. In other words, of all men alive.[16]

Meulan and his brother, Henry, Earl of Warwick, were sons of Roger of Beaumont, who had declined to stay with William the Conqueror in England, and retired to his estates in Normandy. In the 1090s, both Meulan and Henry were stripped of their lands in Normandy by Duke Robert in retaliation for their support of William Rufus. After which, not unnaturally, the brothers were steadfast in their loyalty to Rufus and Henry, and in their hatred of Robert.

Meulan's first battle experience was at Hastings, although he was young at the time if we take his date of birth as 1050. He became a seasoned soldier, getting plenty of experience in the frequent unrest and uprisings that ensued post-Hastings, not only in England, but between the two Williams and their brother, Robert in Normandy. By the time Henry came to the throne, Meulan was a leading member of his council and, in 1106, he led a division of the royal army against Robert at Tinchebray, where the duke was taken captive. Meulan is known to have played a central role in government by his signatures appearing on royal writs and charters.

At the time of the investiture controversy,[17] Anselm had withdrawn from his tenure at Canterbury and Meulan was excommunicated by Pope Paschal II, more as a shot across Henry's bow than anything else.[18] The Pope's problem was that he needed Henry's support for a proposed crusade.[19] However, Henry and Anselm met in France to discuss the situation. Anselm agreed to return to the see of Canterbury and Meulan's excommunication was withdrawn. Nobody knows if Meulan was involved in these discussions, or in persuading Henry to meet Anselm, but it is not beyond the bounds of possibility.

Meulan's lands in England were substantial to the extent that some thought it scandalous. He was granted the Grandmesnil properties in Leicestershire. Ivo of Grandmesnil supported Duke Robert against Henry in 1101. In 1103, he was in bother with the king again and asked Meulan to mediate. An agreement was reached because Ivo wanted to redeem his character by going on crusade.[20] He went off on crusade on the understanding – plus a payment of 500 silver marks – that Meulan would look after his estates. Also included in the agreement was that Ivo's young heir would marry Meulan's niece, daughter of the Earl of Warwick, and, should Ivo not return, his heir would inherit the Grandmesnil lands.

What actually happened was that as soon as Ivo had sailed over the horizon, Henry appears to have created Meulan the Earl of Leicester, and he appropriated Ivo's lands. And yet, this has never been absolutely confirmed. There is no actual proof that Meulan was ever created Earl of Leicester. The confusion may have come about because Ivo's brother was also called, guess what? Yes, Robert. And, taking into consideration that Henry was very careful about the rights of his nobility, the reference to Robert, Earl of Leicester, may well mean Ivo's brother and not Robert of Meulan.

Between 1109 and 1111, the French king Louis the Fat sought to force Henry to pay him homage as a vassal.[21] Henry, with Meulan's help, delayed and procrastinated until 1113 when Henry and Louis met at Gisors. Louis gave Henry sovereignty over Maine, Brittany, and Bellême, but he neither did homage to the French king nor admit to being a vassal.

It is true that Meulan was instrumental in making Henry's reign one of long periods of peace, interspersed with short wars, unlike the reigns of his two predecessors.

In 1114, there was a new dispute between the Sees of Canterbury and York. Henry and Meulan favoured York until they switched sides in 1116. This was probably because Canterbury was the wealthier of the two sees and trouble was brewing again in Normandy. At some point between 1116–1118, Meulan retired. It is known he signed no charters after February 1116. He died, aged around 75 years old, having become a monk at the ancestral monastery of the Beaumonts at Préaux. This was the first in a double blow for Henry because he also lost his queen, Matilda in 1118.

Robert of Meulan's legacy was proving that most wars and disputes are more easily settled by the pen than the sword. He was clear-sighted about the long-term effects of his decisions. It is notable that Henry adopted Meulan's theories in this respect, because the last 15 years of his reign were peaceful.

Eustace Fitz John

Eustace Fitz John was one of the most important people on Henry I's council. He was the Lord of Malton and Alnwick and rose from obscurity to be prominent in the government of northern England. Fitz John came from an Anglo-Norman family, of what we might now call middle class. He did not inherit any land. His possible date of birth was around 1088. He grew to be very wealthy, but this owed more to his royal service than to any inherited wealth.

Eustace began to sign royal charters, possibly as early as 1114. This would fit in with when Robert de Meulan retired from court. He is known to have attested to over 25 of Henry I's charters between 1119 and 1133. Away from court, Eustace was one of the leading royal officials and justices in northern England. He is known to have heard petitions from people in Yorkshire, Northumberland, Carlisle, Westmorland, and Durham. Being in royal service brought Eustace various benefits including exemptions from the payment of Danegeld – a kind of land tax paid to the king of Denmark. He also secured royal custodian positions and royal lands in the parish of Bamburgh, close to the castle, which was also entrusted to him. When Ranulf Flambard died in 1128, it is likely that Eustace may have been one of the men who took control of the vacant see of Durham. Between 1129 and the early 1130s he was farming lands in Yorkshire on very favourable terms.

Royal patronage also gave him a head start with regard to marriage. His first marriage was to Beatrice, daughter of the Lord of Alnwick. It enabled Eustace to control the major barony in Northumberland centred in Alnwick and also probably gave him the control of Caythorpe, near Grantham, and the rest of the Lincolnshire tenancy that went with it. Some historians also believe he became lord of the valuable manner of Malton in the North Riding of Yorkshire, but Malton was almost certainly a direct gift from Henry I, and nothing to do with his marriage.

His second marriage after the death of his first wife, was to Agnes Fitzwilliam, the sister of the Constable of Chester, through whom he acquired further lands in the East Riding of Yorkshire. And in 1144 or 1145, this second marriage gained Eustace control of the office of Constable of Chester. It is clear that once Eustace established himself as a loyal servant to Henry I, the king then granted him offices, custodianships, and lands in the north of England so that he would help keep the area secure and peaceful for the king.

When Henry I died in December 1135, Eustace and his fellow royal servants were confronted by Stephen, who had rushed to England, rather like the previous two kings, to seize the throne. It is clear that the important people in Henry's council were very suspicious of Stephen. He attempted to win them over by offering them the positions they had held under Henry, but they refused to obey his letters, because they had sworn an oath of loyalty to King Henry's daughter, the Empress Matilda.

Eventually Stephen became impatient and threatened them, at which point, after gaining a promise of safe conduct, they met with the new king, who agreed to all their requests. They then paid homage to him with the addition of a voluntary oath that they gave themselves wholly to his service. Stephen kept his promises to Eustace and the others with regard to retaining their positions.

In the summer of 1136, King David of Scotland invaded the North of England. He captured the castles of Carlisle, Wark, Norham, Newcastle, and Alnwick. He was not able to take Bamburgh Castle. It is not known if Eustace Fitz John submitted to David during this time, but the castle at Alnwick was almost certainly in Eustace's possession at the time. King David may have believed that the allegiance the Northern lords swore to him was wholehearted, but there was a plot hatched by King David to ambush Stephen and it is clear that Stephen was made aware of it. It is doubtful if it was Eustace who made this known to Stephen because Stephen forced Eustace to give up Bamburgh castle. The chronicler Richard of Hexham, states that Eustace had long secretly favoured King David.

However, this is not necessarily true. The consistency of Stephen's treatment of suspect courtiers had a lot to do with the problem. According to Ailred of Rievaulx, another chronicler, Eustace had shifted his allegiance from Stephen because he had been forced to give back the castles King Henry had entrusted to him. Eustace, being offended, went to Stephen's enemies in order to get that particular wrong righted. Of course, there is also the theory that Eustace might have been having second thoughts about his allegiance to Stephen because not only was he a close associate of King David, who supported the Empress Matilda, Eustace had actually promised Henry I, he would serve the Empress.

What is clear is that between 1136 and 1138 there was a serious breach of trust between Stephen and Eustace. Stephen deprived him of Bamburgh, and probably Tickhill and Knaresborough, too. It is possible that he took refuge with Scots. However, Stephen could be pragmatic as well as indolent, so he accepted the status quo and recognised Eustace as a power in the north of England. Around about 1144, Eustace obtained lands mostly in Cheshire, Lancashire, and Yorkshire from Ranulph II, 4th Earl of Chester. There is no clear indication that he was ever permanently reconciled to King Stephen until the settlement between Stephen and the Empress Matilda in 1153, when the former agreed that the latter's son, Henry, would succeed to the throne upon his death.[22]

When Henry II, Empress Matilda's son, acceded to the throne following Stephen's death in 1154, Eustace developed a very good relationship with him. He attested the king's new charters. Eustace was killed in an ambush at the battle of Ewloe, in Flintshire on campaign with Henry against the Welsh. His legacy is one as a great monastic patron. He patronised Gloucester Abbey, as well as the Augustinian priory at Bridlington. He founded his own abbey at Alnwick and favoured the order of Gilbert of Sempringham in Lincolnshire. He founded a Gilbertine priory in Malton, and a nunnery at Watton, just north of Hull in the East Riding of Yorkshire.[23]

Stephen, Matilda, and the
Anarchy 1135–1154

FOR A UNIQUE take on King Stephen, we need look no further than *1066 and All That*: 'The moment Stephen came to the throne, it was realised that he was a mistake and had been christened wrong; thus, everything was thrown into confusion.'[1] W. C. Sellar and R. J. Yeatman are no kinder to Matilda: 'Stephen himself felt quite uncalled for, and even his Aunt Matilda was able to take him in when she began announcing that she was the real King. Stephen, however, soon discovered that she had been mal-christened, too, and was unable to say for certain whether her name was Matilda or Maud.'

The plain fact is that, had William Adelin not gone down with the *White Ship*, Stephen would never have become king of England.[2] David Crouch makes the point that by the time Stephen was born, the world had accepted that one of the greatest powers in it was the Anglo-Norman realm.[3] It dominated every part of the world in which he grew up, although he did not travel beyond it until he came of age.

Stephen never got to know his father. Stephen Senior decided to go on crusade along with his brother-in-law, Duke Robert of Normandy, but disgraced himself by panicking and absconding from the army he was supposed to be leading during the siege of Antioch. Feigning illness, he deserted the field and abandoned the crusade, leaving his men to whatever fate God decided for them. It transpired they didn't need him anyway because they defeated the Turks. However, upon arriving home, Stephen Senior found his reputation so severely tarnished by his cowardice that rather than stay and face it out, he returned to Palestine and died there in 1102, when Stephen Junior was about six years old.

The most important person in young Stephen's life was his mother, Adela of Normandy, daughter of William the Conqueror. She brought him up until he was of age and had him educated. That he was brought up among women may well account for the fact that he was more than happy in his later years when fighting the Civil War with the Empress Matilda, to delegate a lot of his royal power and duties to his own queen, also called Matilda, just to confuse the issue.

Stephen was then sent to the court of Henry I, one of the cultural and political centres of Europe at that time. It might have been a centre for spiritual and literary excellence, but it had the morals of an alley-cat. Stephen found a young woman with whom he established a long-term relationship and had a son called Gervase and also a daughter. The nickname he gave his mistress was Damette, which means 'little lady'. When Stephen married Matilda, he followed custom and practice and set Damette aside, but it is possible that he arranged a marriage for her, since she had other sons who were known as Gervase's brothers.

When Stephen received news that Henry I was on his deathbed, it may have come as a shock because although the old king was 67, he had been well and vigorous until then. It is possible that Stephen and his elder brother, Count Theobald, had already agreed a strategy to seize the throne. What is uncertain is which brother was supposed to seize it. The nobility in Normandy expected it to be Theobald, since he was the elder.

Henry died during the evening of Sunday, 1 December 1135. Some historians have theorised that if Stephen received the news on Monday, possibly via a relay of horses, he might well have taken ship on Monday afternoon from Wissant and would have been in Kent as early as 3 December. However, David Crouch maintains it is unlikely he moved that fast.[4] We know that Stephen was very pious so it is more than likely he would have organised the appropriate services for his uncle's soul before crossing the Channel.

Warned by Robert of Gloucester, illegitimate son of Henry I, and the Empress Matilda's half-brother, Dover shut its gates against Stephen. He managed to land notwithstanding, and although he travelled as far as Canterbury, discovered that it too had closed its gates against him. He was forced to ride on to London, where he was received with joy. The city had been in something of a confused state since Henry I's death and, as is usual when a crisis of this nature happens, it was a very uncertain time for trade and commerce. The city fathers knew Stephen. He was popular with them and with the people. Although Theobald was his elder brother, the English did not know him, and Stephen, either by accident or design, chose the right moment to ride into the city and ask the people if they wanted him to be their king. Everyone responded with enthusiasm and the city's people were the first to acknowledge him as their monarch.[5]

Stephen of Blois, reigned from 1135 to 1154. He had been a favoured nephew of Henry I and fully expected that he would be accepted as monarch over the more legitimate claims of his cousin, Matilda. He argued that preserving order in England was more important than the oath he had sworn to support Henry's daughter.[6]

Empress Matilda, Henry's only remaining legitimate child, not unnaturally, disagreed. This led directly to a civil war that lasted almost 20 years – frequently known as the Anarchy. The two insuperable problems were firstly that Matilda, although considered by some to be the legitimate heir, was a woman and therefore, by default, not considered to have the necessary qualities to be monarch in her own right. But it was her personality that really swung the pendulum against her. She was proud, arrogant, and haughty. She managed to alienate most of the people who had sworn fealty to her because of her high-handed attitude. This was, of course, the normal attitude to strong women in power, but in Matilda's defence, she was trying to gain what was hers by right, and by fealty sworn by her father's nobles.

By contrast, Stephen was much more easy-going. And a man. He was popular with the English nobility, having spent some of his childhood at the court of Henry I, who had also given him land in England, Normandy, and the county of Boulogne.[7] William of Malmesbury described him thus 'when he was count, had by his good nature and the way he jested, sat and ate in the company even of the humblest, earned an affection that can hardly be imagined'. The resulting war led the contemporary Peterborough chronicle, to describe the 20 years of conflict with the words 'they said openly that Christ and his saints slept'.[8]

Stephen was born around 1096/7. In common with the other English magnates, he pledged to support Henry's daughter as a successor to the throne. Many English nobles were reluctant to accept a woman ruler and Henry's Norman subjects very much resented Matilda's marriage to the Duke of Anjou because the Angevin family were considered to be enemies of Normandy. Stephen took advantage of this when he crossed the English Channel to claim the crown, whereupon, not just Londoners, but leading lords and bishops welcomed him. He also promised the Pope that papal influence would become a significant factor in English politics. Upon hearing this, the Pope also supported him.[9]

As a man, Stephen was brave and energetic. He was also very affable and mild mannered. All of which is lovely, except it meant he did not provide the iron-hand leadership, his three predecessors had wielded over England. He imported Flemish mercenaries in an attempt to build a party loyal to himself. But this simply alienated the nobility.

Two things happened in 1138, neither of which was to prove advantageous for Stephen. The first was that he supported Theobald of Bec as a candidate for Archbishop of Canterbury against his own brother, Henry of Blois, the then Bishop of Winchester. (And, speaking of the bishops of Winchester, we will meet several of them in the next few hundred years, also called Henry.) This particular Henry never forgave his brother for the slight, especially as he believed Stephen had timed his final decision to coincide with Henry being away on other business. It is more than likely that this was the deciding factor in Henry's decision, in 1141, to support the Empress Matilda.

The second event was that due to the barons' dissatisfaction with Stephen's governance, Robert, Earl of Gloucester, Empress Matilda's half-brother, invaded England on her behalf. Initially, Stephen won several battles, but he then arrested Bishop Roger of Salisbury and his family, believing they were fomenting treason. This lost Stephen the support of the church.

Matilda seized her opportunity and came over to England in September 1139 to stake her claim to the throne. In either what might be regarded as an exaggerated display of chivalry or monumental stupidity, Stephen had Matilda escorted to Bristol. She then set about bringing most of western England under her banner.

At the Battle of Lincoln in 1141, Stephen was captured and imprisoned in Bristol Castle, the south-west being the heartland of Robert of Gloucester's operations. Matilda immediately rushed to London to claim her rightful prize. However, her arrogance and complete disregard for anyone save herself, upset the citizens of London so much they rebelled against her. They were not happy that she seldom used the term 'queen' but kept her title of 'empress', something that had, being pedantic, died with her first husband; it obviously sounded much more significant than 'queen'. Sometimes she referred to herself as the 'Lady of the English', which is even more inaccurate, when one considers she was married to Henry VI, the Holy Roman Emperor at the age of 12, and when he died, returned to Normandy, and married Geoffrey, Count of Anjou. Thinking she could now depose Stephen and be crowned, her haughty attitude lost her the support of just about everybody in authority, including Bishop Henry, Stephen's brother. The tide of opinion turned against her.

In the meantime, during his imprisonment, Stephen's queen, Matilda, and the king's chief lieutenant, William of Ypres, remained faithful to him, along with most of the county of Kent. The Empress was driven out of London. She was never crowned and took up residence in Oxford. And so, for a while, the two sides jockeyed for position but nothing much happened. Stephen held London and the south-east; the Empress held Bristol and the south-west. Presumably, the north did as the north has always done and went its own way.

Everything changed when Robert of Gloucester was captured at Stockbridge while King Stephen was still imprisoned in Bristol. Robert had always been Matilda's main strength and stay. His detention led to a stalemate. The Empress was forced to accept an exchange of prisoners. Stephen was restored to the throne and enjoyed a second coronation on Christmas day 1141, but he was crowned at Canterbury this time.[10]

The war was not won by any means, but Stephen now became more determined and resolute. He retained the upper hand, taking advantage of the situation when in 1142, Robert journeyed to Normandy to gain support from the Empress Matilda's husband, Geoffrey of Anjou. Geoffrey was too busy trying to gain control of Normandy and refused to help. During Robert's absence, Stephen pounced and besieged the Empress at Oxford Castle. She escaped, allegedly being lowered from St George's Tower, dressed in a white cloak to camouflage herself against the snow. She crossed the frozen River Isis and walked six miles to Abingdon.[11]

Although Stephen remained king, he was never totally in control of his country. He became a little paranoid and frequently arrested people on suspicion, including Geoffrey de Mandeville, Constable of the Tower of London, and Earl of Essex. De Mandeville's support was akin to modern revolving doors, in that he would support whoever appeared to be in the ascendant. However, gradually, Stephen managed to wear down the opposition and this was underscored in 1145 when Robert of Gloucester's son, Philip, swore fealty to him.[12]

In October 1147 Robert of Gloucester died and that took the heart out of the Empress Matilda and her campaign. Her cause was taken up by her son Henry of Anjou, but he did not have the necessary resources to support a sustained campaign. Eventually, the war did not so much end as fizzle out. Stephen was almost a broken man by this time. He had come to the throne as strong, resolute, and affable, but was now uncertain, suspicious, and haunted. His policies were continually thwarted by Theobald, Archbishop of Canterbury, who refused to accept Stephen's involvement in church affairs. Theobald soon found himself in exile, but Stephen realised that he had to work with Theobald in order to keep the peace. Stephen wanted his own son, Eustace, to succeed him, and he needed Theobald's approval for this, but Theobald refused it.

The death of Stephen's queen in 1152 further broke Stephen's spirit. In 1153 Henry of Anjou brought a force to England and fought to establish his right to the throne. In August 1153, Eustace also died and Stephen's ambitions were all but finished. He therefore negotiated with Henry and signed the Treaty of Wallingford in November 1153, acknowledging that the Empress Matilda's son was his heir and would succeed him to the throne.

Less than a year later, Stephen died of appendicitis at Dover Castle, although he was also in great pain from bleeding piles. He spent his final year living mostly in Kent, which had always remained loyal to him, and was buried alongside his wife and his son at Faversham Abbey, which he had founded in 1147.

Fun Fact – for us, if not for Stephen!

Stephen became king because Henry I's only legitimate heir died in the White Ship disaster. Stephen was due to sail on the ship, but had to miss it because he was suffering from a bout of diarrhoea.

William of Ypres

William was born before 1104, the illegitimate son of Philip, Lord of Lo, and grandson of Robert, Count of Flanders. In 1119, and between 1127 and 1128, he made unsuccessful attempts to succeed to his grandfather's title.[13]Although he was known to King Stephen before the latter came to the throne, William did not appear at court until around 1136. He had been expelled from Flanders in 1133 and that may be when he came to England. Not much is known about his career before 1140, but he cannot be considered as solely a military professional because his other activities as a significant royal presence in Kent and his position at court preclude this.

He was a Flemish aristocrat by birth. His grandfather, Count Robert, and William the Conqueror's wife were brother and sister, thus making William and Stephen related. This caused problems for the English and their perception of him. He was vilified as a foreigner and for being a mercenary. At this point, though, the general opinion in England of Flemings was not overly hostile: that came about during the next reign when Henry II came to the throne.

His alleged ruthless streak when in authority made him unpopular. Gervase of Canterbury, a late twelfth-century chronicler, described him as being typical of Flemish mercenaries who he labelled 'hungry wolves'. In 1133, William had led a failed revolt against Count Thierry and fled to the neighbouring county of Boulogne, then governed by Stephen of Blois, who was to become the King of England two years later.

It is generally agreed among historians that he was in royal service by 1136, but his first confirmed presence at King Stephen's court is in 1138, in a royal charter.[14] From this date onwards, William's presence at court becomes more visible. He is alleged to have had a personal quarrel with Robert, Earl of Gloucester in 1137, possibly because William was becoming more prominent at court. Stephen granted him significant lands in Kent and he was assigned the governance of the county, almost to the status of an untitled lord, probably because Kent was such an important barrier between London and Normandy/Boulogne. Given Stephen's uncertain hold upon the throne, he needed someone with a proven track record of strong leadership to maintain that buffer. Some historians have suggested that William was made Earl of Kent, but there is no confirmation of this.

William commanded Stephen's forces when the Empress Matilda invaded, and nowhere was he more effective than after the Battle of Lincoln, in 1141, when Stephen was captured and then imprisoned at Bristol.[15] When he knew the battle was lost, William withdrew his forces from the field, something for which he was heavily criticised. However, he immediately marched to Queen Matilda and together, they set about ensuring Stephen's early release. He is also known to have been involved in burning Wherwell Abbey, when the abbess gave sanctuary to the Empress' forces, who were attempting to fortify it. He plundered Abingdon Abbey on the order of King Stephen, who was demanding a contribution from the monks there. William allegedly broke open their treasure chest with a hatchet and seized the sum Stephen had demanded.

In 1143, it is also alleged that William threatened to burn St Albans, but was pacified by a valuable gift from its treasury.[16]

With Waleran de Meulan holding Worcester, Stephen's steward, William Martel sitting at Sherborne, and Matilda and William of Ypres holding London, the Empress' forces were confined to the south-west.[17] By this time, the Empress' adherents were more than a tad fed up with her. Henry of Blois, Bishop of Winchester, returned his allegiance to the King. There followed a few skirmishes and, at Stockbridge, Robert, Earl of Gloucester was captured.

William lost his sight in the late 1140s, which ended any continuance of his military activities and may have played a part in Stephen considering making the Empress Matilda's son his heir, something that became inevitable when Eustace died in 1153. William is known to have endowed monasteries in Flanders and also the Cistercian house at Boxley in Kent, possibly in repentance for the outrages at Abingdon and St Albans. When the abbey of St Bertin in Flanders burned down in 1152, he paid virtually all the expenses of rebuilding it.

When Henry II came to the throne, he had no use for William, who, though he tried to hang on to Kent, was eventually forced to leave England and retire to Flanders, spending the last seven years of his life at the monastery of St Peter at Lo. He died on 24 January 1165.[18]

Most historians know him as an effective commander and it is interesting that another effective commander, Winston Churchill died exactly 800 years to the day after him.

William d'Aubigny (Aubigné)

He was born around 1109, son of William d'Aubigny and Maud Bigod, the daughter of Roger Bigod of Norfolk. He was loyal to King Stephen and was created Earl of Arundel around 1138 and then Earl of Lincoln.

He is known to have appeared at court as an acknowledged earl at the Christmas festivities in 1141 when Stephen had his second coronation following his captivity. In 1143, as Earl of Lincoln, d'Aubigny granted two charters confirming the donation of land to the abbey of Affligem in Brabant. He also built Castle Rising in Norfolk. He is the first proven supporter of the Order of St Lazarus of Jerusalem and granted that order land at Wymondham. He also built a leper hospital near his castle in Norfolk.[19]

Sometime after 1139, d'Aubigny married Henry I's widow, Adeliza, who, although she sheltered the Empress Matilda, when the latter invaded England in 1139, had always been one of Stephen's supporters, and had – presumably unknown to the Empress – already promised to marry William. Stephen, acting entirely in character, maintained he did not make war on women and the Empress' release was negotiated by Henry of Blois.[20] However, when we look at other sources, d'Aubigny gained the earldom of Arundel by his marriage to Adeliza, and, according to 'sign of the times', he gave shelter to the Empress, but thereafter was completely loyal to Stephen.[21]

In 1141, he attested to one of Stephen's charters as the Earl of Sussex, and it was under this title that he witnessed a charter to the abbey of Barking. By this time, the earldom of Lincoln had passed to William de Roumare, presumably because of d'Aubigny's adherence at that time to the Empress.

He was instrumental in arranging the Treaty of Wallingford in 1153 and became a favourite of Henry II who held him in high esteem. He commanded

Henry's army in 1173 when that king's sons all rebelled against him. Later that same year, he helped defeat the Earl of Leicester, who, had invaded Suffolk. Henry confirmed d'Aubigny as earl of Arundel and Earl of Sussex. He was sent to remonstrate with the French king in 1164 for giving shelter to Thomas Becket, but failed to persuade Louis to hand Becket over to Henry.

William died on 3 October 1176 and was buried at Wymondham Abbey.

We cannot leave this section having only mentioned two of Stephen's favoured courtiers, and not mentioned the Empress Matilda's strongest adherent, her half-brother, Robert, Earl of Gloucester.

Robert, Earl of Gloucester

Robert Fitzroy was born around 1090, the illegitimate son of Henry I of England and half-brother to Empress Matilda, the king's only remaining legitimate child after the *White Ship* disaster. He was her foremost military commander and loyal adherent during the Anarchy. Although not known for certain, it is possible he was the eldest of Henry's many illegitimate children.[22] In 1119, Robert was married to Mabel FitzRobert, who brought with her the honours of Gloucester and Glamorgan and lands in Normandy. After the *White Ship* disaster, Henry made Robert Earl of Gloucester.

When the widowed Empress Matilda returned to court in 1126, Henry began to clear the way to ensure that she would succeed him, since it was clear by then there would be no children from his second marriage to Adeliza.[23] At this time, Robert of Gloucester was given charge of the captive Duke Robert of Normandy, something urged upon Henry by his daughter, Matilda and King David of Scotland. By trusting Gloucester to hold the duke, Henry then made plans to negotiate an Angevin alliance by marrying Matilda to Geoffrey, Count of Anjou, thus uniting Normandy and Anjou. The marriage duly took place, but Henry was also strengthening the coterie around his daughter to ensure that she would succeed him on the throne of England.[24]

Robert was one of the last – and the most lukewarm – nobles to give his fealty to King Stephen and one of the first to turn against him.[25] The chronicler, William of Malmesbury's depiction of Robert was according to Patterson, 'inaccurate, mendacious, and unreliable, and that its author is unworthy of being called an historian.'[26] However, it appears clear that Robert was actively supporting his half-sister from the time she returned to England in 1126.

What really put the cat among the pigeons was when Henry I and Geoffrey fell out over the possession of castles on the Norman/Angevin frontier. Robert's first loyalty was to Henry and although Henry was successful in his campaign, he died before he could heal the breach with his daughter and her husband. What then complicated things still further was that, upon hearing of Henry's death, Geoffrey immediately invaded Normandy, hoping to take advantage of the situation. At that time, Robert was in Normandy. Upon hearing that Stephen had taken the throne, he took Henry I's treasure from the castle at Falaise and left. This indicates he was still loyal to his half-sister because, had he favoured Stephen, he would have held the castle for the new king.[27]

To pile complication upon complication, the Norman lords were dithering about whom to support, so Robert waited on events. Some on both sides favoured the Empress' young son, Henry, but King David negotiated a treaty with Stephen, which took everyone by surprise. Eventually, Robert swore fealty to him. It was only when Matilda herself invaded England, and was given safe passage to Bristol by Stephen, that Robert came down on the side of his half-sister.

He commanded her forces at the Battle of Lincoln, which gave Matilda the upper hand. She went to London in supposed triumph while Robert escorted Stephen to Bristol. However, the king's adherents worked tirelessly for his freedom, their efforts greatly aided by the Empress' arrogant and alienating attitude. At the Rout of Winchester, her forces were defeated and Robert was captured.[28]

Without him, the Empress was powerless. However, true to character, she refused point blank to exchange Robert for the king. She offered 12 earls and some gold, but would not surrender Stephen. Queen Matilda contacted Robert of Gloucester's wife, who had been given charge of the king's captivity at Bristol. Since both women wanted their husbands freed, they bypassed the Empress altogether. Stephen and Robert were released.[29]

After that, the war went on with neither side gaining any advantage. The only people who suffered were the commons because the nobility began building and fortifying castles and more or less doing as they pleased without let or hindrance. Then, in 1147, Robert died at Bristol Castle. He was buried at St James' Priory in Bristol, which he had founded in 1129.

Deprived of her most able and loyal supporter, the Empress lost heart. She returned to Normandy.

THE HOUSE OF PLANTAGENET 1154–1485

Preamble

The House of Plantagenet is the dynasty whose tenure on the English crown lasted for over 300 years, from 1154 to 1485. Strictly speaking, the dynasty lasted up to the death of Richard II in 1400, at which point, Henry IV, son of John of Gaunt, formed the House of Lancaster, followed by Edward IV and the House of York. However, all the monarchs up to 1485 had Plantagenet blood running through their veins. So, for the purpose of this book, which is not an academic tome, I will call all of them Plantagenets.

Their name was taken from the common broom bush – Latin name *Planta Genista*. Its bright yellow flowers are alleged to have medicinal qualities, helping the heart and circulation. They were also worn in battle to encourage abundance, strength, and courage.

The origin of the dynasty is buried in ancient European myths of water and wood sprites, and the female demon who seduces men in dreams – the succubus. In some quarters, the Plantagenet monarchs were called the 'Devil's Brood'. It helps the legend along when you realise the number of monarchs from Henry II to Richard III is...wait for it...13! The number 13 is long thought to be unlucky, because Judas Iscariot was the 13th disciple to sit down at the Last Supper.

Gerald of Wales was a courtier and friend of Henry II and his son, Richard I. Gerald is alleged to have told the tale of how the Angevin royal family came into being. It would have made a worthy addition to those stories told by the brothers Grimm. The story goes that the unnamed count, (possibly the grandfather of Count Fulk the Black), was hunting in the depths of the Black Forest one day. It had to be the *Black* Forest, didn't it? He encountered a 'lady of unearthly beauty but mysterious origin' called Melusine, and married her there and then. (It's always good to have a priest in your retinue for these spontaneous occasions.)

Melusine bore him four children, but she either refused to go to church, or would leave before the consecration of bread and wine. Her husband became distinctly annoyed about this, because she obviously wasn't going home to check on the Sunday roast. He ordered his knights to grab her next time she tried to leave church early. They tried, but she slipped out of her cloak, grabbed two of her children, and flew out of a church window. As you do. I wonder if that is why old churches were built with windows that do not open.

I digress. Again. Melusine left behind two of her four children. One of them was either the grandfather or the father of Count Fulk the Black of Anjou. He was a charming fellow. Having caught his wife, Elizabeth of Vendôme, in flagrante with a goatherd, Fulk had her burned in her wedding dress in the marketplace in Angers in front of the cathedral. A few days later, Angers itself was torched, nobody knows by whom, although fingers were pointed straight at Fulk. I told you he was a charming chap. Nobody knows what happened to the goatherd either, which is probably just as well.

Fulk – known as the Black Count – had a track record of robbing, destruction, and rape when on campaign. His son, Geoffrey – known as The Hammer – was a chip off the old block – sorry, couldn't resist that. They sound like contestants in a wrestling ring, and that probably is not too far from the truth of the matter. Geoffrey rebelled against his father, who not only defeated him, but put a saddle and bridle on him and made him crawl around begging for mercy. It is also said that Fulk went on pilgrimages to Jerusalem, where he made his servants flog him through the streets as he begged for God's forgiveness. The citizens of Anjou, known as the Angevins, decided the Devil's blood ran in his veins. Gerald of Wales is said to have frequently told this tale to Richard I, who is alleged to have replied, 'We come from the Devil and we'll end up by going to the Devil.' Very apt when you consider some of the monarchs who have graced the English throne.

The Plantagenet monarchs were known for red-gold hair, ferocious tempers, quarrelling with their nearest and, obviously, not so dearest, and generally not just wanting their own way, but fighting, relentlessly and without mercy to ensure they got it.[1]

Henry II

DURING THE LAST half of the twelfth century, the monarchs of England ruled a vast collection of territories, which stretched from Hadrian's Wall in Northumberland across to Ireland and then down to the Mediterranean. This great empire came into being because of the marriage of Geoffrey of Anjou to the Empress Matilda, daughter of Henry I. Henry had arranged this marriage when his daughter returned as the widow of the Emperor Henry V, to the court in England. When Geoffrey and Matilda married, he was 16 and she was 26. It is quite ironic to consider that when their son Henry Plantagenet, also known as Henry FitzEmpress, married, his wife, Eleanor of Aquitaine, was also ten years older than him.

Many historians have posited that this marriage was brokered by Henry I in order to satisfy his grand design of an empire emanating from his reign. But there is also the fact that Normandy had long been under threat from its neighbouring territories, and during Henry I's lifetime, Geoffrey of Anjou made several attempts to conquer Normandy. So, the marriage between Matilda and Geoffrey may well have been a pragmatic move on Henry I's part. What it actually meant was that the two states previously administered by different magnates were now joined together and logically speaking, were stronger because of it.

Christopher Warren Hollister argues that England and Normandy shared a single ruling class that could not be governed satisfactorily by two independent rulers, and this must have been part of Henry I's thinking when he brokered the marriage between his daughter and the Count of Anjou.[1] Henry had a tough job on his hands. And part of his difficulties was the attitude of the first Plantagenet monarchs to England. Up until Henry III, they all regarded themselves as Norman, Angevin, or even Poitevan, but not English. England was there to be used as a money pit for their European territories and for building, but it was not home. Even John, who lost most of the lands in Europe never regarded himself as English.[2]

King Henry II and his family are probably known to some people, through the 1968 film, *The Lion In Winter* starring Anthony Hopkins and Katharine Hepburn. Many people may have considered that it was well over the top in terms of performance and content. However, in its portrayal of the family disharmony, it actually told the truth.[3]

Henry II was born in 1133. He was the eldest son of Geoffrey and Matilda, and despite the latter's struggles during the civil war against her cousin, Stephen, her son Henry had inherited all his titles by the age of 21.[4] During his childhood, he had visited England frequently, the first time being 1142, at the age of nine with Earl Robert trying, once more to gain the crown for Matilda. She had been captured but escaped from Oxford. Earl Robert's problem was lack of money, so he changed his policy to support the young Henry until the latter was old enough to take command.[5] Henry's father was, in the meantime, trying to gain control of Normandy, which he did in 1144, and was recognised as Duke of Normandy by the French king. Henry tried to win England again in 1147, but was defeated. His mother and uncle refused him money to get back home, so Henry applied to Stephen for funds. Stephen, often a soft touch, sent him the money. He tried again in 1149, at which point, Stephen's main objective became capturing and eliminating him. However, Henry eluded all Stephen's efforts and reached Bristol.

When his father, Geoffrey, died in 1151, Henry was then recognised, after a bit of to-ing and fro-ing with King Louis, as Duke of Normandy and swore fealty to the French king. It was probably at this event Henry met Louis' then queen, Eleanor of Aquitaine. The marriage had never been desperately harmonious, and, although Eleanor gave birth to two daughters, Louis was convinced she would never give him a son. By the time of Henry's visit, the marriage was on its way out, and Louis had set his mind on an annulment. Nobody will ever know for certain what happened between Henry and Eleanor, but the instant Louis presented her with the annulment in 1152, she fled to Poitiers, knowing that, as a now free, rich, 28-year-old woman, and with the duchy of Aquitaine once more in her hands, she was a target for kidnapping and forced marriage. Indeed, one of her pursuers was Henry's younger brother, Geoffrey. Once in Poitiers, she sent an urgent message to Henry, about to embark on an invasion of England. He immediately cancelled his plans, rode in very short order to Eleanor, and they were married less than two months after her marriage to Louis had been annulled. Louis was incandescent. Partly because of the haste, but mostly because they did not ask his permission. It was a rift never to be healed.[6]

In 1153, Henry once more invaded England, but this time, there was little appetite for battle. It was bitter winter, there was a famine, and, not to put too fine a point on it, everybody was sick to the back teeth of all the fighting. Long story short, it was agreed with Stephen that Henry would be his nominated heir, bypassing Stephen's son, Eustace. Eustace, understandably, was very bitter and set about rampaging through Cambridgeshire trying to entice Henry to engage with him. And failing miserably. Eustace died suddenly, allegedly struck down for damaging St Edmund's Abbey, but whether his death was divine intervention or human intervention, it happened very conveniently for Henry. Within a year, he was king of England, with a wife who had produced one son, and went on to produce four more, as well as daughters for dynastic marriage purposes.[7] You can hear Louis grinding his teeth, can't you? It was obviously Eleanor's fault she didn't give him a son, and then she gives the upstart Henry five of them!

There is no doubt that Henry II was a complex character. He had all the arrogance and self-justification he inherited from his haughty mother, an extremely intelligent, quick-witted mind, and an unassailable belief that he was always right. And, to be fair, he usually was. For this reason, he is one of the best kings England ever had. There is also no doubt that the implementation of law and order in England was completely transformed by him.

England was completely exhausted after years of internal conflict. There had been a rash of fortifications built by barons, without the permission of the monarch. The barons had also descended into factions for each side, and this trickled down to the lowest echelons of English society – the peasants. The nobility had been involved on both sides of the divide and this left their villeins and the lowest orders at risk from any predations on their lords' lands by an opposing lord. Whilst the nobles may have been in some ways shielded from this by their private militia, their tenants were not. Crops – the lords' and the tenants' – would be at risk of destruction and anyone who tried to prevent that would be cut down without mercy.

What Henry II inherited upon Stephen's death in 1154, was a land that was not only exhausted with fatigue, but also exhausted for money. As things stood when Henry succeeded to the English throne, the legal system was immensely complicated. Decisions made were frequently without logic, and it was cumbersome and slow. Henry's approach to solving these problems was that the law should be a practical thing and should rest on intelligent responses to purely practical problems. Whilst the problems might not be new, they had never before come under scrutiny. Henry needed to know not just what needed to be done, but also how it could be done better. In this context, laws required to be shaped with logic to be efficient and effective.[8]

To give one example of how complicated the legal system was, there was a proliferation of different courts. Which court a man took his case to was only partially dependent on the nature of that case. It also depended on his status and on the nature of his tenure. So, while villeins might bring cases into the Hundred Court, another man might bring in the same case to the Shire Court and a clergyman would bring his case into the Ecclesiastical Court. That said, William the Conqueror had declared an edict that ecclesiastical courts were the proper place for things which only concerned the cure of the soul. The main issue with ecclesiastical courts was that anything that concerned a man of the church was liable to be hijacked by them and this raised their status to that of being parallel to other forms of law. However, secular courts were frequently blurred in their demarcation lines and several courts could compete for cases within the same sphere of law. All in all, it really was a mess, and Henry knew he had to sort it out.[9]

Henry was intelligent: he spoke Latin and French, and understood English, although he may not have been able to speak it. He was very well educated and had a quick and subtle mind that was excellent at solving problems. Of course, the previous 20 years had rendered the English exchequer virtually empty, so Henry applied his mind to remedying that deficiency, by instituting reforms. In fairly short order, the royal revenues were restored. His legal reforms earned him the title of 'the Father of the English Common Law'. He did not, of course, create common law since many of the tenets of the English Common Law had been actively applied since Roman times. He was responsible for the institutions and innovations that brought common law to a place whereby peace was restored in England. The chronicler *Gerald of Wales wrote:* 'He had at his fingertips a ready knowledge of nearly the whole of history and also the practical experience of daily affairs'.

Of course, there were the downsides to his character. The most evident of this was his uncontrollable temper. He is once alleged to have rolled around the floor of his bedchamber screaming with rage and stuffing his mouth with rushes torn from his bedding. This followed one of his attendants, having praised the king of Scotland in Henry's presence. That said, he did have a sense of humour. It is alleged that Bishop Hugh of Lincoln caused him to laugh by teasing him about the illegitimacy and loneliness of his ancestors. He was well able to divert arrows aimed at his pride, but when it came to questioning his royal authority, he took no prisoners.[10]

The most famous and enduring row of his entire reign was his prolonged animosity towards and feud with Thomas Beckett. Beckett, of lowly birth was irritatingly pompous and self-aggrandising. He once lectured Henry by saying, 'temporal lords should be obeyed, but not against God: as St Peter says we ought to obey God rather than men'. Henry is alleged to have instantly responded with the words, 'I do not want a sermon from you. Are you not the son of one of my peasants?' Beckett started off as one of Henry's most loyal friends and adherents. He was made chancellor because he was very good at collecting money, and at that time, Henry needed money to fill the empty royal coffers. What happened after that is in many ways a clash of two very similar personalities.

Henry's devious mind thought that he could bring both state and church under his rule, and that the best way to do this was to make his good friend and chancellor, Thomas Beckett, the Archbishop of Canterbury. Which he did. But then Beckett 'caught' religion, and, in an act which Henry for ever after believed to be treason and disloyalty, stood up for the rights of the church against the state. That was the main cause of their disaffection and we all know how it ended. More of the irritating archbishop later.

Although personality-wise, Henry was inferior to his genial predecessor, Stephen, in his abilities as a king, he was infinitely superior. L. F. Saltzman declares that the bulk of his English subjects were strongly prepossessed in his favour, and the church was on his side. The more important barons did not care who was king so long as their titles and revenues were confirmed. The lesser lords, and especially the peasants, were exhausted, made infinitely poorer by the 20 years of civil war. They welcomed a strong ruler who could curb the lawlessness that had broken out because Stephen had been completely incapable of doing that.

Henry was a very active man. He spent long hours in the saddle. He loved hunting and seldom sat down unless he had to. He was short and sturdy with, according to Saltzman, coarse hands and a freckled face. He did not care one whit for his dress and how he appeared but he could demonstrate an immense degree of courtesy and charm which made him formidable.[11]

Despite his ferocious temper, he mostly ruled his hot headedness with a cool, calculating mind. He had no great affinity for religion but was not impious. In the same way his morals could be lax, but he was not completely immoral. That said, he was known to be lusty and there is no evidence that any of his numerous mistresses were unwilling. He was emphatically a strong man but his major weakness, which was in the end to prove his ruin, was his affection for his family.

W.L. Warren perhaps encapsulates King Henry's view of how to run his now large empire best: 'He conceived the future of the Angevin dominions not as an empire but as a federation.' Henry was to be deeply disappointed, however, for his arrangements demanded strong fraternal affection, younger brothers' acceptance of their portions, and cooperation with their eldest brother, all of which his sons lacked. Henry's periodic proposals for changes in the succession fuelled their resentment of him and their jealousy of each other.

In other words, he saw himself as chairman of a family consortium, but his alone was the power to rule.[12]

His attitude to power cannot be unconnected to the events of his childhood. His mother had constantly struggled to gain the crown of England her father had wanted her to wear. One of Henry's major faults, and the one thing that destroyed him at the end of his life, was that he would never cede an ounce of land or give any responsibility to his sons. His attitude was that he was always right because he was the king.

In 1170, he made his eldest surviving son, Henry, co-regent, something unknown in England, and the latter's name became Henry, the Young King, but King Henry allowed him no power. When he made Richard Duke of Aquitaine, he permitted him no power whatsoever, even though Aquitaine was only connected to Henry by his marriage to Eleanor, who was vociferous that it was not Henry's to rule. As can be imagined, his sons, Henry, the Young King, Richard, Geoffrey, and to a lesser extent, John, found his stance unbearable, especially as, in character, they were similar to their father.[13]

In 1173, Henry proposed that his youngest son, John, should marry the daughter of Humbert of Maurienne who had no sons. As part of the agreement, Henry agreed to give John the castles of Chinon, Loudun, and Mirebeau, which prompted Henry, the Young King to rebel since he held them at the time and refused to give them up. In this, the younger Henry was egged on by King Louis, former husband of Eleanor and the young king's father-in-law. Eleanor sided with her sons against her husband and sent her sons Richard and Geoffrey, to the French court. The rebellion failed. The sons submitted, being presented as boys flexing their muscles. No such luck for Eleanor. Rebelling against one's husband was against the natural order of things. Henry captured and kept her imprisoned for 16 years until he died.[14]

In 1182, the whole situation got out of hand. His elder son, Henry the Young King, again threatened revolution against his father, whilst at the same time, being at war with his brother Richard. The younger Henry wanted all of his father's lands, including Aquitaine. Richard not only wanted to dismember the family federation, he would never give up the sovereignty of Aquitaine. This situation was exacerbated when Geoffrey joined his brother, Henry against Richard, who was then supported by King Henry. It is said that during this campaign, Henry the Younger and Geoffrey attempted to have their father killed.

By 1183, the younger Henry was perpetually short of money to fight Richard. He travelled through Richard's domain robbing shrines to pay his mercenaries but died of a fever on 11th June. Urgent messages were sent to his father, detailing the seriousness of his son's malady. King Henry thought they were a trap and ignored them, but both he and Queen Eleanor were devastated by the Young King's death. Geoffrey then allied himself with his youngest brother, John, and both went to war against Richard.

The last six years of the reign were somewhat chaotic. Henry tried to make Richard submit to his wish that John – called Lackland because he had no lands – should be given Aquitaine. Richard listened and asked for a few days to think about it. At which point, he slipped away and rode at full speed for Poitou, sending his father a message that nobody save himself would rule Aquitaine.

When King Henry was trying to mediate between the king of France and the Count of Flanders, John joined Geoffrey and they tried to raise Aquitaine against Richard, failing miserably. Richard retaliated by raiding Brittany, which belonged to Geoffrey. King Henry ordered all his sons to come to England for a meeting. In December 1184, a peace agreement was made between all of them. But, as can be imagined, it was superficial and had no chance of lasting given the personalities of all the participants. Henry then gave John charge of Ireland, but he only succeeded in alienating everyone, making fun of the Irish chieftains and pulling their beards.

By forcing Richard to cede power for Aquitaine to his mother, Eleanor, Henry at last prised it from his son's hands. In July 1186, Geoffrey died after being wounded at a tournament. He left a young son, Arthur. This left Richard and John as Henry's remaining sons. Richard had long been betrothed to Alice, daughter of Louis VII, but there was a long-standing rumour that she had been seduced by King Henry. Richard then attempted to get Henry to acknowledge him as his heir at the conference of Bonmoulins. Henry refused. Father and son were seen to walk off in different directions.[15] Henry immediately strengthened his defences in Anjou and Aquitaine. There were further rumours that he would name John as his heir.

In June 1189, Richard came armed to a conference in Le Mans, at which point, Henry immediately rode out, heading for Chinon. Richard pursued but was beaten back by a rear-guard left behind to protect the king. By this time, Henry was a very sick man. He began making arrangements to go on crusade, but asked for, and received, a list of the knights who had gone over to Richard's side. The last name on the list was John, his favourite son. The shock was such that he declined very quickly and died in early July 1189.

Richard, in the same way that King Henry had not believed his son, Henry, was ill, refused to believe his father was on his deathbed. It was only when a messenger sent by William Marshal gave him the news that he believed it. He travelled to his father's tomb at Fontevrauld Abbey. After saying a short prayer, he called William Marshal to attend him and went to take charge of his inheritance.[16]

Fun Fact

He was called Henry Curtmantle. Known to be on the short side, Henry wore an equally short cloak when the custom for kings was to wear a long flowing cloak. He may well have worn his cloaks short because he spent so many hours on horseback and a shorter cloak would not impede his movement.

William Marshal

There is no way this book *cannot* include a brief biography of William Marshal. Known as 'The Greatest Knight', for over 50 years he served five kings, Henry II, Henry the Young King, Richard I, John, and Henry III. His first biography *Histoire de Guillaume le Marechal* was written between 1225 and 1250 within a few years of his death and is regarded as an accurate account of his life.[17] It is also regarded as one of the best sources for depicting knightly chivalry: 'Here one can see chivalry as a living institution rather than as a mere inspiration for chivalric romances.'[18] For a fictional biography of William, I recommend 'The Greatest Knight' by Elizabeth Chadwick, who used the *Histoire* extensively for her account.

William, born 1146 or 1147, was the landless younger son of John Marshal, an adherent of King Stephen during the Anarchy, before changing sides to support the Empress Matilda. In order to pull John into line, Stephen ordered him to bring his young son to court as a hostage for his father's loyalty. When John reverted his allegiance to Matilda, Stephen would have been expected to have the young William executed, but he could not bring himself to do that to a child.

By the mid-1160s, William was a regular tourney competitor, in the household of Guillaume de Tankerville. During this time, he became a tourney champion, although in his early years, he did not always manage to make money by ransoming the knights he defeated. Through the Tankerville connection, he became known to Eleanor of Aquitaine, Henry II's queen, and when accompanying her in 1168, foiled an ambush attempting her abduction, only to be wounded and taken prisoner. After some months, Eleanor paid his ransom, and William was appointed to her household becoming familiar with her sons, Henry, Richard, Geoffrey, and the young John.

In 1170, William was appointed to be a tutor to Henry, the Young King, in the matter of arms. He remained loyal to the younger Henry through the revolt of Henry II's sons, but in 1182 was accused of having an affair with the Young King's wife, Marguerite. Given what we know of William's knightly code of conduct, it is unlikely he committed adultery, but may have been showing a degree of arrogance that led to false accusations.

He was dismissed from the younger Henry's service, later being cleared of all charges. William then returned to the younger Henry's court, being present at the latter's rampage of plundering religious shrines of gold and money. Soon after the defilement of the shrine at Rocamadour, the Young King died, probably of dysentery.

Before his death, the Young king asked Marshal to fulfil the vow he, Henry, had made and go to Jerusalem. On his former master's behalf, William did so, staying away for two years, before returning to the service of Henry II. He was given the wardship of Heloise of Kendal and control of her lands. During his time looking after Heloise's properties, William founded the priory at Cartmel.

During the last days of Henry II, when he was at war with his son, Richard, William was part of the rear-guard protecting the king as he fled Le Mans. Richard attempted to pursue his father, but Marshal unseated him, killing his horse, and making the point that he could have killed the prince had he so desired. He was, allegedly, the only man ever to unseat the Lionheart.

After Henry's death, Marshal was appointed to serve the new King Richard I, who in recognition of his loyalty gave him permission to marry the heiress Isabel de Clare, and take control of all her lands. They made a powerful couple, even though he was well over 40 at the time and she was in her late teens. There is ample evidence to indicate the marriage was very happy, and, at a time when noblemen took mistresses as a matter of course, there is no evidence that William did. They had five sons and five daughters.

When Richard departed for the crusades – he was another king who used England as a money pit spending only around four months in the country during his ten-year tenure on the throne – William was appointed as one of the council looking after the country. He found life difficult when John began plotting to usurp the throne, saying that Richard was dead and he should now be declared king. William stayed true to his oath of fealty to Richard.

When Richard died, many of the English nobility believed the throne should pass to Richard's nephew, Arthur, son of John's elder brother, Geoffrey, who had died in 1186. However, William supported John as king and gave his fealty to him. This caused him serious problems throughout John's reign, especially when William paid the French king, Philip II homage for his lands in Normandy. John took offence, causing William to leave court and go to his lands in Leinster, returning only at John's express command. He fell foul of John again when the latter waged war on the Braose and Lacy families, but he managed to steer his way through the maelstrom. Throughout the Barons' War, William remained loyal to John, who knew he could trust him to support the accession of his young son, Henry, after John's death.

This William did against serious opposition.[19] John died in October 1216 at Newark Castle. William took the young Henry III to Gloucester and held his coronation there, but instead of a crown, a coronet allegedly belonging to Henry's mother was used. And, since Stephen Langton, Archbishop of Canterbury had been told to leave England until the Barons' war was over, the nine-year-old was crowned by various prelates.[20]

By this time the French Prince Louis, supported by John's disaffected barons, was holding London. The French also held Lincoln.[21] This led to the now 70-year-old William, aided by Nicholaa de la Haye, Sheriff of Lincoln, attacking the invaders and expelling them from the city in 1217. For more details of William's leadership at the Battle of Lincoln, I recommend, Sharon Bennett Connolly's excellent biography of Nicholaa de la Haye.[22]

William died in May 1219 at the age of around 72, but before his death fulfilled a vow he had made some 30 years previously in Jerusalem, to become a member of the Knights Templar. He is buried at the Temple Church in London.

Thomas Becket

Of course, the huge elephant in the room when we are considering Henry II, has to be Thomas Becket, Archbishop of Canterbury. Gallons of ink have been spent writing about this most haughty of prelates, but no account of the reign of Henry II would be complete without mentioning him.

There was a good deal of strife between King Henry II and the church over the responsibilities of the ecclesiastical courts. And this led to the biggest scandal of his reign. He made his good friend, Thomas Beckett, chancellor, and therefore responsible for the rule of law, which was in a state of confusion and disarray after the Anarchy. However, the church kept interfering in legal matters that Henry thought were nothing to do with the church. With his quick and decisive mind, the king decided the best way to bring everything into some semblance of cohesion, logic and competence, was to support Thomas Beckett as the new Archbishop of Canterbury.

Beckett was quite as wily and intelligent as his king. He was, in some ways, very similar in character and although he came from the lower echelons of society, he grew pompous, overbearing, and with a superior attitude that put everybody's backs up. What actually happened was akin to the poacher becoming the gamekeeper and knowing all the tips and wrinkles known to poachers. From the moment Beckett transferred his allegiance solely to the power of the church, it was inevitable there would be a huge clash between monarch and prelate.

Thomas Beckett was born on 21 December, the feast day of St Thomas the apostle, in either 1119 or 1120 in Cheapside, London. His parents were of Norman descent, his father being either a small landowner or possibly a petty knight. His mother's family are believed to have originated, near Caen. By the time Thomas was born, his parents were living in London, his father's income generated by monies from rented properties in his ownership. He also served as sheriff of the city of London at some point.[23] One of Thomas' father's wealthy friends often invited the young Thomas to his estates where he discovered hunting and hawking. At the age of ten, he was sent to Merton Priory in Surrey and later attended a grammar school, possibly the one at St Paul's Cathedral. When he was around the age of 20 he spent some time at the University of Paris, but he did not study canon or civil law and his skill at Latin was always fairly basic.[24]

At some point during his education, his father suffered a financial reverse and Thomas was then forced to earn his living as a clerk. Later he gained a position in the household of Theobald of Bec, the Archbishop of Canterbury. He went on several missions to Rome for Theobald, and in 1154 the prelate created Thomas, Archdeacon of Canterbury. He was also given other ecclesiastical offices, including a number of benefices at Lincoln Cathedral and St Paul's Cathedral, and also the office of Provost of Beverley. In these posts, he was extremely efficient and this led Theobald to recommend him to Henry II for the vacant post of Lord Chancellor. Thomas became Lord Chancellor in January 1155.

King Henry sent his eldest son, Henry, to live in Beckett's household, since it was the custom at that time for noble children to be fostered into noble houses. As chancellor, Beckett was more than competent at enforcing the traditional sources of royal revenue exacted from all landowners, including those from the church and bishoprics. In 1162, when Theobald of Bec died, Beckett was nominated as Archbishop of Canterbury by a royal council of bishops and noblemen. It is not inconceivable that Henry hoped his friend would continue to put royal government ahead of the church, but Beckett became wholly engrossed in his new duties as archbishop. Although elected on 23 May 1162, he was not ordained as a priest until 2 June 1162 and on 3 June, he was consecrated as the Archbishop of Canterbury by Henry, Bishop of Winchester.[25]

The rift between Henry and Beckett began to grow when the new archbishop resigned his chancellorship in an effort to give himself time and energy to recover and extend the rights of the church. This led to a series of conflicts with King Henry, including the jurisdiction of secular courts over English clergyman. Antipathy between the two men accelerated and attempts by the king to turn the other bishops against Beckett began in 1163, when the king sought approval of the traditional rights of royal government with regard to the church. This led to the Constitutions of Clarendon – see later – a series of assemblies of the higher English clergy at Clarendon Palace in 1164. Beckett was officially asked to agree to the king's rights in terms of government and royal government and told that if he did not agree he would have to face the consequences.

Henry sought less clerical independence and a weaker connection with Rome, and used his skills to persuade the clergy to agree to his suggestions. Everyone agreed except Beckett. Eventually, even he said he was willing to agree to the substance of the Constitutions of Clarendon, but he refused to sign the documents. Henry then summoned him to appear before a council at Northampton Castle to answer allegations of contempt of royal authority and malfeasance in his running of the chancellor's office. He was convicted of those charges, stormed out of Northampton, and fled to Europe.

Henry pursued him with a series of edicts targeting not just Beckett but also the archbishop's friends. However, Louis VII of France had never forgiven Henry II for marrying Eleanor of Aquitaine only two months after the annulment of their marriage. The French king gave Beckett his protection and he spent nearly two years at the abbey of Pontigny. Henry continued to threaten him from a distance. Beckett fought back by threatening Henry and the bishops with excommunication and an interdict. He tried to get Pope Alexander III, to support him, but Alexander favoured diplomacy over direct action.

In June 1170, Henry's heir apparent, Henry the Young King, was crowned at York. This action breached Canterbury's privilege of coronation, and in November 1170, Beckett excommunicated the Archbishop of York, the

Bishop of London and the Bishop of Salisbury, who had all taken part in the 'illegal' coronation.

By December 1170, Henry II was celebrating Christmas in Normandy, and fulminating against what he perceived to be Becket's treachery. It was here that he is supposed to have said, 'Will no one rid me of this turbulent priest?' However, that is not actually what he said. A contemporary biographer, Edward Grimm, wrote his words as, 'what miserable drones and traitors, have I nourished and brought up in my household, who let their Lord be treated with such shameful contempt by a loan low born cleric?'[26]

Regardless of what Henry actually said, the net result was that four knights, Reginald FitzUrse, Hugh de Morville, William de Tracy, and Richard Brito on set out to confront Beckett at Canterbury. To give him his due, the instant Henry found out they had galloped off, and why, he immediately sent people after them but it was too late. The four had already sailed for England. According to the accounts of the monk, Gervase of Canterbury and Edward Grimm, the knights put their weapons under a tree outside the cathedral, hiding their armour under their cloaks before entering the cathedral. They told Beckett he must go to Winchester and give an account of his actions. Beckett refused. The knights retrieved their weapons and rushed back inside to kill him.

By this time Beckett was about to celebrate Vespers and his fellow monks tried to lock themselves in so that Beckett would be safe. However, he said to them that it was not right to make a fortress out of a house of prayer and ordered them to unlock the doors.

The four knights ran into the room crying, 'where is Thomas Becket traitor to the king and country?' They found him in the monastic cloister near the stairs leading up to the choir of the cathedral, where the monks were already chanting Vespers. Beckett is alleged to have said, 'I am no traitor, and I am ready to die.' At which point they murdered him.[27] When the monks prepared his body for burial, it is alleged that they found Beckett had been wearing a hair shirt under his archbishop's garments, which at that time was a sign of penance.

Henry II's response was immediate and, probably, utterly sincere. He was horrified.

Beckett was made a martyr and less than three years after his death, in 1173, he was made a saint. In 1173, his sister was appointed abbess of Barking as reparation for the murder of her brother, and in 1174, Henry humbled himself in public penance at the tomb and at the church office at Dunston's, which became the most popular pilgrimage site. Henry prostrated himself in front of the shrine that had been built to the murdered archbishop, spending the night in prayer and tears, not even getting up to go to the bathroom. It was the single most appalling thing that had happened to him during his reign, probably only to be superseded by the revolt of his wife and sons. He regularly visited the shrine when he was in England to demonstrate his sorrow and grief.

Becket's assassins fled north to Knaresborough for about a year. They were not arrested and Henry did not confiscate their lands, but he did not help them when they sought his advice in 1171. The Pope excommunicated all four. They travelled to Rome where the Pope ordered them to serve as knights in the holy lands for a period of 14 years. They obeyed and their penance inspired the creation of the Knights of St Thomas, which was formed in 1191 at Acre, the only military order native to England with a chapter in that city.

The monks were afraid that Beckett's body might be stolen, so his remains were placed beneath the floor of the eastern crypt of the cathedral with a stone cover over it. Two holes were bored through the stone so that pilgrims could insert their heads and kiss the tomb. In 1220, Becket's bones were moved to a new gold-plated, bejewelled, shrine behind the high altar in the Trinity Chapel. This shine became a magnet for pilgrims and has remained so to this day.

The Constitutions of Clarendon

As has been noted, Henry II stood very much on his honour, and held on to his possessions with a very tight grip. When he could not subdue Thomas Becket and felt that the clergy were getting above themselves, he called together a meeting in 1164, attended by most of the higher echelons of clergy, and the barons, to hammer out the limits of their remit within the boundaries of his domain. What he wanted set down in stone was a recognition of the 'customs, liberties and dignities of his predecessors' to be maintained as they had been in the time of his grandfather, Henry I and before.[28]

Basically, what Henry demanded was an agreement with his clergy and nobles that anyone found with a letter from the Pope or an archbishop declaring an interdict on England, was to be regarded as a traitor; that no member of the clergy or any clerk could come to England without an official letter permitting him to do so, or he would be imprisoned, and that anyone who obeyed any such interdict would be exiled with his whole family.[29]

There were a dozen or so points which were presented to the assembly. They included:

- That any controversy between laymen, or laymen and clerks regarding church patronages were the responsibility of the King's Court.
- That churches 'of the lord King's fee' could not be bestowed without his consent.
- That any clerks transgressing those rules were answerable to the king.
- That bishops and archbishops could not leave England without permission from the king.
- That nobody who held lands granted by the king could be excommunicated without his consent (see the problem this caused for Robert de Beaumont later).
- That any appeals should go upwards through a designated hierarchy and finally, to the king.
- That should an archbishopric or bishopric be vacant, its revenues and expenses became the responsibility of the king, and the king not only had the right to approve new appointments to vacant sees, the newly appointed candidate had to swear fealty to the king.

We must now look at two of Henry II's ministers in the earlier part of his reign. They had both been active in the courts of Henry I and Stephen. The year between the Treaty of Winchester in 1153, which agreed that Henry would succeed Stephen, gave the former plenty of time to sort out his household as Duke of Normandy. It was a useful time to make changes that would ensure his succession would be more palatable to his new ministers and other people of power in England. One of these was Theobald of Bec, the Archbishop of Canterbury who was very apprehensive about the young Henry's companions, known to be anti-clerical.

Immediately after his coronation, Henry appointed three men who had been in the service of King Stephen. He selected Richard de Lucy to be in charge of the royal administration. And as co-justiciar, Henry also appointed the second Earl of Leicester, Robert de Beaumont. The latter was at that time, probably the most powerful baron in England.[30] Henry's other appointment was Thomas Becket.

Robert of Leicester

Robert de Beaumont, 2nd Earl of Leicester – nicknamed Le Bossu or The Hunchback – was one of twins, born in 1104, his brother being Waleran, Count of Meulan. When their father died, Robert took over the English estates, but still retained lands in Normandy, while Waleran concentrated on the French holdings. Both brothers had fallen from favour after Stephen's captivity in 1141. However, it appears that Robert was always the practical one, and when he matured, revealed excellent statesmanlike abilities. Robert also realised that should the already 20-year-old civil war be allowed to continue, the barons themselves had quite as much to lose as the crown did. He tried to intercede in the private wars between barons in England, but knew the only solution was to support Henry in 1153 while the latter was still Duke of Normandy.[31]

Robert received schooling at the abbey in Abingdon and trained for knighthood at the court of King Henry I. He was said to be precocious in his degree of learning at school. As a co-justiciar, he was both prudent and discreet. His social position as Earl of Leicester ensured that he had a prominent position and he frequently appeared in public as Henry II's deputy. W.L. Warren opines that it is unknown if there was any formal division of duties between Robert and Richard de Lucy. He goes on to say it would not be surprising if Richard de Lucy provided professional expertise to the partnership and was more active, directing the administration. This left Robert free to concentrate his political judgement on situations, dealing with the barons and presiding over public sessions of the king's court when Henry was absent. The two apparently worked in complete accord.[32]

Robert was well placed for high office, but not simply because of his eminence. He had a lot of experience of government that had been acquired in his youth at the courts of Henry I and Stephen. However, Henry II was as unlike his predecessor as it was possible to be. Although Henry appointed Beaumont and de Lucy as justiciars, this most energetic of kings did not always cede them the powers they were permitted by tradition. One example of the latter concerned a wood owned by the abbey of St Albans, but that had been worked by the family of Peter of Valognes since the days of William the Conqueror. This is a tale of three Roberts. Robert of Valognes, the petitioner of the family, Abbot Robert of St Albans, and Robert Beaumont, Earl of Leicester.

Successive abbots had renewed the privilege of working the wood to the first Peter's descendants. In 1158, Abbott Robert, heard that the latest incumbent, called Peter like his ancestor, was on his deathbed. Abbot Robert sent two monks to ask for restitution of the wood. Peter readily agreed that his family held the wood, not by hereditary right, simply by the generosity of St Albans Abbey, and on his deathbed, made it over to the monks. That night Peter of Valognes died and Abbott Robert took possession of the wood.

Peter's successor was his brother, yet another Robert. He was reluctant to let go of the wood his family had held for almost a century, but his pleas to Abbott Robert were in vain. Robert of Valognes went to King Henry, then in France, and petitioned that the wood be handed back to his family. Because Henry was concerned about getting his barons' support, he gave Petitioner Robert a writ saying that he was not to be unjustly deprived of possessions that his ancestors had held. On his return to England, Valognes confronted Abbot Robert with the king's writ.

Abbot Robert then pointed out that there was no question of hereditary right involved in the matter and he refused to return the wood. Petitioner Robert was somewhat aggrieved, as you can imagine, so went to Robert Beaumont, Earl of Leicester and drew the earl's attention to the last words of the king's writ to the abbot which read, 'and unless you do it, Robert Earl of Leicester shall do it, lest he is further vexed for want of right'. The earl instructed the sheriff to summon Abbot Robert to answer the complaint, but the abbot did not consider he needed to be judged by Earl Robert and sent one of his monks instead. Now it was the earl's turn to be aggrieved. He summoned the abbot again, but the latter refused to appear. In his role as justiciar, the earl pronounced judgement – that the wood should return to Petitioner Robert 'by judgement of the Royal Court'. He instructed the sheriff of Hertfordshire to put Valognes in possession 'by Royal authority'. Are you still with me?

This is really where the whole thing should have ended. Except that Valognes reckoned he would only be allowed to enjoy the wood for a short time, so he started harvesting the timber at a rate of knots. This upset Abbot Robert because irreparable damage was being done to the wood, which indicates he had not yet given up the fight. Abbot Robert hastened to Earl Robert – which is ironic since he hadn't believed the earl worthy enough to pronounce judgement earlier in the dispute – and asked him to stop the wood being destroyed. Perhaps in a spirit of 'chickens coming home to roost', Earl Robert simply repeated his former judgement. With his nose now seriously out of joint, the abbot hot-footed it to Queen Eleanor and begged her to send a writ to Valognes condemning the damage he was causing. She did so, and Valognes did stop cutting down the wood for a while. But not for long.

Meanwhile back at the ranch…sorry, in the meantime, Abbot Robert had sent messengers to the Pope to whinge to him about what had happened. A letter came back from the Pope addressed to Theobald of Bec, Archbishop of Canterbury and Hilary, Bishop of Chichester, instructing them to require Valognes to restore the wood or 'do full justice to the monks within 30 days'.

If he failed to obey, the prelates were ordered to excommunicate him. But they were stuck between a rock and a hard place because King Henry II had forbidden his bishops to pronounce sentence of excommunication on any of his barons. Finally, after *many* delays and to-ing and fro-ing, caused by people not turning up at court when ordered to and using other delaying tactics, the wood was finally judged to belong to the abbey and therefore it was Abbot Robert's. Hurrah, or boo-hiss, depending on your viewpoint.

The reason that this is an important judgement is that although Robert Beaumont was a co-justiciar, and therefore allegedly had the power to hear pleas of this this kind, decide and pronounce on them, and issue orders which had the force of royal authority, he could only act on specific instructions from King Henry. This is another aspect of Henry's character in that he kept a firm hand on all his possessions. Because, in truth, most of the wasted time was due to Henry not being in England. But even then he did not allow his justiciars their rights in making decision in his absence.[33]

Earl Robert married Amice de Montfort and they had four children. He founded numerous religious establishments, including Leicester Abbey in 1144. The earl filled the office of justiciar for nearly fourteen years until his death, and earned the respect of the emerging Angevin bureaucracy in England. His opinion was quoted by learned clerics, and his own learning was highly commended.

Robert died on 5 April 1168, probably at Brackley in Northamptonshire. His entrails were buried at the hospital in Brackley. On his deathbed, he was made a canon of Leicester and was duly buried in the cathedral he founded, north of the high altar.[34]

Richard de Lucy

Richard de Lucy was born in 1089, his mother being the niece and heiress of William Goth. Henry I's papers refer to both Richard and his mother around 1130. The de Lucy family originated in Normandy in a town called Domfront, which was close to the area in which Henry I had many connections and this is probably what initially brought the family to that king's attention.

The first mention of Richard is in *The Book of Fees* around 1212 and states that Henry I granted land from his own holdings in Suffolk to Richard de Lucy.[35] The family held other lands in England. How and when they acquired them is not known, however, it seems clear that the de Lucys had strong roots in Normandy and hereditary lands on both sides of the

Channel. Richard achieved some prominence during the early years of Stephen's reign and witnessed his first known charter for King Stephen in Oxford in 1136.[36] Although it is not known for certain, it is possible that he came straight into Stephen's household from that of Henry I, or there is a possibility that he was serving Stephen before the latter came to the throne.

What is clear is that Richard was very knowledgeable in military matters fairly early in the reign, because in October 1138, he was in command of the garrison at Falaise and successfully repelled Geoffrey of Anjou's siege. He appears to have spent most of the rest of the reign in England, frequently in attendance on Stephen.

What made him particularly useful to Stephen, was the fact that much of Richard's estates were in Norfolk, Suffolk, and, most especially, in Kent. Since those counties adjoined the centre of Stephen's power in London, he was a useful and valued member of the king's court. So much so that Stephen granted him further lands in Essex and Sussex. He was granted the manor of Chipping Ongar and built a castle there, encouraging the development of the town and generally being mindful of his responsibilities to the locality. Such was his standing with other barons, especially in Essex, he married two of his daughters to prominent Essex barons. These were very desirable and useful political links as well as being a sure sign of Richard's status in the royal service.

Unlike Robert de Beaumont, who was very supportive of Henry, Duke of Normandy's claim to succeed Stephen after the latter's death, Richard de Lucy was among the courtiers who did not, initially, have that level of loyalty to Henry. That said, he had a long history of being staunchly faithful to the monarch, and Henry, when he became King Henry II, valued this and recognised it. In fact, during the peace treaty between Stephen and Henry in 1153, Richard was made guardian of the Tower of London and Windsor Castle. And when Henry succeeded Stephen, Richard handed both castles over to Henry without any problems. That may have been because his son was being held as a hostage for his good faith.

The new king appointed him co-justiciar along with Robert de Beaumont, second Earl of Leicester, and this raised his status quite dramatically, as well as providing Henry with an experienced and very effective administrator. Although he was never officially the designated Sheriff of Essex under Stephen, he submitted accounts for the county farm for 1155, which included the three months before Henry's coronation, and paid more money into the royal coffers than any other sheriff in that year. His accounts were very detailed and this demonstrated his familiarity with government and stability within government, something that Henry was very anxious to restore after 20 years of civil war. Richard became one of Henry's most useful and valued courtiers, high in the king's favour.

In 1158, Richard was relieved of his duties in Essex, probably because King Henry preferred to have him on hand at all times, concentrating on his job as justiciar. It was in this role that his fame and influence grew. He worked closely and harmoniously with most of the leading barons and nobles at Henry's court. These included, of course, Robert Earl of Leicester and Thomas Beckett. But he had connections with numerous lords, building solid support within the court structure.

He did not get forget his family and it is known that he supported his brother, Walter, to become Abbot of Battle Abbey in 1139 under Stephen's rule. The brothers were reasonably close, but Walter had much less ambition than Richard. And this, allied with Richard's reluctant to press too hard to raise his brother's profile, may have contributed towards the fact that he was not known to press for family honours. Any kinsman who are known to have been elevated, only benefited now and again, if at all, from their connection with him.

His brother Walter, still the Abbot of Battle, died in 1171 and Richard attended him in his final illness and then became the protector of Battle Abbey. He safeguarded its privileges during the four-year vacancy before the next abbot took office. So influential was Richard that when he eventually asked Battle Abbey to give him the church of Wye in Kent for his son Godfrey, the monks tried to stop this from happening and took their case to a church council. However, no churchmen present at the council wanted to argue the abbey's case for fear of incurring Richard's displeasure. Meanwhile Godfrey, his son, was a canon of Exeter and Richard, clearly recognising the usefulness of education available in continental schools for a man destined for a career in the church, sent him to study abroad.

Richard took his responsibilities seriously and amply demonstrated the trust in which Henry placed him. Justice being one of Richard's chief concerns, in 1166 he was sent with Geoffrey de Mandeville, Earl of Essex on the first of the revived judicial eyres. (An eyre was a circuit travelled by itinerant justices to hear cases and inspect the holdings of the monarch's vassals.)

Henry was so frequently absent from England that the burden of government fell upon Richard and Robert de Beaumont. That burden grew heavier as Henry sought to tighten his control over his kingdom with new procedures and declarations of royal authority. One of these innovations being the Constitutions of Clarendon. Richard is alleged to have been one of the authors and he was excommunicated for it in 1166. He had also been instrumental in Beckett's election to the see of Canterbury a few years earlier, but then incurred the enmity of the Beckett supporters.

After the death of Robert de Beaumont in 1168, Richard continued to run the administration of government for another decade. The last ten years of his life were in fact the most illustrious of his career. Gervase of Canterbury called him, 'the most powerful man in the kingdom'[37] and in 1176, according to chronicler, Roger, of Howden, he was the king's most cherished courtier. Even that did not stop Henry taking the castle at Chipping Ongar away from him to emphasise the intensity of the king's determination to confiscate castles from barons who might pose a threat to his throne.

During the first revolt of Henry's sons in 1173, Richard led the loyalist forces in England and he negotiated a truce with the King of Scotland. He became the person to consult in any legal controversy, and his writings and opinions were still being referred to and acted upon long after he died in 1179. Also in 1173, Richard was made Constable of Salisbury Castle. He also held lands in Wiltshire and was heavily involved in the military affairs in that county. In 1175 he was Sheriff of Worcestershire. There was a proliferation of up and coming younger de Lucy's in the 1170s, and although nobody can say that they were all related to Richard de Lucy, it was a fairly rare name at that time. So there is some evidence to suggest that the younger family were gaining power in influential circles.[38]

In 1178, Richard founded at the house of Augustinian canons at Lesnes (or Westwood), which was dedicated to the Virgin and Richard's erstwhile colleague, now a saint, Thomas Beckett.

Richard retired as a justiciar in the summer of 1179 and then became a canon at Lesnes, dying there a few months later.[39]

Richard I – The Lionheart

RICHARD WAS BORN in September 1157, the third son of Henry II and Eleanor of Aquitaine. As a junior son, he was not expected to succeed to the throne. However, his eldest brother, William, died in infancy and Henry, the Young King, died in 1183, six years before Henry II.

In appearance, Richard grew to be tall—possibly around 6'2/3". His hair was red/gold like his father's and his eyes were grey. He was graceful with an athletic build, although in his later years he became somewhat hefty. He is known to have had a love of poetry and music, and of fine clothing – attributes probably inherited from his mother, Eleanor of Aquitaine. Richard is generally acknowledged to have been his mother's favourite child. He is known to have spoken French and Occitan, which is the old language of Provence. He also inherited, in full measure, the infamous Plantagenet hot temper,[1] with Richard Heiser describing him as a boastful, southern, French, absentee, monarch.[2] His temper, of course, caused him to always be at odds with his father and brothers. He was also known as Richard Yes-and-No, possibly a reference to his habit of terse responses to questions.[3] Although he was born in England, and spent some of his childhood in England, his preferred home was his territories in France.

At the age of 11 he was given the duchy of Aquitaine, and enthroned as duke in 1172. In 1169, his father betrothed him to Alys (Alice), half-sister to Eleanor of Aquitaine's daughters by Louis VII of France, and sister to Philip II of France. Aged eight, Alys was sent to England and by 1177, the Pope threatened to excommunicate Henry if the marriage did not go ahead. It didn't. Not only that but rumours soon spread Henry had taken Alys as a mistress and had a child by her.

Richard was always fascinated by military matters and knightly behaviours. He learned very quickly how to control the aristocracy of Poitou and Gascony but had few filial feelings towards his father. Having joined his brothers in the Great Rebellion of 1173–1174, he finally submitted to his father and received a pardon. Richard was a very harsh overlord and this resulted in the inhabitants of Gascony, calling on the help of his elder brother, Henry, the Young King, and his younger brother Geoffrey to drive Richard out of his duchy altogether. To prevent this, Henry II supported Richard. Then Henry the Young King died very suddenly and the uprising crumpled.

With the death of the younger Henry, Richard became heir to England, Normandy, and Anjou. His father wished him to yield Aquitaine to his youngest brother, John. However, Richard, definitely his father's son, refused to surrender the duchy in which he had virtually grown up and even appealed to the young Philip II of France for aid. In 1189, he openly joined forces with Philip to drive Henry into submission and harried him to his death.[4]

Upon Henry's death, one of Richard's first actions was to free his mother, Eleanor of Aquitaine. Eleanor then announced Richard's betrothal to Berengaria of Navarre. However, virtually as soon as Richard had been crowned, he embarked for Jerusalem to fight in the crusades. Not one to be put off anything upon which she had decided, Eleanor, around 65 years of age, travelled to collect Berengaria from Navarre. Richard repudiated his betrothal to Alys, and when his mother arrived in the Mediterranean with his new bride, Richard married her in Cyprus. This infuriated Philip II, who then fell out in a big heap with Richard, but, in an effort to salvage something, offered Alys to Prince John. Eleanor stopped that, too.

On crusade, Richard conquered Sicily and Cyprus besieged Jerusalem, which was held at that point by Saladin. Richard is known to have caught sight of Jerusalem's 'glittering roofs' but Saladin defeated him. Richard's lieutenants fulfilled their vow of paying homage at the Holy Sepulchre, having been given safe conduct by Saladin, but Richard did not go, presumably because he had been defeated by Saladin and wanted no favours from an infidel.

He then diverted to recapture the city of Acre and fortified other coastal cities, which ensured that Christianity survived in the region for at least the next hundred years. Richard decided to sail back to England. But bad weather forced him to land at Corfu.[5]

The Byzantine emperor objected to Richard's annexation of Cyprus on his way down to the crusades, so Richard then set sail again with just four attendants, but his ship was wrecked and he was forced to land and undergo a hazardous over-ground journey through central Europe. Shortly before Christmas 1192, he was captured by Leopold of Austria. Leopold believed Richard had arranged the murder of his cousin, Conrad, and he had also offended Leopold by throwing down the latter's standard from the walls of Acre.[6]

Leopold of Austria sold Richard to the Holy Roman Emperor, Henry VI, and the latter demanded a ransom of 150,000 marks (roughly £99,000 in

2024) – literally a king's ransom. It was, of course, raised from English taxes because most of the early Plantagenet kings regarded England as a cash cow. The money was raised mainly by Richard's mother, Eleanor, but later on England was again taxed to pay for Richard's protection of his lands in France against Philip II of France, now his implacable enemy.

It is also said that during his captivity, he first gained the soubriquet, 'Lionheart' when he came across a maiden being threatened by a lion. Richard is said to have used 40 silk handkerchiefs to subdue the lion, before reaching down its throat and pulling out its still beating heart. He then sat down, added salt to the heart and ate it. Nobody has ever explained where the silk handkerchiefs came into the equation, but the lion was allegedly let loose by the emperor to kill Richard. This legend spread very quickly and cemented Richard's reputation as a fearless warrior.[7]

Whilst he had been in captivity, his younger brother John had caused problems at home, spreading rumours that Richard was dead and he should be crowned king. He went so far as to ally himself with Philip II to offer the Holy Roman Empire Emperor 80,000 marks (about £53,000 in 2024) to keep Richard a prisoner. Henry refused the offer because he needed more than that to assert his rights over southern Italy, so he continued to hold out for the full ransom demand. The money to rescue Richard was transferred to Germany by the emperor's ambassadors, but 'at the Kings peril'. This means that, had it been lost or stolen on its journey to Henry, Richard would have been held responsible. He was finally released in February 1194 and Philip II sent a message to John which said, 'look to yourself; the devil is loose'.[8]

Richard is known to have been a valiant and fairly competent military leader as well as extremely courageous. However, he was in many ways a military failure. He was reckless and egotistical to his own detriment.[9] Perhaps had he been less arrogant with Leopold of Austria and the Holy Roman Emperor, his imprisonment might have been shorter and less arduous – at one point he was held in chains. He spent most of the last five years of his reign, protecting his French lands. He died from an arrow wound that went gangrenous in 1199, whilst besieging the castle of Chalus.

His opinion of his younger brother John was dismissive and certainly not something that would persuade the younger brother adhere to him. When told that John had tried to usurp his throne. Richard is alleged to have said, 'forgive him. He is merely a boy.' At this point, John was actually 27 years of age.

Richard is also known to have been concerned solely with money and boasted that he would sell London if the price was right. This pronouncement along with other lands and preferments he had sold led much of the population to believe that the Jewish moneylenders were to blame for the fact the king appeared to be selling England. This led directly to attacks on the Jews and the massacre at Clifford Tower in York in 1190.[10]

Richard was not as good as his father at judging character. He inherited most of his councillors from Henry II, but his own choice as justiciar, William de Longchamp, was so unbearably arrogant he offended everybody and their cat! Longchamp was forced to flee, ending up on the beach at Dover disguised as a washerwoman and being pursued by a sailor. One has to wonder about the state of the sailor's eyesight. More of Longchamp later. Nicholas Vincent opines that Richard, as well as John, was responsible for the collapse of the Plantagenet empire in France.[11]

So why has this amazing legend of a heroic conqueror come down through the last 1,000 years? The fact that he is known to have been obsessed by defeating Saladin and reclaiming Jerusalem for the Christians has to be a large part of his reputation. The struggle of the intrepid and fearless monarch protecting Christendom against the infidel – the age-old struggle of good vs evil. Recently, his reputation has been more rigorously examined, but nobody can deny that Richard the Lionheart is still regarded by most people as one of the best monarchs England ever had.

It is difficult to write of Richard's 'favourites' since his overwhelming obsession was fighting. So I am covering the two most well-known of those he left in charge of England while he was absent.

Fun Fact

Richard embodied the chivalric code and the ideals of knighthood, believing in the importance of honour, loyalty, and courage. He became not just a role model for knights but his code of chivalry became his legacy in medieval European culture.

William Longchamp

William Longchamp was elevated to royal chancellor, then Bishop of Ely, and finally to chief justiciar in June 1190, at which point, Richard the Lionheart ordered everyone to obey his new appointee. At about that time, it was made known that the Pope had made Longchamp his legate for Britain because the Archbishop of Canterbury was, at that time, on crusade. Longchamp exercised so much power and 'forged his spiritual and secular authority into a formidable two-edged sword'. One chronicler stated that the justiciar had 'three tides and three heads' and that 'he had become Caesar and more than Caesar'.[12] To emphasise that power, the king made it known that after following Prince John's release from his oath to remain out of England, he would only be allowed back into England if Longchamp said so. Richard's degree of trust created an unbelievably arrogant and ambitious underling, who rode roughshod over everyone. In the end it proved his downfall.

Longchamp was apparently quite short in stature and compensated for it with an unbelievable degree of hubris, counting on Richard's affection and presuming on the king's goodwill. It was also said his haughtiness nearly equalled that of royalty. The general opinion was he had been elevated beyond his social station and was regarded as an upstart. Longchamp's major vulnerability was his immense pride. The following example of his treatment of Bishop Hugh of Durham is a perfect example of his behaviour.

He ousted Bishop Hugh of Durham from the government at a time when Hugh was a fellow justiciar, who had been chosen by Richard. What cemented Longchamp's total power was his possession of the Royal Seal of Absence, which meant that while Richard was absent from England, Longchamp had complete control of the administration of the realm. Bishop Hugh of Durham had failed to control bouts of anti-Semitism in northern England at the time of Richard's accession, and Longchamp used this as another reason to oust him.

After the Council of Nonancourt in March, 1190, Longchamp immediately returned to England, and Bishop Hugh followed a few days later. Longchamp used Hugh's delay to exclude him from the exchequer at Westminster, after which he went up to Yorkshire and punished those guilty of the massacre in Clifford's Tower. By doing this, Longchamp usurped Hugh's authority in the North. He went further by sending an armed force to York, sacking the sheriff, and deciding on punishments and imprisonments.

When he heard what had happened, Hugh set out from Westminster to confront Longchamp and demand that he respect Hugh's royal commission as a justiciar of the North. Longchamp proposed they wait a few days before discussing it further. At that subsequent meeting, Longchamp outmanoeuvred Hugh by showing documentation he held authority from Richard confirming everything that he had done was legal. Bishop Hugh was stripped of his acquisitions and made to surrender his own son as a hostage. Despite the fact he was a cleric, Hugh followed many of his colleagues in having illegitimate children.

Finally, Hugh appealed to Richard, who ordered restitution of all his properties, except Windsor Castle, but left Longchamp as sole justiciar. Now in complete control, Longchamp carried out all the functions of government without let or hindrance. To give him his due, he was speedy and effective. One scholar quoted him as being 'plainly an efficient superintendent of Royal business'. He was also very energetic, making sure that everything was carried out efficiently.[13]

He reintroduced shrievalties and made further adjustments to the roster by removing sheriffs, replacing them with men from his own household.[14] In the end, men from Longchamp's household occupied 13 counties, so the spread of his rule across England was considerable. He also supervised royal castles. Many of the constables of those castles were also his men. He was given the keys of the Tower of London and Dover Castle by Richard. He named a member of his own entourage as constable of the Tower. He also put his brother-in-law in charge of Dover Castle.

He tried to replace Gerard de Camville at Lincoln Castle with one of his own supporters, but the opposition he encountered was so determined, his attempt failed. At the centre of Longchamp's belief was that he must retain control over all castles, since any conflict which might arise would inevitably centre on those fortifications that could be held by the opposition. So, he spent a large amount of money making sure as many castles as he could were in good order and had 'his' people in charge of them. There is some evidence that the castles receiving his attention indicate he was aiming to undermine Prince John, who had vast holdings given to him by Richard, making him the greatest lord in England. What supports this view even more is that all the renovated castles were located either in or very close to those John either owned or which were owned by his associates. Longchamp seems to have regarded Prince John as his nemesis for his behaviour towards the king's brother was threatening and aggressive, if not provocative, and totally the wrong thing to do to someone who regarded slights at every touch and turn, *never* forgot them, and bided his time before taking his revenge.

Longchamp worked extremely hard to raise as much money for the royal coffers as he could, and virtually every penny he raised was sent to Richard for the crusades. He was very effective in defending law and order. This is demonstrated by the fact that the Jewish community for the remainder of his tenure as justiciar was secure because of the effectiveness of his actions. He also committed to holding councils and filling vacancies in the English church and his leadership here does seem to have been mainly well-received because the bishops of England banded together to sign a petition seeking a renewal of his appointment as Legate to the Realm in 1191.

Longchamp is only known to have held one ecclesiastical council – in the autumn of 1190 – and although he tried to use it as an opportunity to display his own power, the less than harmonious relationship between monastic cathedral chapters and prelates surfaced. It was not resolved until the Council of Westminster, which then obeyed instructions from the Pope.

He attempted to fill any vacancies in monasteries with his family. His brother Henry was appointed to Crowland Abbey in Lincolnshire in 1190, and he tried to install another brother, Robert, as Abbot of Westminster in 1191. John encouraged the Westminster monks to renege on the agreement to appoint Robert and elect their own abbot. Longchamp imposed an abbot upon St Guthlac's in Herefordshire, but the monks ejected his appointee and threw the man out together with his bedding.[15]

The reactions of the monasteries to Longchamp are a good indication of the mood towards him by the kingdom as a whole. He was described as more savage than a wild beast and a modern historian wrote that he employed *indelicate vigour*. He became the focus of all the disaffection in England.[16] The causes for his downfall are many, some of them beyond his power to control. Mostly, his innate arrogance and highhandedness doomed him. Richard's absence further undermined him because had the king been geographically closer to England, his backing might have preserved Longchamp's power. However, another factor was that, by the late twelfth century, there was a distinct undercurrent of feeling that wished to sever 'Englishness' from any kind of relationship with the Normans and Normandy.

Of course, Prince John turned all this to his advantage. There were rumours that Longchamp's grandfather had been a peasant. This was raised by two people known to be hostile to Longchamp and associates of John, Gerald of Wales, and Hugh of Nonant, Bishop of Coventry. They asserted that his grandfather had been a runaway serf, but David Balfour argues that Longchamp's grandfather may well have been in the lower ranks of the aristocracy.[17] They also accused Longchamp of ruling England without reference to his associate justiciars, all of whom, were English, presumably believing them to be inferior to a Norman. Both those things were untrue. But John further fed the flames by saying that Longchamp was importing 'foreigners and unknown men' and turning the realm over to them.[18]

The truth is, he did not violate any royal constitution; his behaviour and supreme arrogance alienated everybody with whom he came into contact. That pride heightened the natural xenophobia of the English, so as he progressed through the kingdom, he and his entourage became the target for more and more animosity. As a further example of this, in 1191, when

Walter of Coutances, Bishop of Rouen, arrived from Sicily with Richard's instructions that Longchamp should incorporate him into the inner circle of advisers, Longchamp ignored the order. He claimed he knew Richard better than anybody else and declared the letters Walter bought were fraudulent.

Meanwhile, popular opinion continued to rise against him. He ignored it because his unshakeable confidence in Richard's support made him careless, and his actions then snowballed into disaster. His basic approach to every issue was to use the free hand Richard given him to swat people he considered to be his enemies as if they were flies. He attacked William Marshal's castle at Gloucester, a recent purchase from Richard. This was unbelievably stupid because Marshal was never an overt threat to Longchamp. All Longchamp's actions isolated him from those who might have been able to help him. Marshal was always unfailingly loyal to whichever king he had given his fealty. He would have counselled Longchamp had he been given the opportunity. Complaints against the justiciar were chasing Richard across Europe, but the king was reluctant to do anything, and proved to be two-faced about his actions. On the one hand, he told Longchamp he had all the power he needed to do as Richard wanted him to, whilst at the same time, pretending to hear the protests and granting the wishes of the protesters.

Queen Eleanor of Aquitaine is generally credited with achieving the final breakthrough when she delivered the complaints to Richard in Sicily. It's also said that she might have had a moderating influence on her youngest son, Prince John, in England. However, as soon as she left to collect Berengaria from Navarre and take her to Richard in the Mediterranean, John surfaced and actively undermined Longchamp. There appears to have been a twofold strategy aimed at clipping Longchamp's wings without actually taking his powers away from him unless the situation became untenable. Richard's trust appeared unshakeable, but he fully realised that if he could not preside over a peaceful and tranquil kingdom there were serious difficulties confronting his desire to go on crusade.

Walter de Coutances, Archbishop of Rouen, was given a satchel of letters from Richard to use as he deemed fit. There were instructions regarding the election of an archbishop of Canterbury and a directive that the Lincolnshire manor of Kirton in Lindsay be turned over to William Longsword, the king's half-brother. Two further letters, one addressed to Longsword and the other to William Marshal, commanded that Walter de Coutances be admitted to the regency council as long as he remained in England and that he should be responsible for the election of the new Archbishop of Canterbury. William Marshal's letter instructed him to act upon Walter's instructions.

By the time Archbishop Walter arrived in England, Prince John and Longchamp had faced off before the walls of Lincoln Castle.[19] John saw his position regarding the succession to the throne as being at risk, should Richard die whilst on crusade. It did not help that Richard then declared Prince Arthur of Brittany to be his heir. And that, combined with Longchamp's growing domination of England made Prince John's position untenable. So much so he wrote to the monks of Canterbury and remonstrated with them against electing Longchamp as the new archbishop. By this time John, travelling about the country with a large retinue of barons, was fortifying castles and when Gerard de Camville, Constable of Lincoln Castle, paid homage to John, Longchamp regarded it as an offence against the crown. This was the state of affairs facing Archbishop Walter when he landed on 11 June 1191. Walter had a difficult situation in front of him because he had to restrain Longchamp without overtly going over to Prince John's side.

There was a meeting at Winchester and John, who could not risk being ousted as the Bishop of Durham had been, arrived with 4,000 Welsh soldiers and called on people to join him. Longchamp responded in kind and called out a force of mercenaries to escort him. Under tremendous pressure, a treaty was cobbled together that pushed both opponents away from the brink of outright war. They swore to act honourably, to reconvene in the event of any future conflict, and also to abide by whatever decisions were concluded. Marshal was required to restore Lincoln Castle to Gerard de Camville and John returned Nottingham and Tickhill castles, but, according to Ralph Turner, those castles went to William de Wendeval, and other allies of Prince John. John left Winchester with no more power in government than he had held before, but the agreement gave Walter of Coutances time to assess what Longchamp was really doing. Within days it became apparent a change was vital.

Longchamp had sent orders forbidding Geoffrey Plantagenet, brother to the king and Prince John, to land in England and decreed that no letters from the Pope must enter the kingdom. He sent people to the Continent to prevent Geoffrey from embarking from Flemish ports. This was directly opposing John, who had been trying to encourage Geoffrey to come to England. Longchamp ordered that, should Geoffrey arrive in England, he was to be arrested. This was regarded as a complete outrage. It ended with the Angevin Geoffrey Plantagenet fleeing to Dover Priory for safety and then being unceremoniously dragged from sanctuary to a place of imprisonment, purely because Longchamp declared he must be arrested and imprisoned. It was the final nail in the justiciar's coffin. And not before time.

What then happened was that the Bishop of Coventry contacted John and prodded him to do something about the situation. John summoned the Council at Marlborough, where he made serious complaints that the Peace of Winchester had been broken and his brother Geoffrey had been unlawfully seized. Longchamp was ordered to meet the council. But he sent a representative instead. His arrogance was the last straw and the council was urged to remove him from office. This was significant because it made Walter de Coutances the spokesman for the council – not Prince John. Longchamp heard rumours that John had dispatched troops to London. He fled to the Tower of London, beseeching Londoners to shut the gates to anybody who tried to force their way in. He was received with howls of derision, insults, and accusations that he was a traitor.

The council assembled in the open air in front of the Tower. Those assembled there declared they did not want to have Longchamp reigning over them and he was deposed. He then surrendered to John and the council, defended his work and tried to justify his actions.

He also surrendered the king's seal and fled to Dover so anxious was he to escape from the country. Having disguised himself as a washerwoman in an attempt to remain undiscovered, he was accosted by a sailor – one can only assume the man was unbelievably drunk, or that Longchamp had had time to shave in his headlong flight. Or perhaps it was dark! The sailor tried to woo him and was infuriated when he found out that the person he thought was a prostitute was actually a man. Brings a whole new meaning to the phrase 'Hello, Sailor'.

Longchamp played a part in the deal with the Holy Roman Emperor to release Richard and returned to England with the king. He was made Sheriff of Essex and Hertfordshire, but yet again, fell out with too many people to remain in post. Thereafter, he accompanied Richard on his travels to Europe. Longchamp died in Poitiers in 1197 whilst on a diplomatic mission for Richard to Rome.

Walter de Coutances

Walter de Coutances (or Walter of Coutances) was born in Cornwall, but we don't know when. He probably received an education in a school, possibly in Paris, because he was usually called *Magister*. The chronicler, Gerald of Wales, declared that he was a 'talented courtier'.[20] His brother was already in service at the court of Henry II and this may have greased the wheels and begun Walter's career as a royal clerk. He was a canon – probably an administrative role – in Rouen Cathedral by 1169. By the 1170s, he had risen to prominence as the chaplain for Henry, the Young King, but when, in 1173, the younger Henry rebelled against his father, Walter returned to the elder Henry's service.[21]

He learned the Angevin way of administration under Henry II and was given first the bishopric of Lincoln and then of Rouen. It is sometimes confusing to remember that nationality was of no matter at all in the reign of the Angevin kings, since their territories covered England from the Scottish border, across the Channel and as far south as the Mediterranean. Whether English or French was irrelevant until the later years of Richard, who only spent a few months in England, and then John who lost most of the territories across the Channel, whereupon there was a move towards 'Englishness'.[22]

Back in England, Walter became Archdeacon of Oxford and was in this post in 1176. King Henry sent him on diplomatic missions to the courts of Flanders and France and on his return, he was given administrative charge of Wilton and Ramsey abbeys, both of which required new abbots. This appointment allowed him to collect the revenues from both abbeys in Henry's name.[23]

He became Bishop of Lincoln in 1183, was ordained as a priest, consecrated in July of that year, and enthroned at Lincoln Cathedral in December. He helped the schools in Lincoln, which led to Gerald of Wales accusing him of increasing the debt of the diocese and squandering its resources. He was a curial bishop, which meant that his role was primarily an administrative and court one, the term 'curial' meaning a court that had administrative jurisdiction over civil matters.

In 1184, Walter became Archbishop of Rouen, a post more or less preferred on him by Henry II, who had rejected nominees from the chapter of Rouen Cathedral, before suggesting three English bishops, whilst making it plain he wanted Walter in the post. As usual, Henry got his way. These posts meant that it gave the incumbent an independent way of accomplishing wealth and status while not being completely dependent on the king.[24] The chronicler William of Newburgh states that Walter hesitated to accept Rouen since it was poorer than Lincoln, but Rouen was an archbishopric whereas Lincoln was a bishopric, so it appears that Walter allowed his increased status to overcome the possible reduction in his revenues.[25]

Walter continued to work for Henry II and was appointed to help arbitrate between Henry II and the future Richard the Lionheart – at that time an ally of King Philip II of France – over the latter's desire to cement his inheritance of the English throne, something Richard believed his father would confer on Prince John. Of course, the participants were of much the same character and could not agree on anything. Henry rejected the terms put forward by Richard and Philip, that he should name Richard as his heir and that Prince John should go on crusade with him.

When Henry died in 1189, Walter de Coutances absolved Richard of his sins in rebelling against his father. Richard took Walter with him to Sicily where the new king began the third crusade. The archbishop acted as negotiator between Messina and the crusaders, and later was the guarantor of the peace treaty between Richard and Tancred of Sicily. Then word reached Richard that Longchamp, the justiciar he had left in charge of England was in dispute with Prince John, so Richard sent Walter back to England to sort things out. Poisoned chalice or what!

As a sting in the royal command's tail, Richard released Walter from his vow to go on crusade – for a fee, naturally. Walter returned to England accompanied by Queen Eleanor of Aquitaine. The tale of how that turned out is covered in the segment on William Longchamp. After Longchamp was exiled, around 1193, Walter was made Justiciar. He had a lot of experience in matters pertaining to the Chancery, but not much when it came to judicial problems. At that time, he was also concentrating on raising Richard's ransom. This effectively made the role of justiciar allied more with the Exchequer than with administering justice in England. He issued writs in Richard's name, not his own, stressing that his decisions were made with the advice and consent of the leading nobles, something that aided the transition from the high-handed ways of Longchamp.

Upon hearing that Richard was being held captive, Prince John attempted to persuade everyone that the king was dead and he should be crowned. This was rejected, so John crossed the Channel, swore fealty to Philip II for Richard's territories in France, and then returned to England and incited a rebellion. Walter besieged Windsor Castle. When Prince John heard that Richard was about to be released, he fled to France.

Walter went to the court of the German emperor and became a hostage to ensure that the final payment of the ransom was made. Richard never paid it, and Walter ended up paying 10,000 marks to obtain his release. From that time onwards, he played no part in England's affairs, returning to Normandy and attempting to secure restitution for the losses Rouen had suffered in the war between Richard and Philip. Since Hell would have frozen over before either monarch agreed to that, Walter abandoned Rouen, only returning when both kings needed a guarantor for the Treaty of Louviers. The archbishop subsequently quarrelled with Richard and laid Normandy under an interdict, saying that Richard had built the Château Gaillard on his land without his consent.

After Richard's death, Walter accepted John as the new king despite his personal preference being for Arthur of Brittany. However, John managed to persuade him to change his mind. Little is known of his later years. He died in 1207.[26]

King John

I HAVE TRIED to give some/interesting facts about each monarch I have covered, but that might well be a problem with King John. He is known to most people through film and television screens conspiring – sometimes with the aid of the Sheriff of Nottingham – to usurp the throne from his heroic elder brother, Richard, and being obstructed by the noble, loyal, Robin Hood, usually looking very much like Errol Flynn or Kevin Costner depending on your age![1] John has, and with reason, come down through 900 years with the soubriquet 'Bad King John'. So, just who was 'Bad' King John? In some ways, he is as divisive a character as King Richard III in peoples' opinions. Hollister asks us the question: 'Whose interests would not be piqued by the man who was recently described by a distinguished scholar as 'cruel and ruthless, violent and passionate, greedy and self-indulgent, genial and repellent, arbitrary and judicious, clever and capable, original and inquisitive?'[2]

Let's begin with his birth. John was the youngest child of King Henry II and Queen Eleanor of Aquitaine, born on Christmas Eve, 1167 at Beaumont Palace in Oxford. He was also the youngest of five sons, his eldest brother, William, died at the age of 2 or 3 years, and the next eldest, Henry, the Young King, died in 1183. Geoffrey died in 1186. Three years later, Henry II died leaving Richard and John to succeed him. His nickname was 'Lackland', because he had no territories and was not expected to inherit any, which makes it ironic that he ended up with the entire Angevin Empire, even if he soon lost it.[3]

He became Henry's favourite child when the king's other sons rebelled against him in 1173. At that point, John was six years old, which says more about Henry's dislike of his other sons, rather than any attributes in John's character. And talking of character, John was cynical, feckless, treacherous, and had few, if any, scruples. Like the rest of his family, he had appalling rages and his distrust of people led him to commit the most dreadful acts. He perceived slights at every touch and turn, punished those who he thought were against him, and held grudges like few other paranoid monarchs. One of his most despicable acts was starving Matilda (or Maud) de Braose and her eldest son to death. Her husband William de Braose was a powerful baron and erstwhile favourite of King John. Matilda is also known as the Lady of Hay. In 1208, William argued with John for some unknown reason, possibly to do with money William owed John. But it may also have had to do with Arthur of Brittany. John ordered that William's son – also called William – should be sent to him as a hostage for the elder William's loyalty. Matilda is alleged to have refused and said very loudly that 'she would not deliver her children to a king who had murdered his own nephew'.[4] In very short order, John seized all the castles that belonged to William the elder, arrested Matilda and William the younger and imprisoned them, first in Windsor Castle, but then in Corfe Castle in Dorset. They were allegedly given one piece of bacon and a sheaf of oats.[5] Eleven days later, they were dead.

In appearance, John was built rather like his father, short and stocky. He is thought to have been around 5'5" (around 165cms), and must have felt very inferior to his brother, Richard, who topped 6'. That said, Richard was considerably taller than most people, so John was not noticeably shorter than the average man, around 5'8" at that time. He also dressed in rich fabrics and adored jewellery.[6] He was educated by one of his father's chief ministers, Ranulf de Glanville and was, originally, intended for the church. However, he rebelled against this in true Plantagenet fashion. At the age of nine, Henry II betrothed him to Isabella of Gloucester, who was the grand-daughter of one of Henry I's illegitimate sons. They married but had no children.

Possibly in an effort to compensate for John not having any territories of his own, Henry II sent him to Ireland, hoping he could make him king. However, John acted completely within character – he was known to have an impish sense of humour – and when the Irish chieftains came to pay him homage, he poked fun at them and pulled their beards. Needless to say, they were more than a tad vexed, and promptly rebelled, forcing him to come back to England, humiliated.

Many historians cite the fact that John going over to Richard's side in 1189, when the former rebelled again against his father, was the final blow for the king. He is alleged to have asked for a list of those who conspired against him and the last name on that list was John's, at which point, Henry more or less turned his face to the wall and died.

John's shenanigans when King Richard was at the crusades and during the king's captivity are well documented. He conspired with the French king to offer Richard's captor money to hold onto him. However, when the ransom was paid and the king released, Philip II of France sent John a message that said 'Look to yourself. The devil is loose'.

John was 32 when he acceded to the throne, although some would have preferred Richard's successor to have been Arthur of Brittany, son of John's elder brother, Geoffrey, who had died in 1186. Arthur besieged his grandmother, Eleanor of Aquitaine at Mirabeau in 1200 and John, very speedily, came to her rescue and imprisoned Arthur in Falaise Castle. He did attempt to come to terms with Arthur, but Arthur also had the Plantagenet temperament and refused, allegedly warning John that he would never have another peaceful moment. Definitely the wrong thing to say to John, who does not seem to have been the kind of person who ever craved anything like a peaceful life.

In 1200, John abandoned Isabella of Gloucester, saying that the paperwork had not been accurate when the wedding took place. He immediately married Isabella of Angoulême, by whom he had five children, the eldest of whom became Henry III.[7]

Back to Arthur. Allegedly, John personally murdered Arthur, but, whatever happened, mirroring Richard III – yes, him again – almost 300 years further down the line, the king's nephew was never seen alive again. Most people believe John dumped Arthur's body in the Seine. By 1204, John had lost all his father's French territories. He tried to defeat the Welsh and the Scots, failing miserably with each, and slinking back to England, his tail firmly between his legs.[8]

And then Stephen Langton happened. Pope Innocent III appointed Langton as Archbishop of Canterbury. Langton was known, through his Bible commentaries, to not only distrust the monarchy in general, but making the Plantagenet monarchs his especial target.[9] Unsurprisingly, John didn't want Langton; in fact, he proclaimed that anyone who supported Langton was a 'public enemy'. Langton was voted in by the Canterbury chapter unanimously in 1207, whereupon John expelled them all. This clash between king and Pope led to England being put under an interdict for six years with Langton and the Canterbury chapter leaving England. It also meant that all churches in England were closed – allowing no baptisms, marriages or funerals – and the Pope instructed the king's subjects not to obey John, and excommunicated him.

John caved in – eventually! But things in England did not improve. John's barons plotted against him, so John made his peace with the Pope and agreed that England should be a fief of the papacy, meaning it was a source of income for the Pope. In addition, the barons were gaining more power and becoming very vocal about the restitution of their 'ancient liberties'. And so, at Runnymede, on 15 June 1215, King John was forced to sign Magna Carta. John was more than happy to sign, because he had no intention of abiding by what he considered an insult to his royal prerogative quite apart from signing under duress.

Sadly, or perhaps, inevitably, this did not satisfy the barons for long. They asked Philip Augustus of France to send his son, the Dauphin Louis to come and help them. Louis did, and, in effect for almost a year, England was partly occupied by the French. And in that year, John, angry, depressed, and finally losing his baggage train in the Wash, retreated to Newark Castle, where, on 18 October 1216, he died.

His wish was to be buried in Worcester Cathedral near the shrine of his favourite saint, St Wulfstan. He lies in the central aisle of that magnificent cathedral, in a tomb built later by his son, Henry III. The one thing John did was give England an heir, something none of his other brothers had done, save Geoffrey with the unfortunate Arthur. One wonders if in whatever place he occupied at that time in Purgatory, Henry II applauded this favoured son for carrying on the line.

Fun Fact

Not fun, really, but typical of John. It is alleged that he tried to rape Matilda, the daughter of Lord Robert Fitzwalter. What is interesting is that at some unspecified time in history, Matilda is thought to have been the origin of 'Maid Marian' in the Robin Hood tales.[10]

William Longespée (Longsword), 3rd Earl of Salisbury

William was John's illegitimate half-brother, born around 1167. He was utterly loyal to John and remained so throughout all the troubles John caused and navigated, apart from one short period after the French landed in 1216, but he soon reverted his allegiance to John. William was known as Longespée because he was 'of great physical size and his use of oversized weapons'.[11] Initially it was thought his mother was Henry's most famous mistress 'Fair' Rosamund Clifford, but documents found later confirmed his mother was Ida de Tosney, wife of Roger Bigod, 2nd Earl of Norfolk.[12] Henry freely acknowledged William as his son, giving him the barony of Appleby in Lincolnshire in 1188. In 1196, Richard I bestowed Ela of Salisbury plus the lands and title of Salisbury on the fortunate William.[13]

During John's reign, Salisbury was made sheriff of Wiltshire, Constable of Dover, and Lord Warden of the Cinque Ports among other honours. He was, and remained, one of John's inner circle of trusted advisors and one of the very, *very* few people John trusted. Others included Peter des Roches, Engelard de Cigogné, Richard Marsh, and William of Wrotham. They were contemporaries of John and came to be regarded as his evil councillors.[14]

Around 1213, Salisbury was made Sheriff of Cambridgeshire and Huntingdonshire. He commanded John's troops in Poitou and commanded troops in Welsh and Irish expeditions. In 1214, John sent Salisbury to help Otto IV of Germany, who was intent on invading France. Salisbury, in charge of the right wing of Otto's army, suffered a catastrophic defeat at the Battle of Bouvines, and was captured.

It took some time before he returned to England but when he did, it was to find John and the barons at each other's throats. In common with William Marshal, but few others, Salisbury remained loyal to John through the troubled French occupation in 1216, although after Louis landed, he briefly went over to the French side, presumably because he thought John, having fled England, was a lost cause.[15] He helped Marshal oust the French from Lincoln in 1217 and after the battle was given the titles held by Nicholaa de la Haye for a time. He put his full support behind John's son, Henry III, holding a place of influence in the child king's minority government. Salisbury was appointed High Sheriff of Staffordshire and Shropshire in 1224, but the following year, he was almost lost at sea during a storm while returning to England. By a quirk of fate, he had always been resentful at being forced to give back Lincoln and its castle to Nicholaa de la Haye, but his eldest son married her grand-daughter and the two became in-laws.

William died in 1226 at Salisbury Castle and although there were rumours he had been poisoned, these are nebulous at best. What is ironic is that in 1789, Bishop Barrington of Salisbury ordered James Wyatt, a rival of Robert Adam, to remodel Salisbury Cathedral. At the time of William's death, he had been buried in the Trinity Chapel, at that time the only part of the cathedral that had been completed. The bishop wanted all the tombs moved to the nave.

Quite why Wyatt opened up William's tomb is unclear. It may have been easier to move disassembled, or he may have been simply curious and it was too good an opportunity to miss! When the tomb was opened, the well-preserved body of a rat with traces of arsenic in its system was found inside William's skull, so perhaps the rumours might have had some merit. In a bizarre decision, the rat was put on display in Salisbury Cathedral. It now resides in Salisbury Museum.[16]

Nicholaa de la Haye

We are led to believe that women in medieval times held little power or influence, but powerful women existed just as they do today. Most of the twelfth and very early thirteenth centuries were dominated by the formidable Eleanor of Aquitaine. However there was another lady, lesser known, but equally formidable, and to be admired. With the help of William Marshal, she evicted the French invaders from Lincoln after the battle in 1217, when Marshal was approaching 70 years of age and she was in her mid-60s. That lady is Nicholaa de la Haye and she was King John's Sheriff of Lincoln.[17]

Nicholaa was born around 1150 in Swaton, a few miles south-east of Sleaford, in Lincolnshire.[18] She was one of three daughters born to a Lincolnshire landowner, who also held lands in Normandy. Her father was the hereditary custodian of Lincoln castle, which made her an important marriage prospect, since there were no sons to inherit. Her first marriage was to William fitz Erneis, who died in 1178, and by whom, Nicholaa may have had a daughter.[19] Realising she must marry again to produce a male heir, she married Gerard de Camville and had Richard. Whew, job done.

However, Nicholaa did not have the temperament to sit and sew quietly, popping out children, while her husband looked after everything else. Gerard had legal hold of the custodianship of Lincoln castle on paper, but his wife was very active in running their estates extremely efficiently. So much so, that when Gerard fell foul of William Longchamp, and left to support the then Prince John in 1191, he left Nicholaa in charge of the castle. Longchamp besieged the castle for 40 days before throwing in the towel. Richard of Devizes said that she held out for so long 'without thinking of anything womanly'.[20]

In 1194, Gerard was removed from his custodianship, and only regained it when John became king in 1199. In 1215, Gerard died and Nicholaa claimed her inheritance as a widow. She was officially made custodian of Lincoln castle shortly before the French attacked, staving off occupation by the enemy by buying a truce.

King John visited Lincoln in 1216, at which point Nicholaa asked to be relieved of her duties because she was by this time in her mid-60s. John ignored her plea:

> The King to the archbishops, bishops, earls, barons, knights, freeholders and others of the county of Lincoln etc. Know

that we have granted to our trusty and well-beloved, the lady Nicholaa de Haye and Philip Marc, the county of Lincoln with all its appurtenances, to be in their custody for so long as it may please us. We therefore command that you do heed and obey the said Nicholaa and Philip in all things as the bailiffs of the said county. And in testimony etc. Witness myself, at Newark, the eighteenth day of October, in the eighteenth year of our reign.[21]

She became one of his most trusted, loyal, and fearsome supporters and shortly before he died, John made Nicholaa Sheriff of Lincoln, the first woman to hold such an important post. When John died in October 1216, Nicholaa remained in post, which was fortunate for the late king's nine-year-old son, Henry III.

The barons, Magna Carta notwithstanding, still opposed John's mismanagement and wanted to install the French dauphin, Louis-Philippe as king. Louis invaded despite some reservations on the part of his father and the Pope. With the aid of the English barons, he gained control of parts of England before making his way to London and taking part in a procession to St Paul's. He then captured Winchester, but when John died, many of the barons gave their support to the new child-king, Henry III. The whole mess came to a head when, in 1217, William Marshal took a force to Lincoln to oust the invaders. And here, Nicholaa truly came into her own.

The French occupied the city, being welcomed by the populace, but the castle was still under her control and holding out for Henry III. Nicholaa held out from October 1216 until May 1217.[22] In truth, Louis completely underestimated this formidable little old lady. She never once considered giving in. Eventually, William Marshal brought his forces to Lincoln. There was fighting in the streets for about six hours, but the castle was, finally, liberated. Louis lost half his army, including its commander, the Comte de Perche. The rebel leaders were captured. Nicholaa was the heroine of the hour, since Lincoln held strategic importance for the monarch.

To show his (in)gratitude, four days after the siege was lifted, Henry III removed Nicholaa from all her offices and gave them to William Longespée, the Earl of Salisbury. Seriously peeved by this monstrous act, Nicholaa took her grievance to the court. I can imagine this stalwart woman who had spent most of her life running estates and carrying out her duties for the monarch, standing in front of these men, reminding them that Lincoln would have fallen completely into French hands had it not been for her, and telling them it just wasn't good enough. Whatever, she had a partial success. Although initially, Salisbury was ordered to restore everything, he retained the county, but Nicholaa kept Lincoln and its castle. Salisbury was not too happy about this, even when Nicholaa's grand-daughter, Idonea, by her son, Richard, married the earl's son, William. Salisbury chuntered on about it til he died in 1226.

Nicholaa did not outlive him for long. She died in 1230, probably approaching the age of 80.[23] At which point, all her de la Haye and de Camville territories were inherited by William Longespée II and Nicholaa's grand-daughter.[24] She was buried at St Michael's in her home village of Swaton, where her tomb still lies. Nicholaa has gone down in history as 'The woman who saved England.' In the years after her death, many girls born in the county were named Nicholaa.[25]

Henry III

HENRY III WAS born on 1 October 1207 at Winchester, thus becoming known as Henry of Winchester. You will become accustomed to seeing this form of title, where the birthplace is part of the name. Henry's mother, Isabella of Angoulême, married King John in 1200, when she was around 12 years of age. Henry was their first child of five, two boys and three girls.[1] Little is known of his early childhood, although the name of his nurse, Ellen Dunn, is on record as looking after him and, later in her life, Henry made sure she was well provided for.[2]

Around the year 1212, the Bishop of Winchester, Peter des Roches, was given responsibility for Henry's education.[3] Des Roches proved to be an excellent tutor and it is possible that Henry developed his piety and his reverence for saints under the bishop's tutelage. One of his bodyguards, Ralph de Saint Samson taught the young Henry to ride, and Philip d'Aubigny tried to train him in the art of war – rather less successfully, as we will discover.

In October 1216, Henry became nine years old and just a few days later, his father, King John, died at Newark Castle. He had decreed that his son should succeed him and enlisted the support of Pope Innocent III to ensure it happened.[4] Since London, being held by the French, was unsafe for Henry, he was crowned at Gloucester by the pope's representative, Guala of Vercelli. Some historians declare he was crowned with a gold headband belonging to his mother, Isabella of Angoulême, John having lost the royal crown in The Wash![5] Others say that because the coronation regalia was held by the revolting barons, a chaplet of flowers was used.[6] What is known is that the Gloucester coronation was done very hastily to prevent the barons from crowning Louis-Philippe in London.

A regency council was formed, headed by William Marshal, Earl of Pembroke. And never more was his soubriquet, 'The Greatest Knight', needed more, for England was in a parlous state. Although most of John's disaffected barons had now given their support to the young Henry, the treasury was empty, discontent was still rife, and William and his fellow councillors began the arduous job of putting England back on an even keel.

The first task was to eject the French dauphin, Louis-Philippe and keep him ejected. It helped enormously when Marshal, with his forces including the Earl of Salisbury and aided by Nicholaa de la Haye, defeated the French occupying Lincoln and threw those still left alive out of the city. Shortly after, Hubert de Burgh defended Dover Castle and defeated Louis' fleet in the Battle of Sandwich. For a payment – naturally – Louis agreed to renounce his claim to the English throne in the Treaty of Lambeth in 1217. Having rid England of the French, Henry's fledgling government agreed to honour the tenets of Magna Carta, and, in the 1218 Treaty of Worcester, peace in Wales was restored when Prince Llewellyn ap Iorwerth of Gwynedd, the dominant native Welsh prince, was given enough territory to make him the effective ruler of Wales and defined the border with England, making the country, in effect, a two-state realm.

In 1219, William Marshal died. The regency was then rearranged with a triumvirate of Peter des Roches, Pandulf Verraccio, who was the papal legate, and Hubert de Burgh leading it. De Burgh spent the next few years grabbing as much land, money, and power as he could, after which, he re-took the lands that had been granted to Llewellyn. He also introduced new crown taxes and then attempted to regain the lands that had been formerly held by the Angevin monarchs and lost by King John. Gascony was recaptured during this time, but Simon de Montfort's harsh regime there caused problems for Henry.

In 1225, Henry was accused of breaching Magna Carta by preferring 'aliens' over his own people. The blame was laid at the feet of his favourites for treating his subjects badly. Henry replied with 'only good words and fair promises'. When he decided he needed money to go on crusade, parliament sent the bishops of Winchester, Salisbury, and Carlisle to remonstrate with him. They decided he needed to ratify Magna Carta and in a ceremony, read the articles contained within it. Henry replied: 'So help me God, I will keep all these articles inviolate, as I am a man, as I am a Christian, as I am a knight, and as I am a king crowned and anointed.' Unfortunately, everything went back to normal very quickly, and 'the reasonable expectations of his people were thus perpetually eluded and disappointed'.[7] As king, Henry seems to have been a something and nothing king. He wasn't vengeful, like his father, neither was he outstanding, like his son. It is almost as if he were a makeshift monarch sandwiched between the two. Nicholas Vincent makes the point that Dante didn't include him in his *Divine Comedy* but stationed him among the 'preoccupied' in Purgatory.[8]

In 1227, Henry convened a council at Oxford and declared his independence from the regency, but he still allowed de Burgh to run the country, making him the Earl of Kent and justiciar for life.[9] However, the young Henry was very weak, although in the introduction to his biography, Darren Baker maintains Henry was a 'dynamic and capable king...witty, eloquent, and well informed, had a phenomenal memory and mischievous sense of humour'. He also points out that Henry was prone to making hasty decisions and could be temperamental and devious.[10]

In the end, what marked the downturn of de Burgh's prominence was the return of Peter des Roches. He had been in the Holy Land as part of the Sixth Crusade after having been accused by de Burgh of treason and removed as one of Henry's guardians in 1221. Pandulf was recalled to Rome in the same year, leaving de Burgh in the position of Lord High Everything Else, as Gilbert and Sullivan would have put it. In 1232, des Roches was appointed baron of the exchequer, which basically put him in charge of England's finances and he was able to undermine de Burgh. He also demonstrated an ability to raise taxes for yet another war in France. Des Roches' cousin was appointed treasurer of Henry's household and this signified that the des Roches family was in the ascendant. At that point, Henry completely split from de Burgh, citing rumours that the justiciar intended to interfere in in church affairs.

By now, Henry was almost 25 years old, but instead of standing on his own two feet, he simply gave dominance of the government to des Roches. It was only in the summer of 1234 when the Archbishop of Canterbury, Edmund, of Abingdon, urged him to end his reliance on powerful advisers that Henry dismissed des Roches and finally began to rule in his own right.

His new aim – and an absolute necessity – was marrying and producing an heir. He married Eleanor of Provence and had five children with her. Henry was by this time, known to be very pious and particularly devoted to the figure of Edward the Confessor, whom he adopted as his patron saint.

In 1241, rebels including Hugh de Lusignan – Henry's stepfather – rebelled in Poitou against the rule of the French king. In another attempt to re-gain the old Angevin lands in France, Henry invaded Poitou in 1242, but was defeated at the Battle of Taillebourg. During the battle, Henry's brother, Richard, persuaded the French to delay their attack, giving the king time to escape to Bordeaux. However, Simon de Montfort, who fought a very successful rear-guard action against this withdrawal, was furious with Henry because of his incompetence and told the king that he should be locked up like the tenth-century king, Charles the Simple. The campaign became a disastrous failure and it cost the English Treasury over £80,000 – approximately £114,188,293.47 in 2023. After this debacle, Henry relied on diplomacy rather than warfare.

Henry believed that kings should rule in a dignified manner, surrounded by ceremony and church ritual. He also believed that the status of the crown had been eroded during the years of his father's and uncle's reigns. He tried to use his royal authority to appease those barons hostile towards him. However, his rule became very lax and resulted in a reduction of royal authority in the provinces, and that led, inevitably, to the collapse of his authority at court. This was exacerbated by the fact that he applied charters quite inconsistently throughout his entire reign and alienated many of the nobility, even those who supported him.

The power of the royal sheriffs also declined during his reign. They were now often men appointed by the exchequer, rather than because of their social positions from local prominent families. They focused on generating revenue for the royal coffers and their, sometimes harsh, attempts to enforce fines and collect debts generated a lot of discontent and unpopularity in the lower classes.

Henry travelled less than some previous kings, probably because he had a no empire to speak of. He led a sedate and tranquil life staying at each of his palaces for fairly long periods before moving onto the next one. He became very focused on palaces and houses, and according to John Goodall he was, 'the most obsessive patron of art and architecture ever to have occupied the throne of England'. He extended the Palace of Westminster, one of his favourite homes, and spent more time there than any of his predecessors. He also spent lavishly on the Tower of London, Lincoln Castle, and Dover Castle. He undertook a huge overhaul of Windsor Castle. And, at the Tower of London following a tradition begun by his father, King John, he kept a menagerie which included an elephant, a leopard, and a camel.[11]

However, his overwhelming characteristic was his piety. He was known for public demonstrations of piety and was genuinely devout. He gave generously to religious causes and paid for paupers and orphans to be fed. He regularly went on pilgrimages and sometimes used these as an excuse to avoid dealing with his political problems. He had been supported by the papacy during his early years and this led to him defending the church very diligently throughout his entire reign.

Eleanor of Provence was a decorous and cultured wife, but she proved to be a pragmatic and astute politician. In fact, she was far tougher and more determined than her husband. By the time of the barons' discontent in 1263, she was regarded as interfering and very unpopular. So much so, her barge was attacked by the people of London.[12] At the time of their marriage, she was 12 years old and Henry was 28. He was generous and warm-hearted, giving her gifts, paying personal attention to her, and ensuring her household was firmly established and in good order. She gave birth to their first child, Edward, in 1239 and he was, of course, named after Edward the Confessor. He was followed by four more children.

Henry encouraged his French relatives in the Lusignan family to travel to England and rewarded them with large estates, mostly at the expense of English barons. More nobles from Poitou followed the Lusignans to England. Around two-thirds of them were granted very substantial incomes, many being given estates along the Welsh Marches or in Ireland. It is possible Henry did this as an indication that one day he might reconquer Poitou and restore the rest of what had been the Angevin empire. Other imports to England were the Savoyard relations of his wife, Eleanor. The Lusignans began to foment trouble with the Savoyards. Henry – no exponent of reading the runes – allowed them to do what they wanted.

Soon there was a significant groundswell of xenophobia towards the number of foreigners in England. By 1258, xenophobia had turned to hatred, and the leader in whom that feeling centred was Simon de Montfort. Henry was urged to renege on his promise to the Pope to conquer Sicily and make his son, Edmund, king. Henry refused. In June 1258, the barons tried to force Henry to agree to the Provisions of Oxford, which basically formed a constitution on how the realm should be ruled and administered. In reality, Henry lost all his power and for the next three years, England was ruled by a council. He responded in true Henry fashion by 'disappearing into religious devotion'.[13]

The adherents then fell out, but in 1263, Simon led a rebellion to restore the Provisions. However, by this stage, the barons were completely disunited and, in 1264, Simon was forced to accept Louis IX's annulment of the Oxford Provisions. He didn't accept it for long, attempting to redirect the negotiations. That failed, and in May 1264, he took King Henry and his two sons, Edward and Richard, prisoner at Lewes.

It is at points like this that the observer, from a distance of several hundred years, wonders why some, allegedly intelligent, people don't learn from experience. Henry III grew up in the maelstrom of his father's belligerence, hubris, and downright nastiness. The result was the first baron's war. Worse, it took years after Henry acceded to the throne for England to get itself onto any kind of stable footing precisely because of what had happened during the first 20-odd years of the thirteenth century. But instead of learning just how much trouble the nobility could make for the monarch and determining not to repeat his father's errors, his own arrogance/absolute certainty he was always right/ignorance/whatever, led directly to the second barons' war. This is not the first instance of the king/queen not realising that their actions could put their throne and life in jeopardy, and it is not the first time we shall see this. The saying, 'if you always do what you always did, you'll always get what you always got', is true and several monarchs learned that the hard way.

Having captured the king and his eldest son, Simon then set about trying to make England a more egalitarian realm, by setting up a government based on the Provisions of Oxford. Henry still had the status of king and the authority resulting from his title, but all decisions now rested with his council, led, naturally, by de Montfort. Historians are still divided as to whether he ran a military dictatorship or was the founding father of the English parliament. He extended the shire knights' right to sit in parliament by allowing ordinary citizens from boroughs to be elected. This was the beginning of parliament as we know it today.[14]

What scuppered the whole shebang was that the nobility still weren't happy. The Welsh lords were adherents of Prince Edward – called The Lord Edward – and when the prince escaped, they rallied to his banner. Gilbert de Clare, one of de Montfort's close allies, became unhappy at the latter's power and eminence. De Clare and his brother, Thomas, also joined Edward's forces.

Edward – a completely different kettle of fish from his father – approached de Montfort at Evesham flying the banners that he had captured at Kenilworth from Simon de Montfort the younger. The ruse worked, giving Edward time to put his forces in the most advantageous position. The resulting Battle of Evesham was short, sharp, and almost a massacre. Edward had directed 12 men to find de Montfort and kill him. Some of Edward's forces almost killed King Henry, who was wearing borrowed armour, before they recognised him and escorted him to safety.[15] De Montford was savagely killed – more about him shortly. Evesham and its abbey were pillaged. Robert of Gloucester described it as, 'the murder of Evesham'.[16] Henry immediately took revenge on his enemies, refusing all calls for moderation until the papal legate persuaded him to sign the Dictum of Kenilworth, which allowed the king to fine his rebels so long as he gave them back the lands he had seized. Prince Edward went off on crusade.

Henry's final years saw him becoming more infirm, so much so, he wrote to his son asking him to return, but Edward didn't. At one point, Henry recovered enough to announce he, too, would go on crusade, but he died in November 1272 at Westminster, having reigned for almost 56 years and 19 days, a reign that would not be exceeded until that of James I and VI (57 years and 246 days). Although Edward was declared king, he was in no hurry to come and claim his throne and did not return until 1274.

urder of Thomas Beckett. (Wikimedia Commons)

Simon de Montfort; Gravure, 1690, Heince et Bignon. (Wikimedia Commons)

Queen Anne pleads for the life of Simon Burley. (Wikimedia Commons)

Richard Neville – 'Warwick the Kingmaker'. (Wikimedia Commons)

Above: Statue of William Marshal.
(Wikimedia Commons)

Right: John Tiptoft, Earl of Worcester.
(Wikimedia Commons)

William de la Pole; Chief Baron of the Exchequer. (Wikimedia Commons)

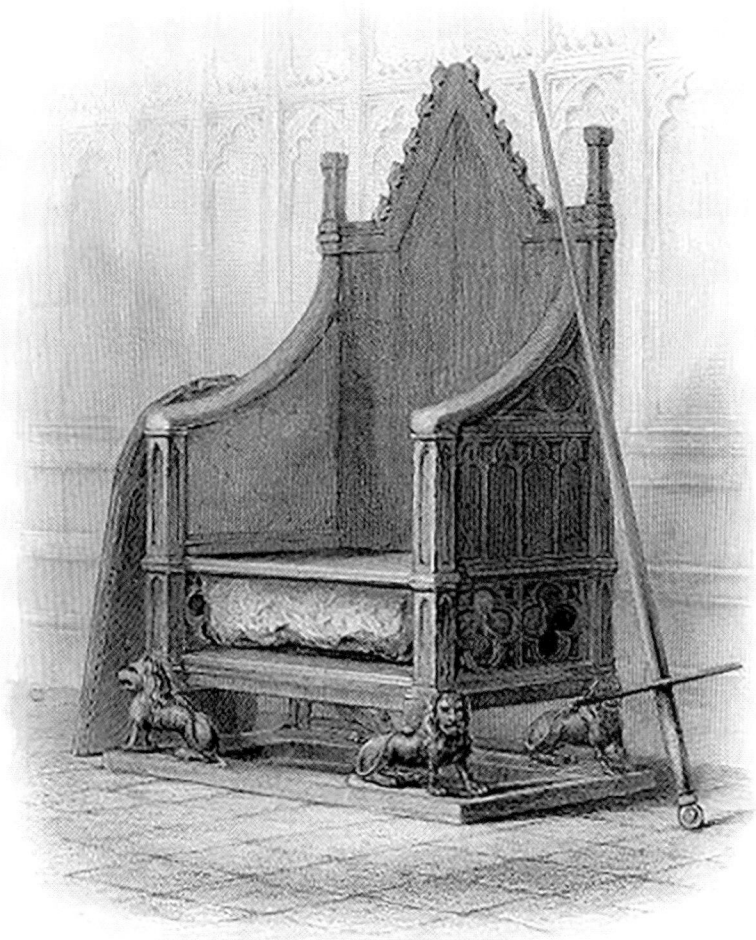

Coronation Chair and Stone of Scone. (Wikimedia Commons)

Crown of Princess Blanche. (Wikimedia Commons)

Henry was buried in Westminster Abbey. His tomb was magnificent and covered in relics. Shortly after his death, a local beggar praying at the tomb, claimed to have been cured of his blindness. For a while, it appeared that the tomb might become a shrine – although perhaps the authorities at the abbey wanted their own version of Becket's pulling power at Canterbury. It is said that Henry's widow believed the beggar, but, upon his return in 1274, Edward I did not. He put a stop to it saying his father had been a good man, but not a saint and that the beggar was a fraud.[17]

Fun Fact

When Henry visited the French king, Louis, he demonstrated his reverence for *all* saints by stopping at every shrine and church on the way to pray and give thanks. Although the two kings were in competition to see who was the more pious, Louis became exasperated with the delays and had every church and shrine on the route closed.[18]

Simon de Montfort

Simon de Montfort was a minor French noble, who rose to become first, a favourite of Henry III, then his brother-in-law, and, finally, his bitterest enemy. In character, Simon was devout – he went on crusade, but he was also a tyrant, a troublemaker and a 'grasping politician', a phrase some might consider tautology. Some historians consider him the founder of the British parliament, although James Maddicott disputes this. He was a major player in public affairs, something observed by the chronicler, Matthew Paris.

Simon was born around 1208, therefore being a contemporary of Henry III, born the previous year. He had no real interest in England but through his grandfather, had a family claim to land in Leicester, the city with which he will always be linked. He rose to prominence in the 1230s probably because of his charisma. What is not in doubt is that he was a mighty military man, effective in the field and with the ability to persuade people and win them over.

In 1238, he married Henry's sister, Eleanor and became even more powerful, not to mention rich. Most of the barons opposed the marriage, partly because they saw him as a foreign interloper, but also his wife was the widow of the great William Marshal's son, and thus held lands all over the place, including Wales and Ireland. The fact that these lands were only Eleanor's for her lifetime left Simon and their family in a precarious position. By marrying her, the barons considered a valuable asset for England had been removed from the negotiating table. The year following his marriage, Simon was made Earl of Leicester. It seemed he had everything he needed: English lands, an English wife, an English title, and he was the king's close relative. What could possibly go wrong? What went wrong was a bitter quarrel with Henry.

The king accused Simon of seducing Eleanor before their marriage, but, worse, Simon had put himself in a perilous financial position, whilst having no money, but naming Henry as guarantor for his debts. The resulting argument led to Simon leaving post-haste for the Holy Land. When he returned three years later, his relationship with his brother-in-law was still frosty, but Henry needed Simon's contacts in France, and more especially, the French court, for diplomatic reasons.

In 1248, Henry sent him to Gascony, which had become unruly, with instructions to put it in order. Not only did Simon spend Henry's money as if it were water, his treatment of the Gascons was unbelievably harsh, so much so, they complained to Henry, who then put Simon on trial at Westminster. Although he was found not guilty, this only served to worsen the relationship between the two. Simon particularly resented Henry's Lusignan relatives.

And he wasn't the only one. A groundswell against the 'foreigners' at court – of whom Simon was, in reality, one – soon led to widespread disaffection with the king. Not only was he not ruling the country properly, giving prominence to aliens, he had spent enormous sums of money on the rebuilding of Westminster Abbey. This led to a concerted effort to generate money for the royal coffers mainly through extortionate taxes raised by provincial sheriffs and justices. Then, in 1254, Henry stupidly became obliged to send troops to Sicily because he had promised Pope Innocent he would fight to gain the throne of Sicily for Henry's son, Edmund. This was purely because the Pope wanted to drive the then rulers of Sicily, who opposed him, from their throne. This act of folly became the final straw leading to the second barons' war.[19]

In 1259, under the provisions of the Treaty of Paris, Henry surrendered his rights in Normandy and Anjou, leaving Gascony as his sole French territory. It marked the end of the Plantagenet empire in France, an erosion that had begun with John and continued under Henry's feckless policies. So, by the time of the second barons' war, the situation had become a fight between English barons and an English king. In a way, this second conflict became a forerunner for the seventeenth-century civil war, because it centred on a monarch vs his barons who sat in parliament. Vincent makes the point that the commonly held view of Henry III is that, like Charles I, he believed in the divine right of kings, wasted money, and had foreign favourites.[20]

The Provisions of Oxford were designed to ensure that the king stuck to the tenets of Magna Carta and governed according to the advice of his barons. One of those barons was, naturally, Simon de Montfort. The Treaty of Kingston was a device to resolve disputes between Henry and his barons, but the Poitevin influence at court soon scuppered that and hostility was, once more, the order of the day.

Simon returned to England in 1263, gathered up the disaffected barons, and after London rose in his favour, he took Henry and Queen Eleanor prisoner, making himself the controller of government, albeit in the king's name.[21] The entente did not hold, and soon Henry was freed. He then appealed to the French king, Louis to arbitrate at the Mise of Amiens, something that Simon eventually agreed to. What Simon did not expect was that Louis' decision would be to renounce the Provisions of Oxford in 1264.[22]

Simon and the barons then declared that the Provisions and Magna Carta were indivisible. At this time, an accident on his horse had left Simon with a broken leg and he was trying to run the country from Kenilworth. With Henry still in France, Simon ordered his elder sons to take a troop of men to 'make war with good conscience'. Richard, Duke of Cornwall, Henry's brother, immediately ordered all the bridges over the River Severn to be broken.

Then Henry arrived home on 4 March and mustered his forces to march to Oxford. At this stage, Simon offered to accept Louis' judgement at Amiens if Henry agreed to get rid of all the foreigners at court – by which he meant the Lusignans and Queen Eleanor's Savoy relatives, but not, of course, himself! Henry refused point blank and conflict became a certainty.

But first, in true Henry fashion, he walked barefoot to St Fridewide's convent, named after a Saxon abbess who had been struck blind after fleeing from a lustful king, who pursued her to Oxford. Allegedly, no king had since dared go near her tomb. So, Henry did, made his devotions and paid the church a pension of £5 to employ a chaplain and pay for candles. Yes, really! There he is facing formidable foe and the possible loss of his country and he decides praying at a shrine and paying for candles is more important.

Meanwhile, in London, the masses were itching for a fight. They ransacked homes belonging to the Duke of Cornwall, emptied his fishpond. I have yet to work out the benefit to the mob of a ransacked fishpond. Anyway, they then rounded up court officials and imprisoned them. Henry was furious. He marched out of Oxford ready for war. The city of Leicester paid him £333 to bypass it, which he did before heading for Nottingham. Then Simon got word that Northampton was under siege, but only got as far as St Albans when he learned it had fallen. Londoners now became panic-stricken, blamed the Jews for everything, and massacred more than 500 of them. The same thing happened in Canterbury. Simon took Rochester, significant because it was a gateway to Dover and Europe. At this point, Henry moved south and caught Simon off guard, whereupon he fled Rochester for London.

Henry learned Simon had vamoosed to London, so he retook Rochester. Things seems to be going the king's way until he received intelligence that Simon had left London and was on his way to confront the king. At the ensuing battle of Lewes, Henry and Edward were captured. Henry undertook to observe the Provisions of Oxford under a caretaker government, but he had to give up his brother, Richard and his son, Edward as hostages.

Queen Eleanor discovered that Edward was being held at Wallingford Castle and encouraged Robert Walerand to attempt a rescue. The warden then threatened to catapult Edward to the rescuers via a mangonel – a sort of medieval stone-throwing catapult. Simon immediately moved Edward to Kenilworth. He continued running his egalitarian regime with burgesses sitting alongside knights, clerics and barons in a national congress, being forced to do that in order to maintain popular support. The nobility was mostly marginalised because they either held themselves aloof or disagreed with his views on how the country should be run – in essence, by them!

In May 1265, Prince Edward dashed for freedom while out riding, aided by a party of horsemen under Roger Mortimer to dissuade any pursuit. He was taken to Ludlow castle and happily agreed that in return for Gilbert de Clare and his allies' support, he would banish aliens and return England to the state of 'the good old laws'. Simon immediately sent out letters in Henry's name denouncing Edward as a public enemy and urging bishops to excommunicate him. But it gave Edward time to consolidate his forces and when Simon tried to manoeuvre his forces, he suffered wholesale desertions. Something had to give and it was Evesham.

Realising he had no other option, Simon decided to fight to the death, and, for a man in his late 50s, he put on a good show, fighting so valiantly, it took a blow from behind to bring him down.[23] When de Montfort was told his son, Henry, had been killed he is alleged to have said, 'then it is time to die'. And die he did, very hard and very bloodily. His final words are alleged to have been, 'Thank God.'[24]

His body was dismembered, his testicles were cut off, and hung on either side of his nose. His head was sent as a trophy to Roger Mortimer's wife – oh, look, darling, what a lovely present! His limbs were sent all over the realm and only his trunk was buried in Evesham Abbey. However, within weeks, there were reports of miracles both at his grave and on the battlefield.[25]

Robert Grosseteste

As a Lincolnshire lass, born and bred, I could not exclude Robert Grosseteste from this book. Also known as Robert Greathead or Robert of Lincoln, he was born in Suffolk, but became a scientist, theologian, and churchman, ending his days as Bishop of Lincoln. The university in Lincoln is named after him, not just because of his clerical connection to the city, but also because of his importance in the development of mathematical and philosophical thought that Roger Bacon, the medieval philosopher, later expanded upon.

Grosseteste was born around 1175, 'humil de patre et matre sum natus' – born of a humble father and mother. When, later in his life, he was in dispute with the chapter at Lincoln Cathedral, he was reproached for being born of peasant stock.[26] From around 1195, he was 'active' in the household of William de Vere, Bishop of Hereford. De Vere received a letter from the chronicler Gerald of Wales extolling Grosseteste, but he does not seem to have received any kind of reward from de Vere before the latter's death in 1198/9. Neither does he seem to have held any important positions in the households of the subsequent bishops of Hereford. We lose sight of him for the next 20 years, but he probably spent time studying in Oxford, and also in Paris during the papal interdict of John's reign and is known to have been a papal judge-delegate around 1216.

By 1225, Grosseteste was a deacon, appointed to Abbotsley in the diocese of Lincoln. This is around the time his scholarship activities and his ecclesiastical activities are mixed. Some argue he taught theology at Oxford, whereas others attest that he used his clerical income to teach at the University of Paris. However, what is clear, is that by 1230, he was teaching in Oxford. At around this time, Hugh of Wells, the Bishop of Lincoln appointed Grosseteste Archdeacon of Leicester and a prebend of Lincoln

Cathedral, while still holding the benefice at Abbotsley. In 1232, he became very ill and resigned all his posts except for the Lincoln Cathedral prebend. This was possibly because of his malady, or because he came to believe that it was wrong to hold more than one ecclesiastical position at a time.[27] In 1235, Bishop Hugh died and the Lincoln chapter elected Grosseteste as the new bishop, although the canons could not initially agree on Hugh's successor. Despite a call from the monks of Canterbury that he should be consecrated there, he was eventually consecrated at Reading.

The Lincoln diocese was enormous at that time, since it encompassed archdeaconries in Lincoln, Leicester, Stowe, Buckingham, Huntingdon, Northampton, Oxford, and Bedford. The energetic Grosseteste, despite an attempt to poison him in 1237, set about reforming the misdeeds of his clerics, including drinking bouts, permitting games in churchyards, processions that led to parish discord, and the behaviour of careless mothers towards their children. In his first year in post, he sacked seven abbots and four priors. This caused much conflict and his own chapter disputed his right of visitation, a dispute that lasted from 1239 to 1245 and ended up with the Lincoln chapter appealing to the Pope.[28]

The canons preached against Grosseteste in his own cathedral, issuing orders that vicars and chaplains should disobey the bishop. Grosseteste excommunicated the proctor of the chapter. The chapter excommunicated his dean, William de Tournay. Eventually, a direct appeal to the Pope was settled at Lyons in Grosseteste's favour. In fact, Grosseteste appears to have argued with all and sundry, including Henry III, about the appointment of John Mansel to Thame. Eventually, Henry backed down because he did not want Grosseteste to leave England and invoke an interdict.

In 1243, Grosseteste became involved again with the chapter in Canterbury, since Boniface, the new archbishop had not yet been consecrated and the chapter claimed they were in charge of events in the diocese. This spilled over into a direct confrontation with the abbot of Bardney who refused to recognise Grosseteste. The latter promptly excommunicated him. In response, the Canterbury chapter assembled 50 priests and excommunicated Grosseteste, who lost his temper and threw the letter, including the seal of St Thomas on the ground. The list of his disputes with all and sundry is endless. In religious matters, Grosseteste adhered to the precepts of Thomas Becket; that secular powers had no place in the church. He upheld the prerogative of the clergy and asserted that a bishop could not disregard the commands of the Pope.

He was known to have a fiery temper and was critical of virtually everybody, stating his opinions no matter who was the subject of them. He was also a pioneer in the progress of literature, science, mathematics and physics.[29] The monk Matthew Paris was not a fan of Grosseteste, but did sum him up as:

> a manifest confuter of the pope and the king, the blamer of prelates, the corrector of monks, the director of priests, the instructor of clerks, the support of scholars, the preacher to the people, the persecutor of the incontinent, the sedulous student of all scripture, the hammer and the despiser of the Romans. At the table of bodily refreshment, he was hospitable, eloquent, courteous, pleasant, and affable. At the spiritual table, devout, tearful, and contrite. In his episcopal office he was sedulous, venerable, and indefatigable.[30]

Grosseteste died in October 1253 and was buried in Lincoln Cathedral in the upper south transept. Allegedly, miracles and legends followed his death. There is an anecdote by Matthew Paris that Pope Innocent claimed the ghost of Grosseteste visited him in the night giving him a wound 'from which he never recovered'.[31] Whatever the truth of that, Pope Innocent IV died within 14 months of the bishop. There were attempts to have him declared a saint, but these were not successful.

Edward I

WE NOW COME to the reigns of three Edwards in succession, all very different from each other. The first being generally accepted as the king who put England together again after the maladministration and weakness of Henry III. He was followed by Edward II, who is alleged to be the worst king England ever had – although he has rivals for that title. Lastly, there was Edward III who was much more like his grandfather than his father, possibly because he did not want to be like his father.[1]

The future Edward I was born during the night of 17/18 June 1239 at the Palace of Westminster and reigned from 1272-1307. His father, Henry III, who idolised Edward the Confessor, named his eldest son after that king, despite the fact that it was considered an Anglo-Saxon name and, was, in consequence, rare. As an adult he was about 6'2" (188cms) in height and towered above most of his contemporaries. His nickname became 'Longshanks', meaning long legs/shins.[2]

Until he ascended to the throne, he was known as the Lord Edward. The other anomaly, of course, is that Edward the Confessor was really the first king of England of that name, so why was the Lord Edward called Edward I? Marc Morris explains that by the fourteenth century, the three previous kings called Edward were considered to have reigned a very long time ago. Even the king after which the Lord Edward was named had been dead for over two centuries, but by 1272, was already known as Edward the Confessor, not as Edward with a number. This didn't matter until Edward I was succeeded by another Edward and then another Edward. So, unsurprisingly, at the end of the fourteenth century, the grandfather, father and son, were respectively known as Edward I, II, and III. And if anyone wanted to be ultra-pedantic, they could add since the Conquest.[3]

Edward's arrival must have been a huge relief for his mother, because she had been accused of bringing foreigners into England, and also being barren. Since she was only 12 years old when she married Henry, and she produced Edward when she was around 16 years of age, this is utter nonsense.[4] Many details of his upbringing are unknown, but he must have received education in military matters. When he was a child, his father had attempted to regain some of the Angevin lands lost by *his* father, King John, with disastrous results. He retained Gascony and named Edward, then around 12 years old as lord of that region.

However, the young Edward really wanted to go on crusade. A rebellion by Alfonso of Castile, who wanted control of Gascony brewed enough for Henry to sail off to fight, but he left the young Edward behind, much to the latter's distress. Henry finally settled the dispute by agreeing to a marriage alliance with Alfonso's half-sister, Eleanor of Castile, provided Henry give Edward lands worth £10,000 a year. Henry gave charge of Gascony to Edward, but in order to meet the marriage demands, he had to give him royal territory in Ireland and Wales, plus the earldom of Chester and important manors in the Midlands.

In the autumn of 1254, Edward and Eleanor were married. He was 15, she 13. Edward had to put the finances of Gascony in order, but his father also wanted money for a crusade, so strife once more broke out. Had Henry left Edward to sort everything out, all would have been fine, but dad kept interfering, so affairs stayed in a state of flux.

The king and queen decided that the newlyweds should be separated for six months. Since Edward and his wife already had a very strong bond, one that was to last a lifetime, the young prince resisted but was over-ridden. Indeed, there is a tale that Eleanor accompanied Edward on crusade and when he was stabbed by a poisoned dagger, his wife sucked out the poison and saved his life.[5]

Eleanor having been sent to England, Edward was supposed to go to Ireland. Instead, he turned up in London to be with his wife and began to test the boundaries of his power. It didn't help that Henry had always been stupidly soft about his foreign relatives, the Lusignans, who were busy fomenting trouble with the queen's foreign relatives, the Savoyards. Edward was wary of both parties, but when Llewellyn ap Gruffudd of Gwynedd rose in Wales, the Lusignans accompanied Edward to put the rebellion down, which he did with arrogance and ferocity, making him extremely unpopular.[6] That said, he showed early promise, both in military matters and administrative skills. He was an excellent planner and while a prisoner of de Montfort in 1265, he escaped from captivity by pretending to try out a few horses and then promptly galloping off on the fastest of them.[7]

However, before the friendship with de Montfort fractured, leading to both Edward and Henry's imprisonment, the prince had supported de Montfort over his father, reluctantly agreeing to the Provisions of Oxford. But when civil war broke out between Henry and his barons, Edward was in Gascony. On his return, he quarrelled with the Londoners who supported the barons and it was his pursuit of the Londoners at the Battle of Lewes that led to Henry's defeat and both king and prince being taken prisoner. Imprisoned in Hereford, Edward escaped and, in the Battle of Evesham in 1265, his absolute loathing of his former friend led him to detail 12 knights to find de Montfort and annihilate him.

Five years later in 1270, when affairs in England had finally calmed down, Edward went on crusade. He was lauded for his courage and energy but achieved very little.[8] He was still abroad when Henry III died in 1272 and seemed in no hurry to get home, although he was informed of his father's death. A royal council proclaimed him king in his absence.[9]

In the 1080s, Robert, the eldest son of William the Conqueror considered himself the rightful king of England after his father, but remained only Duke of Normandy when his younger brother, William stole a march on him. He boasted that 'he would become King of England even if he were in Alexandria when his father died'. Nothing came of that, either. But, when Henry III died, his eldest son *was* on crusade, and was quickly recognised and accepted as being the rightful heir to his father.[10] And this mixture of administrative efficiency and military prowess, plus the fact he was the first king since Richard the Lionheart to actually *go* on crusade and not just promise to go, earned him a formidable reputation as king.[11]

Edward is also known for his parliamentary reforms. He called his first parliament in 1275 issuing orders for the election of two knights from each shire to be elected and two burgesses from each city and town. Thus the 1275 Parliament consisted not just of barons and clerics, but representatives from the lower orders. Successive parliaments were called to listen to Edward's plans for taxes, usually to fight wars. This convention generally led to an acceptance that those who were going to be most affected by having to pay the taxes had to consent to them in parliament.

Edward imposed a tax on the export of wool, at that time England's main source of wealth, in order to pay for the wars.[12] The principle of asking parliament's consent did not become standard practise until the Model Parliament of 1295. He passed a statute enshrining Magna Carta, The First Statute of Westminster, in 1275. Other reforms dealt with law and order, support for traders and merchants, many of them initiated by Robert Burnell, Edward's chancellor.[13]

In 1275, Edward set about sorting out the Welsh situation, mainly because Llewellyn refused to pay him homage. The latter's support in Wales was weak and he soon realised he must come to terms with Edward. Llewellyn was left with Gwynedd as his sole territory. In 1282, the Welsh rose up again, mainly because they wanted their own national identity –

and who can blame them? Whereas, previously Edward's incursion was punitive, this time he was determined to conquer Wales. By 1284, Wales was incorporated into England with an English administration system. Edward also embarked on extensive castle building, many of the castles constructed were built on the concentric design of the crusades.[14]

In 1301, Edward had his son (also called Edward of Caernarvon – I will leave it to you to work out where he was born), declared Prince of Wales, possibly in the hope of appeasing the Welsh but also to give his son financial independence. Incidentally, this young Edward was never meant to be the elder Edward's heir, but all three of his elder brothers, John, Henry, and Alfonso, died, the latter a few months after young Edward was born.[15]

In the 1280s, troubles arose in Europe which led Edward to broker a peace between France and Aragon. He spent three years in Gascony, and took a vow to go on crusade again, but never got there. Up until 1286, relations with Scotland were fairly harmonious. Sadly, when Alexander III died, his three-year-old daughter, Margaret, was his sole heir. The Treaty of Birgham agreed that Edward of Caernarvon and Margaret should marry. At that time, the girl was in Norway. She sailed for home but fell ill on the way and died. This led to a lot of kerfuffle over various claimants to the throne of Scotland – as many as 14! The two leading contenders were John Balliol and Robert de Brus.

The Scottish lords asked Edward to conduct the proceedings to choose the new king but gave him no mandate to adjudicate in the process. Balliol was finally chosen, but Edward kept interfering and trying to stamp his authority on Scotland. The straw that really broke the camel's back was when he demanded Scottish magnates should do military service in the war against France. The Scots allied themselves with the French. Edward nicked the Stone of Destiny and brought it to Westminster Abbey. Problem solved. Err, no, actually.

William Wallace led a revolt against the English and routed the Earl of Surrey's forces at the Battle of Stirling Bridge. Edward soon headed north, doubtless breathing fire and brimstone.[16] This is not the place to go into great detail about Edward's war against Scotland, but I do urge the reader who wants to know more, to read Marc Morris' excellent biography, details of which are in the bibliography. Long story short, his obsession with conquering Scotland led to almost 300 years of intense hatred and savagery.

Initially, Edward was successful but the Scots then refused to engage in battle. They appealed to Pope Boniface VIII, asking him to become the overlord of England. Edward rejected it. Then William Wallace was betrayed, turned over to the English, and executed. At which point Robert the Bruce, grandson of the de Brus mentioned above, who had supported the English, campaigned for Scottish independence. Edward's treatment of the Bruce family was nothing short of brutal. Robert's sister was imprisoned in a cage for four years, as was the Countess of Buchan, who had crowned Bruce. Edward now regarded the Scots as disloyal subjects in rebellion against his rule.

Around 1290, everything went pear-shaped for Edward. His beloved Eleanor died and, two years later, so did Chancellor Burnell, leaving him bereft of two of his most measured and sensible advisors. The wars with Wales and Scotland had virtually bankrupted him and he exacerbated this by refusing to act in a conciliatory manner towards the clergy and his barons, thus alienating them. So much so that when Philip IV tricked the Earl of Lancaster into surrendering Gascony to him, Edward went to try and recover it, but could not find enough barons to support him. By 1290, Edward had also stripped the Jews in England of all their money, at which point he expelled them. Eventually, he made peace with Philip IV by marrying his sister, Margaret.[17]

Edward's last years were spent in physical decline, frequently succumbing to bouts of his ferocious temper – at one point hurling a coronet belonging to his daughter, Elizabeth, into the fire because he was incensed at the cost of the repair made to it. He made one last foray into Scotland, but was racked with dysentery, and died in 1307.[18] There is a tale, told by the chronicler, Froissart, 200 years later that Edward's final orders were that his flesh should be boiled away from his bones and those bones carried into Scotland to remind the Scots he was still invading them, but there is no contemporary account to confirm this.[19] For any reader who is interested in a pictorial account of Edward's life, I recommend Brian Dingle's book, *In the Footsteps of Longshanks: The Places and People of Edward I*.

Edward I was not known for his largesse – the contemporary chronicler, Pierre Langtoft criticized him for it. He believed that, had the king been more generous to his barons regarding lands and money, the wars in Wales and Scotland would have been over quickly. However, Edward did make many land grants in Scotland, especially after Bruce's rebellion in 1306, but before then, he was trying to be sensitive to the political aspects of the situation.

According to Marc Morris, Edward had friends but not favourites. However, he was a charismatic man with ideals that made men flock to him, and he rewarded friends well.[20] By contrast, Deborah Seiler declares that Edward's affections for those around him ensured the continuance of his successful kingship and political stability.[21] The earls saw themselves as being in the top rank of society only slightly below the king, so some magnates didn't like accepting money – they considered it a bit grubby – but they did like accepting gifts of deer from the royal forests, because that reinforced their perception of their social status, since hunting was an integral part of the aristocratic life.

One accusation is that Edward failed to make substantial land grants outside the royal family, but England was peaceful during his reign, so there were no spare rebel lands to be redistributed, although he was generous to those who had been loyal during the 1264/5 period of the barons' war. Since there was very little land to be distributed, the only land left to give away was royal land and Edward spent his time trying to build up the royal estates in adherence to his coronation oath to 'preserve the rights of the crown'. Moreover, the instant he was crowned, he removed the crown and stated he would not wear it again until he had recovered all the lands his father had given away. When he defeated Wales and parts of Scotland, new lands became available that could be granted to loyal barons. One of the winners in this was Roger Mortimer who was granted lands in Wales that he passed onto his son when he died. It was Edward I's attitude to giving away royal land that became a significant factor in 1308 for the hatred directed at Piers Gaveston because Edward II gave his favourite lands left, right, and centre.[22]

Meanwhile, let us look at some of Edward I's loyal friends.

Fun Fact

Well, actually a gory fact – As well as spending a lot of energy trying – with varying degrees of success – to bring the Scots and Welsh under his rule, Edward I is also responsible for one of the most appalling methods of execution. He was so incensed at both Dafydd ap Gruffudd and William Wallace for what he termed their 'betrayal', he invented hanging, drawing, and quartering. Gruffudd was the first to suffer this horrific execution in 1283 in Shrewsbury, followed in 1305 by William Wallace, executed at Smithfield.

Robert Burnell, Chancellor of England

Burnell was the Bishop of Bath and Wells and served as Edward's chancellor from 1274 until his death in 1292. When Edward, then the Lord Edward, went on crusade, Burnell stayed in England to look after his interests. It took the new king almost two years to return after the death of Henry III, so Burnell acted as regent. During this time, Burnell, Roger Clifford, William de Valence, and Otto Grandison, were named as an executor of Edward's will. This emphasised his importance in Edward's life and that he trusted his legacy would be safe in Burnell's hands. He was twice elected Archbishop of Canterbury, but he was known to have, not just a mistress, but one who had borne him four sons – Morris claims more – so the Pope declined to confirm his appointment. Burnell became highly trusted, extremely capable diplomat,[23] with Morris describing him as, 'a man of modest social origins but great ability and seemingly limitless ambition'.

Burnell was born around 1239 in Shropshire, so was a contemporary of Edward. He began work as a clerk in the royal chancery before he moved to the Lord Edward's household as his clerk. In December 1265, Burnell was granted safe conduct on his journey to Wales on Edward's behalf. Later the same year, he went to Ireland with a message from the king and Edward under 'protection with clause', i.e. safe conduct.[24] The following year, the Patent Rolls of Henry III state that Burnell was to be given 'an ecclesiastical benefice of the value of 100 marks if it be a parsonage or dignity, as a reward for his faithful service to himself (Henry)and the Lord Edward'. What does become clear is that Edward worked to raise Burnell's position in the royal household.[25]

Once Edward landed back in England – having escaped an assassination attempt in France on the way home – and had been crowned, he set about sorting out his administration. Burnell was the keystone of this. He was elected as Bishop of Bath and Wells in 1275.[26] Within weeks of his appointment, orders were issued that all sheriffs in England were to be replaced. This was only the first part of a greater scheme; partly that of finding out how much land Edward held in each county and how much revenue and services he could expect from each. But it was more than that. Edward wanted to know about abuses and corruption enacted by sheriffs and bailiffs, so it became an enquiry into rights and liberties. The results led to the Statute of Westminster.[27]

In 1277, Edward I and Queen Eleanor laid the foundation stone for the abbey of Vale Royal, followed by Burnell celebrating mass to a named gathering that included Gilbert de Clare and John de Warenne – more of them later. The fact that these people were named as participating in the installation of the new abbey shows their acknowledged status as being close to the king. They were shown to be occupying the same space as the monarch. Instances like this demonstrate their favoured status with Edward.

In October 1277, Burnell was given the power to 'hear all the complaints and demands of the said Alexander Ide la Puere, lord of Brigerak, in any way touching the king and his person, and to do full and speedy justice therein without cavil or delay'. This is clear evidence of the trust Edward gave his chancellor, but at the same time demonstrating that, in this instance, the Lord Bergerac, was to receive justice for his complaint, even if the two of them were not friends.[28]

The Burnell family held land in Shropshire and in 1284, Robert obtained a licence from Edward to fortify his house in Acton Burnell. The king had held a parliament in the house in 1283, so possibly the granting of the licence was a given, but Edward's Welsh campaigns frequently meant he travelled through Shropshire and at those times, he stayed with Burnell. The house itself was probably never meant to have any kind of defensive purpose, but merely to look impressive. Burnell did, however, build the adjacent church, probably employing the best masons – he was a bishop, after all.[29]

As the reign got into its stride, the older generation was dying off leaving three people in their prime at the head of government. Edward himself, aged 35, his wife Eleanor, aged 33, and Robert Burnell. By this time, all had plenty of experience of politics, war, government and life, but were all still young enough to tackle the problems that lay ahead. The only fly in Edward's ointment was that his eldest sons, John and Henry had died and so had the next son down, Alfonso. This left only Prince Edward of Caernarvon, the Prince of Wales. He, too, left something to be desired. Quite a lot as far as his father was concerned.

Burnell died, unexpectedly, in October 1292 at Berwick on Tweed. His body is buried in the nave of Wells Cathedral, but his heart was interred at Bath Abbey.[30]

John de Warenne

John de Warenne was the 6th Earl of Surrey. A prominent nobleman straddling the reigns of Henry III and Edward I, he was known to have changed sides twice during the Second Barons' War, but ended up on the side of the king. He was known for his boastful arrogance and penchant for violence – so it is not surprising he got along with Edward!

De Warenne was born in 1231, his maternal grandfather being the great William Marshal. When he was a child, his father died and John then became a royal ward, being put under the guardianship of Peter of Savoy, one of Queen Eleanor's uncles. In 1247, he married Henry III's half-sister, a Lusignan, and the marriage created a deal of discontent in the English barony since they resented a penniless foreigner marrying into the English nobility. He is known to have accompanied the Lord Edward on his journey to marry Eleanor of Castile in 1254. When the conflict between Henry III and his barons arose, de Warenne sided with Simon de Montfort in 1260; however, he returned to the royalist side three years later.

De Warenne was besieged by de Montfort at Rochester Castle until it was relieved by Edward. When Henry and Edward were taken prisoner after the Battle of Lewes, he fled to France with Queen Eleanor, following which, his lands were confiscated, but eventually restored. He returned to England in time to fight for the king and the Lord Edward at the Battle of Evesham.[31] He spent many of the years following Henry's death, accompanying Edward I on his campaigns to Scotland and Wales.[32]

There is a fanciful tale that, when Edward called a parliament at Gloucester in order to determine which lords were holding lands they did not own and to which they held no right – *quo waranto*, which means the 'owner' has to show by a warrant or franchise that they own the disputed claim – de Warenne is alleged to have drawn his 'rusty sword' declaring it was all the warrant he needed for his right to hold his lands, supposedly saying: 'My ancestors came with William the Bastard, and conquered their lands with the sword, and I will defend them with the sword against anyone wishing to seize them.' This arose from a suit against Alan de la Zouche regarding land and a certain manor, which de Warenne thought he would lose. He is alleged to have entered Westminster Hall and attacked de la Zouche and his father before fleeing to Reigate where he was besieged by the Lord Edward. He submitted, paid a fine and was pardoned.

This has long been thought to be apocryphal since its sole evidence is in one source, the chronicle of Walter Hemingbugh of Guisborough. Arguments against the tale being true include the fact that the *quo waranto* (whose warrant?) proceedings did not deal with the lands held by magnates but the franchises they held, something that Edward had – wrongly – declared was a sole royal prerogative. However, it would have been within character for de Warenne, if it were true.[33]

In 1296, he was appointed Guardian of Scotland.[34] However he returned to England a few months later saying the climate was bad for his health.[35] In 1297, Edward wanted to fight in Flanders. Few of his lords were enthusiastic, but de Warenne was willing. By then, he was 66 years-old, but his loyalty to Edward was absolute. The only thing he did not enjoy was responsibility. When appointed Guardian of Scotland, he left within a few months, citing health reasons, but offered the post to anyone who would accept it.

According to Walter of Guisborough, he spent most of his time in the north of England. Indeed, when Berwick was retaken, Marc Morris states unequivocally that de Warenne 'continued to linger in England'. However, he soon realised he needed to go to Berwick, which he did and then marched his army to cross the Forth at Stirling, where William Wallace awaited him. The Heminburgh chronicle tells us that Wallace said, 'Go back and tell your people that we have not come for the benefit of peace but are ready to fight, to avenge ourselves, and to free our kingdom.' And avenge themselves they did. De Warenne fled back to England.[36]

De Warenne was defeated by William Wallace at the Battle of Stirling Bridge and fled south to York. Edward still maintained trust in him, sending him back to Scotland in 1298, when he re-took Berwick-on-Tweed – the town that was for quite some time in medieval England, a negotiating pawn for successive kings, and which changed from English to Scottish and back again with boring regularity. Which probably explains why, although it has been officially English since 1482, Berwick still fields a football club in the Scottish League.

Later in 1298, together with Edward, de Warenne was a commander during the Battle of Falkirk, an English victory. In 1300, he led a cavalry unit near the estuary of the Cree, ordering his men to charge at the Scots, causing them to flee.

He died aged around 73, in 1304 in Kennington and was buried in Lewes Priory.[37] With his first wife, Alice of Lusignan, half-sister of Henry III, de Warenne had three children. His daughter, Alice, married Henry Percy, father of the 1st Baron Percy. Isabella, married John Baliol, who subsequently became King of Scotland. Their son, William, predeceased his father, leaving a son, also called John.[38]

Henry de Lacy

Another friend and confidant of Edward I, Henry de Lacy was born around 1249/1251, the son of Edmund de Lacy, Baron of Pontefract, and, more importantly, grandson of Margaret de Quincy, Countess of Lincoln, who owned important estates to which he was heir.[39] He was educated at Henry III's court and became friendly with the Lord Edward. When Edward ascended the throne in 1272, Henry was given the post of Chief Councillor.

The argument for his birth year being 1249 is supported by documents in 1296, saying he was 'in his forty-seventh year'.

He succeeded his father in July 1257. In 1269, he was in dispute over pasture lands with John de Warenne, Earl of Surrey. The quarrel escalated and an appeal to arms was prevented by King Henry. At the trial that followed, de Lacy came out the victor. Following his appointment of custodian to Knaresborough Castle in 1272, he was knighted at the wedding of Edmund, Earl of Cornwall, and, shortly after, received full admission into the earldom of Lincoln. During the next few years, he served in Wales, besieging and conquering the castle of Dolforwyn. He was also one of the escorts to Alexander III of Scotland when the latter visited England in 1278 and, in 1279, was joint-lieutenant of England while King Edward was absent.

When Edward went to Gascony for three years from 1286, de Lacy accompanied him. Upon their return, he and Robert Burnell were appointed to hear complaints against Ralph Hengham.[40] Hengham was a notable assize judge, who at that time was accused of false judgement and false imprisonment. He was imprisoned and fined an enormous amount – mostly because he had the money to pay it – but later pardoned by Edward.[41]

De Lacy was an important presence in the Scottish deliberations over the succession in Berwick and, in 1293, went to France as part of a deputation negotiating a peace treaty. On his return, he was sent to Wales to try and relieve the castle at Denbigh, which belonged to him, but his own Welsh servants helped defeat him and he only just escaped. In 1296, he was among a force that yomped down France towards Gascony, besieging and pillaging where and when they could. He did not return to England until 1298 when he accompanied Edward to the Battle of Falkirk, and he was again in Scotland in 1300 at the siege of Caerlaverock.

During the following years, he travelled frequently on the Continent on missions for King Edward and was present when Edward died on his way to Scotland in 1307. He was loyal to Edward II until the advent of Piers Gaveston, although, for a time, he did support Gaveston even when the 'upstart Gascon' was made Earl of Cornwall. However, Gaveston, not known for his humility, showed such ingratitude to de Lacy that the earl became one of his bitterest enemies, especially after Gaveston referred to him as *boele crevée* (burst-belly). There is also evidence that he had a conflict over his loyalty to Edward II and the policies enacted by Edward I. He joined Thomas, Earl of Lancaster and the party that opposed Gaveston.[42]

In 1310, Edward II made de Lacy guardian of the kingdom when the king went to Scotland. He is known to have spent Christmas 1310 at Kingston in

Dorset, but returned to his London townhouse early in 1311, where he died in February. He was buried in the lady-chapel at St Paul's.[43]

Henry de Lacy married twice, first to Margaret Longespée, the daughter of William Longespée the younger by whom he had two sons. The elder drowned in a well at Denbigh Castle, and the younger fell from a parapet at Pontefract Castle to his death. Henry's second wife was Joan FitzMartin, but they had no children. He is known to have had an illegitimate son, mother unknown, who was named John. De Lacy's grave and monument in St Paul's were destroyed in the Great Fire of London in 1666, but his name appears on a monument documenting the important graves lost in the conflagration.[44]

Edward II

FIRST OF ALL, let's get the elephant out of the room. 'Everybody' knows that King Edward II was killed in September 1327, on the orders of Roger Mortimer. 'Everybody' also knows Edward was killed by being held down whilst a red-hot poker was shoved up his anus into his intestines and that his resulting screams could be heard from miles away. 'Everybody' is wrong. The ex-king – by this time, he had been forced to abdicate – was certainly not murdered in this horrendous fashion. It is a legend that grew among fourteenth-century chroniclers, much as unfounded, incorrect stories are bandied about in the media about the British royal family today.

Edward II was born in Caernarvon Castle in April 1284. Known as Edward of Caernarvon, he was the youngest child of Edward I and Queen Eleanor of Castile, but their fourth son. (One wonders if, with this medieval penchant for naming sons of X, where X is their place of birth, we should be delighted none of them were born in Crapstone in Devon or Giggleswick in North Yorkshire.) Edward's three older brothers died in childhood, the last of them, Alphonso, when Edward was only four months old.[1]

When Edward was 16, his father made him Prince of Wales. He became popular in Wales, but because of his predilection for close male friends, he was never popular in England.[2]

From the time he was around 15 years of age, he accompanied his father on the latter's Scottish campaigns. When Edward I died on his way up to Scotland for yet another foray to vanquish the Scots, he left his son a sea of troubles. Foremost among them was the issue of Scotland.[3] But that was not all. The duchy of Gascony was still in turmoil, the barons were sick to the back teeth of all the war campaigns and the taxes raised to wage them, the relationship with France was hostile, and Edward I had left enormous debts, possibly around £200,000.

One problem he could solve. He married Isabella of France in 1308 and relations with her father, Philip IV (*Le Bel)* eased somewhat.[4] By this time, Edward was 24, tall, handsome, and powerfully built. His bride was, literally half his age. They were the modern equivalent of a golden couple on whom rested so many hopes and expectations. According to the anonymous author of the *Vita Edwardi Secundi*, Edward had been endowed with every gift, including the hand of Philip IV's exquisite daughter.

However, Edward was not the stuff of which kings are made. Before his father's death he was a source of disappointment. Although he rode well and displayed courage, he was not the born soldier his father had been. In fact, he preferred digging ditches and thatching roofs to going on campaign. He enjoyed rustic pursuits such as swimming and rowing.[5] He was not well thought of as a monarch. Indeed, Ian Mortimer tells us that Dr McKinnon began his biography of Edward III, written in 1900, with the words: 'A more complete ninny than Edward II has seldom occupied a throne.'

Mortimer goes on to say that Edward II was not stupid or obtuse. He was a very pious man, a believer in the saints, had a keen sense of humour, and was a man who loved to be generous. However, in some ways he resembled his father and could be cruel, intolerant and slow, if ever, to forgive. He was capable of 'huge affection' and was not that interested in military or formal bonds.[6] He was by no means averse to women, having fathered a child called Adam before his marriage to Isabella.[7]

However, the friend of his heart – some say the love of his life – was Piers Gaveston, a man who was witty, dashing, clever, physically strong, and thought nothing of humiliating the great lords of England who grew to loathe him.[8] I shall sketch Gaveston's story now, because, since he was the most famous of Edward's favourites and the man the king appeared to truly love for the whole of his life, I did not want to include him in the next section of trusted courtiers, purely because so many historians have told his story in great detail.

Gaveston joined Edward's household in 1300 after serving under Edward I as a soldier for three years. At this time, Edward was 16 and Gaveston, 19. They quickly grew close, so much so that, in 1305, when Prince Edward was in dispute with Edward I's treasurer, the father stopped his son's allowance and banished Gaveston from England.[9] In 1306, Edward I knighted his son. Soon after, Gaveston, back from his temporary banishment, was knighted by the prince. And really, this is where Edward's and Gaveston's history merge so completely for the next few years, they present as one soul. Edward made his friend Earl of Cornwall, and married him to Margaret de Clare, sister of the Earl of Gloucester and Edward's niece.[10]

A contemporary described their relationship as Edward adopting 'Gaveston as a brother' and cherishing 'him as a son'. In return, Gaveston gave Edward confidence to be himself, unconventional though that might be. Mortimer maintains that he did not want to be a model prince but an individual.[11] Such was the general alarm at their relationship that rumours began, which have never been quashed, that Edward was a 'sodomite'. If that were the case, he was not the first and would not be the last monarch to be thus accused. Whatever the truth of the matter, it was incontrovertible that when Piers was not around, Edward was completely lost, and had been from the moment he ascended the throne.[12]

Thankfully, Gaveston stayed behind when Edward married Isabella, officially as keeper of the realm; in other words, the regent. Although he stayed out of the way for the marriage ceremony, when Isabella was crowned, Gaveston, was up front and central: 'Decked out that he more resembled the god Mars than an ordinary mortal.' If Isabella had not worked it out before, she certainly did then, especially as it was Gaveston who sat next to Edward at the coronation feast, not his new queen. Isabella was most put out, and made her displeasure plain. She was even more aggrieved when she and her French uncles found out Edward had given all the wedding presents from the French royal family to Gaveston.

So besotted was the king with his favourite, he paid no heed to events north of the border, where Robert Bruce was making hay while the sun shone. So fed up were his barons, they demanded Gaveston's removal, threatening force if their demands were not met. Edward might have held out against them, but when Isabella's father threatened the full might of France against him, he had to capitulate. Gaveston was banished again.[13]

Edward then set about mending fences with his nobles and muttering about another foray into Scotland. But it was all a blind to hide Gaveston's return and reinstatement as Earl of Cornwall. However, instead of learning from his mistakes – here we go again! – his return made the Gascon even more obnoxious and insolent to the English barons. By 1310, Edward sent Gaveston away for his own safety and had to agree that a body of lords – known as The Ordainers – should run the country. Edward, outwardly obedient, began arrangements to march north. In reality, he was intent on misdirection. Whilst he marched north to deal with Scotland, he was obeying his nobles, getting out from under the constraints of The Ordainers, and, most important of all, removing Gaveston from danger whilst having him at his side. Once more, Isabella found herself in a crowded marriage of three.[14]

Naturally, it all fell apart and Gaveston once more took the well-trodden path into exile. However, this time it was different. Because Edward was incandescent that the nobility were treating him as if he had an IQ of three.

He moved north to York and summoned Gaveston to return to his side. By January 1312, Edward was in a cleft stick. Henry de Lacy, Earl of Lincoln, and a loyalist, had died the previous year. The nobles were determined to see the back of Gaveston. Permanently.

It is unclear whether Isabella, by this time 16 years old, and now old enough for a sexual relationship with her husband, became pregnant for political reasons of her own or because Edward and Gaveston thought it might be a good idea. By the end of April 1312, Edward, Gaveston and Isabella – a late arrival possibly due to the early stages of pregnancy – were in Newcastle on Tyne. Whatever the circumstances, the earls were adamant Gaveston must go. When the king learned they were on their way and breathing fire, the three of them left everything and fled to Tynemouth Priory. Edward and Gaveston then left Isabella there and travelled by sea to Scarborough, believing she would be safe from the earls' wrath. She travelled south by road to York where she was reunited with Edward, who had left Gaveston safely behind fortified walls at Scarborough Castle. Many historians have accused Edward of abandoning her, but this did not happen until 1322 when she was in danger of being captured by Robert Bruce's army at Tynemouth.[15] By a promise of safe conduct, Gaveston agreed to accompany the earls south. However, Guy Beauchamp, Earl of Warwick, known as the Black Hound of Arden, broke his word and after a kangaroo court, had Gaveston summarily executed on Blacklow Hill.[16]

Of course, the earls believed that once Gaveston was gone, Edward would do his duty; turn his mind to governing his kingdom and go to war with Scotland just like dear old dad. What actually happened was that Gaveston's discarded corpse was taken to the Dominican friary at Oxford, where Edward ordered it to be embalmed and dressed in cloth of gold until he could get permission to bury it, since the Archbishop of Canterbury had excommunicated Gaveston. And eventually, the earls worked out that Edward would watch, wait and destroy them whenever the opportunity occurred. The only thing that lifted his spirits was the birth of the future Edward III in November 1312.[17]

All should, in theory have now been sweetness and light, but Edward proved to be one of those who refused to learn from his life's experiences. He had lost Gaveston, yes, but now he had a son, and Edward was all about family. Not just that, the nobility had to acknowledge that he now had an heir, something that might have given them cause to wonder if God was on the king's side and not theirs.[18]

The king immediately declared his baby son, Earl of Chester, a title he had had to wait until he was 16 to achieve. Then in 1313, Robert

Bruce demanded allegiance from any remaining supporters of John Balliol, upon threat of losing their lands. Edward could not let this pass, and marched north. He decided he must hurry to relieve Stirling Castle which was under siege. However, Bruce foresaw this and laid his plans accordingly. In the Battle of Bannockburn, which lasted two days, the English were routed and went into full retreat. English losses were considerable. Although Edward had fought with courage – one chronicler described him fighting 'like a lioness deprived of her cubs', Bannockburn was nothing short of a mortifying setback, and one from which Edward never recovered.[19] Eventually, 14 years later, in the Treaty of Edinburgh-Northampton, the English crown recognised that Scotland was a fully independent country.[20] If you listen carefully, you might be able to hear Edward I spinning in his huge tomb in Westminster Abbey!

From then on, life for Edward deteriorated in a relentless downward spiral. Between 1314 and 1316, the weather was consistently dreadful. Crops rotted in fields all across Northern Europe and perhaps as much as ten per cent of the population starved to death or died of disease. In 1315, Edward finally had Gaveston buried at Langley Priory in Hertfordshire and that year, he also became very fond of an Oxfordshire knight called Roger Damory – more of him later.

Throughout this time, Edward was on good terms with his queen; they were seldom apart and wrote to each other when they were. An eyewitness stated Edward loved Isabella and he frequently gave her lands and paid her expenses. She, in turn, interceded with him. Although few of their letters survive, he called her 'his dear heart' and she called him 'my very sweet heart'.[21]

In 1318, Robert Bruce captured Berwick and Edward failed to recapture it. He still held Thomas, Earl of Lancaster responsible for the murder of Gaveston, Warwick having died in 1315. The relationship between Lancaster and Edward deteriorated. Then around 1320, Hugh Despenser the Elder – Edward did not at this point trust Despenser's son, also called Hugh – rose high in the king's affections. The barons, obviously suffering a severe, if accurate bout of *déjà-vu*, attacked Despenser lands and forced father and son into exile.[22]

Lancaster was one of the main proponents of, yet again, forcing the king's friends into exile. But this time Edward acted. He sent Isabella to Leeds Castle where she demanded entry, knowing it would be refused. In the subsequent scuffle, several of her men were killed. That gave Edward the excuse he needed to take military action. This alarmed Lancaster who began mustering his own army in the north. The Despensers returned and were pardoned by the royal council. After a foray into Wales, Edward confronted Lancaster's forces at the Battle of Boroughbridge. Lancaster was captured, given a summary trial and beheaded. Edward then embarked on another (failed) incursion into Scotland. This time, his illegitimate son, Adam, was killed, and Isabella only just managed to escape Bruce's army at Tynemouth, fleeing by boat.

The Despensers became utterly rapacious. There were also disagreements with Charles IV of France. Failing to come to any agreement, Charles invaded Gascony. Edward, in retaliation ordered all French people in England to be arrested and seized Isabella's lands. Not only that but he took their children away from her and gave them up to the guardianship of Hugh Despenser's wife. Their marriage had deteriorated since 1322, mostly because of the actions of the Despensers and the fact that Edward was besotted with them. In March 1325, it was agreed that Isabella and their eldest son, Edward, would travel to France to personally intervene with her brother, Charles. However, when the negotiations were finalised, Isabella not only stayed in France, so did the young Edward.[23]

In 1322, Roger Mortimer, a Marcher lord, was imprisoned in the Tower of London. He escaped in 1323 and fled to the Continent. By 1326, it was clear Mortimer and Isabella had begun a relationship. Then in August 1326, Isabella betrothed the young Edward to Philippa of Hainault. In September, Isabella, complete with an invasion force, arrived in Suffolk. By this time, affairs in England were perilous for the king, and in October, he left London heading for South Wales. A few days later, the elder Hugh Despenser was executed in Bristol, by being hanged in his armour. By November, Edward was a prisoner.

Things were now set for the denouement. In January 1327, Edward II was deposed by parliament. His eldest son became Edward III. In April 1327, Edward II – now relegated to being Edward of Caernarvon again – was moved to Berkeley Castle from Kenilworth. Two months later, the Dunheveds succeeded in freeing him, but only temporarily.[24]

And here is where the real mystery, rumour and legend begins. The only contemporary account of Edward's death, from Adam of Murimuth, just says that Edward was suffocated by Thomas Gourney and John Mautravers on 22 September. It is only later that the chronicler Holinshed and Sir Thomas More, with the help, at the end of the sixteenth-century, of Marlowe's play, *Edward II*, that perpetuate the myth about the red-hot poker, doubtless as a reference to the alleged homosexual relationship with

Piers Gaveston.[25] The poker that was stated right at the beginning of this section, being a lie!

The records, including chancery rolls, show Edward was treated well and fed well at Berkeley. The stories that he was ill-treated came from the pen of Geoffrey le Baker, writing 25 years after Edward's death. Baker was yet another contemporary chronicler who never let the facts get in the way of a good story. But he had an ulterior motive because he was agitating for Edward to be made a saint, so writing about how appallingly the ex-king was treated was all grist to his canonisation mill. He alleged that, while being taken to Berkeley, Edward was forced to wash and shave in dirty ditch-water, and, after his arrival at the castle, was housed in a charnel house – a place where skeletal remains are stored.[26] All lies, but a good story.

Officially, Edward died around 21 September 1327, at Berkeley, on Mortimer's orders. In late September, according to one chronicler, a group of knights, abbots and burgesses viewed Edward's body *superficially*. The body was moved to Gloucester where, on 15 December, his funeral was held. A month later, Edward III and Philippa of Hainault were married in York.[27]

Fun Fact

That Edward and his wife were happy for quite some time, is well attested in the records and chronicles. Edward actually saved Isabella's life at one point. The silk hangings in the pavilion where they were sleeping caught fire. Edward grabbed Isabella and rushed outside, despite the fact that they were both naked.

Sir Roger Damory: Baron d'Amory

Damory was born around 1280, the younger son of Sir Robert D'Amory. He held manors in Oxfordshire, Hertfordshire, Lincolnshire, and Yorkshire. He fought in the Battle of Bannockburn, obviously making a good showing, and quickly becoming a trusted member of Edward's inner circle, since, in 1317, Edward gave him the manors of Sandal in Yorkshire and Vauxhall in Surrey. Acting completely in character, the king showered him with gifts and lands and Roger married Edward's niece, Elizabeth de Clare.[28] Roger was called to attend parliaments between 1317 and 1321 and during this time became Lord d'Amory. He was a prime influence at court until Hugh Despenser the younger supplanted him, at which point, he joined the rebellion against the king in 1321/2. He captured Gloucester for the rebels, then burned Bridgnorth. He was part of the force that besieged Tickhill Castle and took part in the Battle of Burton-on-Trent.

At this point, his lands were confiscated and orders were given for his arrest. He was with the forces against the king when, possibly being wounded or ill, he was left behind at Tutbury Castle, where he was taken prisoner in March 1322.[29] At his trial, Roger was accused of false allegiance and being a traitor, killing the king's people and plundering the country; of besieging Tickhill (Tykille) and then going to Burton-on-Trent, with his banners unfurled – signifying a readiness to do battle – but fleeing when he saw 'the well-armed and mighty approach of your liege lord and his battalions, which you dared not meet and could not hinder… for which this court finds that for the treason you should be drawn, and for the robberies and murders, hanged'.[30] However, Roger cheated the executioner by dying *of illness* two days later. He was buried at St Mary's, Ware in Hertfordshire.

Sir William Montagu, 2nd Baron Montagu

William was not as much a favourite as Damory, but he still held great influence at court between 1316 and 1318. He was born around 1275, his family being prominent in Somerset, Dorset, and Devon. William spent a great part of his life in Scotland. He was at the siege of Stirling Castle with Edward I in 1304 and knighted by him in 1306.

In 1311, he was tasked with examining the defences of various castles around England, being appointed Keeper of Berwick Castle in 1314. He travelled with Edward II and Queen Isabella to France and, on his return, seems to have been Edward's roving trouble-shooter in Scotland, Wales and Bristol, where he settled grievances between the town's burgesses and the Constable of Bristol Castle.

In 1316, he became steward of Edward's household, on an income of 200 marks (£132 in 2024), but the following year, Edward made him 'King's Bachelor' and granted him several manors in lieu of the 200 marks. In 1318, he was appointed the keeper of Abingdon Abbey, but in November of that year, Edward sent him to Gascony as Seneschal – sort of major-domo – allegedly because Thomas, Earl of Lancaster accused Montagu of conspiring against him with Roger Damory.

In 1292, William had married Elizabeth de Montfort who gave him four sons and seven daughters. However, his eldest son, John, predeceased his father.

William died, still in Gascony, in October 1319. His grave site is not known for certain, but it was possibly at Bisham Abbey.[31]

The Dunheved Brothers

Not that much is known about Stephen and Thomas Dunheved.[32] However, they were real people, best known for trying to rescue Edward II from Berkeley Castle in 1327. Tanquerey comments that prior to the escape attempt, Stephen Dunheved had been accused of 'divers felonies', but avers that these were probably trumped-up charges to enable the arrest of those conspiring against Queen Isabella. A little while later, a letter patent was issued to Thomas of Berkeley Castle to arrest both Thomas and Stephen Dunheved.

Thomas Dunheved was a Dominican friar and eloquent preacher, who had, allegedly, been sent by Edward II to Rome to obtain a divorce from Queen Isabella. This has since proved to be false, but he was made a papal chaplain. He apparently let this go to his head and the Pope warned the Dominicans in England to keep an eye on him.[33] Upon his return to England, he heard that Edward had been imprisoned in Berkeley Castle and vowed to set him free. However, the conspiracy was unearthed and Thomas found himself in prison at Pontefract. He 'attempted to escape but that failed and he was thrown into a horrible cell where he died'.[34]

Stephen Dunheved had been lord of Dunchurch in Warwickshire but was accused of an indeterminate crime and abjured the realm – i.e. took himself abroad into exile. However, he returned when Edward pardoned him and joined the king's household as a valet. At that time, he was also ordered to seize all Roger Mortimer's lands and chattels, since the latter was in the Tower of London.[35] After the rescue attempt, he was also arrested, taken to Newgate and subjected to 'severe confinement'. Two years later, he escaped and was rearrested in 1329, at which point any mention of him disappears.[36]

So let us come to Edward's time at Berkeley. Thomas Berkeley married Roger Mortimer's daughter, later imprisoned by Edward II in a nunnery, so Edward was not Berkeley's favourite person!

In March 1327, Kenilworth was attacked by a group of men attempting to free Edward and the attempt was led by the Dunheved brothers.[37]

As far as the Dunheveds are concerned, nobody knows when they died. It is possible that Thomas might have taken part in the Earl of Kent's plot to free Edward in 1329/30 – when the latter is supposed to have been dead for two years.[38] However, Stephen, after his escape from Newgate, would have taken part in any plan to release Edward in 1329-30, so possibly both brothers were in the plot. Sadly, though neither of the brothers appear in any records after that.[39]

Edward III

ADAM RUTHERFORD, A twentieth-century geneticist, has claimed that it is 'virtually impossible' that a person with a predominantly British ancestry is not descended from Edward III. According to his calculations, 'almost every Briton is descended between 21 and 24 generations from Edward III' who had 13 children and an estimated 321 great-great-grandchildren.[1] Edward III is one of the most interesting monarchs England ever had. Ian Mortimer describes him as 'the perfect king'.

He was born at Windsor Castle in November 1312 and, although his parents had married as part of a diplomatic initiative, the marriage was, in general, happy until its last years. Edward was created Earl of Chester when he was less than two weeks old and from that moment on, had his own household. We do not know a lot about his early years, but the Bishop of Durham became a mentor to him.

He spent a lot of his childhood in the middle of the tensions and arguments between Edward II and the Despensers on one side and the barons on the other. When, in 1325, Charles IV of France, Edward II's brother-in-law, demanded homage for Aquitaine, Isabella took the young Edward to the French court, ostensibly, to negotiate a peace, but in reality to escape her husband and the overweening Despensers. In France, she met Roger Mortimer, becoming quickly obsessed with him. They returned to England with an army, summoned parliament and had Edward II deposed, putting her son on the throne as Edward III.[2]

He was crowned in February 1327. At the time, the new king was just 14 years of age with his mother under the malign influence of Roger Mortimer. Almost immediately, Edward was made aware that he was a figurehead with no real power. Mortimer became increasingly arrogant and high-handed (surprise surprise), making him extremely unpopular. But what was the final straw for the young king, was Mortimer's treatment of his uncle, the Duke of Kent. Kent believed Edward II was still alive under guard in Berkeley Castle and launched a bid to free him. Mortimer, increasingly aware that his power base was dwindling, and that he and Isabella were under threat, arrested Kent on a charge of treason. The resulting trial was nothing to do with what Kent had done, but rather the degree of power Mortimer wielded.

Edward III was powerless to stop his uncle from being executed. However, when the earl was led out to execution, the captain of the guard refused to behead him and so did all his men. Mortimer had to find a latrine cleaner, already sentenced to death, to agree to perform the execution in return for his life.[3] From that moment on, Edward was determined to avenge his uncle of Kent. If you want to read one of the most thrilling beginnings to any biography, try the Introduction to Ian Mortimer's *The Perfect King* (details in the Select bibliography). It gives a blow-by-blow account of how Edward's adherents crept up a secret passage in Nottingham Castle and took Mortimer prisoner.[4]

Edward then issued a proclamation announcing he had taken the government of England into his own hands. The first item of business was Mortimer's trial. He was charged with

> accroaching to himself the royal power, stirring up dissension between Edward II and the queen, teaching Edward III to regard the Earl of Lancaster as his enemy, deluding Edmund of Kent into believing that his brother was alive and with procuring his execution, accepting bribes from the Scots for concluding the disgraceful peace, and with perpetrating grievous cruelties in Ireland.[5]

Edward made sure Mortimer was bound and gagged during the trial, just as the late Duke of Kent had been. He was found guilty and sentenced to be dragged to the gallows at Tyburn, wearing the black clothes he had worn at Edward II's funeral, and hanged.[6] Mortimer's adherent, Sir Simon Bereford was also executed, but Sir Oliver Ingham, another accomplice, was pardoned. Mortimer's lands were taken by the crown.

But what to do about his mother? The Pope wrote two copies of the same letter – to ensure at least one of them reached Edward – begging him to show mercy to Isabella. She voluntarily gave up all her estates and, for the next few months, kept a low profile, sensible girl. She was given some of her manors back and, regularly visited by her son, lived in retirement, dying in 1358.[7]

At last, Edward was king in his own right, but he had huge problems. Already, rumours were flying around that Edward II was still alive. Edward III decided that since Mortimer had devised the death of Edward II, the new young king would maintain that his father was dead and that he had been murdered on Mortimer's orders. All the ringleaders of the Berkeley Castle murder had fled, leaving only Lord Berkeley, who stoutly denied he even knew the former king was dead. Edward held him in custody for a while and then released him.[8]

At this time, Edward was 19 years old. He was described as shorter than either his father or grandfather, both of whom had topped 6', but with fine proportions, long hair and a flowing beard. He was courteous and gregarious, with a love of fine clothes, delighting in the ceremony of being king. Edward loved magnificent buildings and it is to him we owe much of the embellishments of Windsor Castle and St George's Chapel, as well as improvements to Westminster Abbey. He also had a great love of chivalry including the cult of King Arthur, and is responsible for the round table still on display at Windsor.

Unhappy with the peace with Scotland signed in his name but without his consent in 1328, Edward repudiated it and in 1333 marched north and won the Battle of Dupplin Moor. Later he besieged Berwick and defeated the Scots at Halidon Hill, but ultimately, it was, as trying to defeat the Scots always had been, futile and costly.

His marriage to Philippa was a happy one and the fact that they had so many children was greeted as the epitome of royal achievement. Nine survived to maturity, although they lost their daughter, Joan, in the Black Death epidemic. However, the very fact that they had so many children, became a problem later on because it created a situation where there were so many branches of the family, it ultimately led to the deposition of Richard II and was a significant factor in the Wars of the Roses.[9]

Then we come to the Hundred Years' War. Edward started it by invading Flanders in order to assert his claim to the French throne. However, the French principle of salic law meant he couldn't claim the throne of France. BUT, the English royal family was French in origin, so that gave him his excuse to lay claim to titles and territory in France. The whole thing became a battle between the House of Valois – Philip VI of France and the House of Plantagenet – Edward III of England. The conflict lasted for 116 years and ended in France keeping everything except Calais.[10]

Life in England was made worse in 1348 by the Black Death, which originated in China, spread west to the Mediterranean and then swept through Europe like wildfire, leading to social and political chaos. It reached Bristol first, spread east and north to Scotland and Scandinavia. The immediate disaster was to trade and agriculture because so many people died. The lack of labour led to wage rises for both artisans and ordinary working people. The French chronicler Froissart stated that one third of Europe's population died. In England, it was calculated that by 1400, the population was half what it had been in 1300. Whole villages vanished.[11]

Despite all this, Edward continued to involve the English armies in European business. In 1346, he had landed in Normandy marching across France, but not intending to fight the French until he had met up with his Flemish allies. At Crécy, all that changed, and the English army defeated the much larger French one. He then laid siege to Calais for a year before it surrendered. From that point on, Calais was English territory until Bloody Mary lost it in 1558, a loss that possibly hastened her death.

Nevertheless, the effects of the Black Death, especially regarding labour shortages, put a stop to Edward's gallop for about ten years. He concentrated on getting England back on its feet with legislation such as the Statute of Labourers, which tried to regulate wages against the argument of supply and demand.

During this time, Edward tried to raise the nobility of war, making the tenets of chivalry become almost like a national identity and thus uniting the king with his nobles. It was Edward who introduced dukedoms for the royals, thus creating a new order of chivalry. At Windsor, he held a feast lasting several days where there was jousting and the announcement of the Round Table of King Arthur, where lords had to take an oath.

By the mid-1350s, his eldest son, also called Edward, but better known as the Black Prince, had earned his military spurs and in 1356, he led the outnumbered English army to victory at Poitiers and not only routed the French army, but captured King John II and his son, Philip.

Towards the end of his reign, Edward suffered losses and internal political discord followed. He had always been bored by affairs of state, preferring to go on military campaigns, leaving the day-to-day running of England to his close confidants, who now began to die off. So, he turned to his sons instead. This led to conflict between the Black Prince and John of Gaunt, the latter being very unpopular. There had been military failures in Europe and these were exacerbated by people's discontent with taxes, especially given complaints about the royal household expenses. Then the Black Prince died in 1376, leaving his young son as the aging king's heir. The Good Parliament of 1376 passed legislation to deal with the corrupt royal council, John of Gaunt being a particular target. He was forced to acquiesce to their demands, but the following year, by which time he was the young Richard II's guardian and Regent of England, he reversed the legislation, dismissing the new council and restoring some of the old councillors.[12]

At some point in the 1360s, Edward's aging eye had lighted on Alice Perrers, one of Queen Philippa's household ladies. More of her later. However, it is true to say she took advantage of his increasing mental infirmity to make herself a very rich woman. When Edward died of a stroke in June 1377, it is said she stripped the rings from his fingers before fleeing the court.

For centuries, historians have claimed that Edward was the 'flower of kings past, a pattern for kings to come, a clement king, the bringer of peace to his people'. He is described as an ambitious warrior, unscrupulous, selfish, extravagant and ostentatious.[13] However, in more recent times, his reputation has suffered as the king who started the Hundred Years' War for no better reason than vainglory; who reigned over the 1348 epidemic of Black Death that decimated the population; who taxed the country to the verge of bankruptcy so he could continue his ultimately useless military forays; and whose final years were spent with a rapacious mistress who took advantage of his descent into senility, before dying and leaving England with a child as king. It was the beginning of the descent that led to the Wars of the Roses some 80 years later. Edward III was also the most recent king from whom the future Henry VII, 100 years later – the king who put an end to the Plantagenet line – could claim direct descent.

Before we leave Edward III, let us quickly look at the still much-debated death of Edward II, because his death came to haunt Edward III's successor, Richard II. And for this section, I am leaning entirely on the points raised by Ian Mortimer.[14]

Every single contemporary chronicle states Edward died at Berkeley Castle in 1327. Mortimer points out that everything we read about the past has been written by somebody who read it, saw it, or heard it. Everything has been filtered by those who wrote it down, something Mortimer categorises as 'events can't write'. It comes down to certainty and with that comes a need for proof. And with that comes the difficulty because so many things cannot be proven absolutely.

So, we have two theories: that Edward died in 1327 or he didn't. In the first theory, we have to take into account contemporary chroniclers who wanted to toe the official line and not fall foul of the royal family. We have, for example, Geoffrey le Baker who claims William Bishop was an eye-witness to Edward's murder. But Bishop was not actually at Berkeley at the time.

Official records produce a mass of evidence to say Edward died at Berkeley, but they do not all hold water and they all stem from one announcement, by Lord Berkeley, of Edward's death. Berkeley was Mortimer's son-in-law and Mortimer was running England at that time. I'll leave that one with you, especially because, in 1330 when Mortimer was dead, the relevant parliament roll states that Berkeley said he knew nothing about Edward's death 'nor did he ever know of his death until this present Parliament'. The thick plottens!

Evidence that Edward II was still alive in 1330 comes from nine documents.[15]

These documents were recorded by respected, credible, people on both sides of the political divide. This is not the place to go into too much detail, but I would suggest the interested reader starts with Ian Mortimer's blogs and his biography of Edward III.

Fun Fact

Edward III was an innovative monarch. In 1337, he created the duchy of Cornwall with the aim of providing the heir to the throne with an independent income. He also founded the Order of the Garter in 1348.

Sir Walter de Manny (or Mauny)

Walter was born in Mauny, not far from Rouen in about 1310. Not much is known about his childhood, but he was in the household of William I, Count of Hainault and the count's brother may well have looked after Walter and his brothers. He first came to England as a page in the household of Queen Philippa on her marriage to Edward III in January 1328. He is known to have been either a friend or an acquaintance of the chronicler, Froissart, who described him as the 'Queen's esquire carver, and Keeper of the Queen's Greyhounds'.[16]

Walter was present at the Battle of Dupplin Moor and acquitted himself well. In the same campaign, when Edward besieged Berwick, Walter captured a pirate called John Crabbe, who then adhered to Edward's service and was known to be an expert in fighting sea battles. Manny was made Admiral of the Northern Seas in 1337. At that time, this meant the north Atlantic, the Irish Sea, the North Sea, the Baltic and the White Sea.[17] He also accompanied Edward on his campaigns into Europe, distinguishing himself at the Battle of Sluys and proving to be a bold and able commander of troops. He went to the aid of Joanna of Flanders against Charles of Blois, who was besieging her.

Walter was captured by the enemy in 1346 and thrown into prison, but quickly escaped and joined Edward in the siege of Calais. When Edward wanted to put the burghers of Calais to death, he joined Queen Philippa in successfully pleading for their lives. In 1349, the French tried to regain Calais, and Walter is believed to have fought alongside Edward and the Black Prince.

He was often sent by Edward on diplomatic missions as a negotiator, and was made responsible for the safety of John II, who had been captured and was a prisoner in Calais. In Edward's later years, Walter fought with John of Gaunt in France and was his second in command.[18]

About 1335 he married Margaret, daughter of Thomas Plantagenet, Earl of Norfolk, a son of King Edward I. She was Countess of Norfolk in her own right and outlived Walter by many years. In 1397, Margaret was created Duchess of Norfolk by Richard II, Edward III's grandson.

In 1347, Walter was summoned to parliament as a baron. Two years later, after the worst of the Black Death was over, he bought land near Smithfield, had it consecrated and designated it a burial site for the huge numbers of plague victims. Nearby he bought ground from the Bishop of London, and built a chapel called Newchurchhaw and also founded a Carthusian monastery called *La Salutation Mère Dieu* (the House of the Salutation of the Mother of God), leaving instructions in his will that he should be buried there. This later became the site of the charterhouse, whose monks resisted Henry VIII during the dissolution of the monasteries, and who were starved to death, their prior being hanged, drawn and quartered at Tyburn. The almshouses are still occupied, but the school was relocated to Godalming in 1872.

In 1359, Walter was made a Knight of the Garter and was awarded lands in England and France. He died in 1372 without leaving a son. His daughter, Anne became baroness de Mauny, but when her only son died, the barony became extinct.[19]

John Beauchamp

John played a major role in Edward III's military endeavours, but he is frequently overlooked because of his elder brother, Thomas, Earl of Warwick, who was a commander at Crécy and Poitiers. John was not as go-getting as his brother, but he was favoured by Edward III and Queen Philippa. He dipped into the land market now and then, but never displayed any overt signs that he wanted to be a huge landowner, unlike most of his contemporary nobles. He was also uninterested in continuing his line, since he never married, but that was not for want of opportunity. He was granted the hand of Margaret, widow of John de Bohun, 'if she will marry him'. Obviously, she didn't. She preferred to go on pilgrimage to Santiago, and John is not known to have tried to ever find anyone else to marry.

He was really a military man, first and last. He thrived in the atmosphere of campaigns and military strategy, seeming to care for very little else. The second son of Guy, Earl of Warwick, he has, as far as historians are concerned, always lived in the shadow of his elder brother. Notwithstanding, he was an important part of Edward's military campaigns. The seventeenth-century writer William Dugdale calls him 'a man of singular note in his time'.

The first record of him appears in the Exchequer rolls for 1331, and he is listed as having paid 100 shillings for a farm near Bromsgrove and Norton in Worcestershire. Later he received a grant to hold Bromsgrove and Norton for eight years at a rent of £10 per annum. This appears to have been the beginning of him being granted lands that had been forfeited, and it may be that he began his rise after Roger Mortimer's lands were seized That said, his brother, Thomas' wife had been Mortimer's daughter, so the grant of land may have had something to do with Edward's desire to heal rifts.

He was granted various manors and lands throughout his life, which seems to have been a concerted effort by the king, queen and their eldest son to raise John's social and fiscal level to the status that would be expected of him in the fourteenth century. These gifts not only gave him a recognised place in the nobility of England, but also raised his profile when he was a captain in the French wars.

What is also known is that Queen Philippa seems to have become almost like a business partner to John. He, along with two other knights, is known to have owed her £2,520 in 1337 – roughly £2,700,150.34 in 2023.[20] It is not known why he owed her this much money, but it was possibly to help his upcoming military service.

As well as Queen Philippa and the Black Prince, Edward of Woodstock, became one of John's patrons This possibly dates from the time of the Battle of Crécy, when he was a royal standard bearer, and the prince was a battle commander. Their connection may also date from the founding of the Order of the Garter in 1348. At this time, the prince would still have been in his teens and John would have been in his 30s, so it is difficult to define the precise nature of their friendship. But it is not beyond the bounds of possibility that Beauchamp was something of a mentor and it must have stemmed from his proven capability as a military captain and administrator. A bond was made between them for £332 15s 6d (roughly £432,000), and the prince ordered a gift of 2 tuns of wine to be delivered to Beauchamp.

Further gifts followed, including 'a cloth of Turkie' and an order that John be given 'the best mare' at the stud in Risbergh.

John died in 1360, still perhaps acting as an occasional member of the Black Prince's household because he is listed as a witness on one of the latter's charters. He was buried in the old St Paul's Cathedral, which was destroyed by the Great Fire of London.[21]

Alice Perrers

Alice Perrers was the much-hated mistress of Edward III. The chronicler, Thomas of Walsingham, described her as, 'a shameless, impudent, harlot... of low birth'. Obviously he didn't like her very much, but then, neither did most people.

She was ambitious, with two great disadvantages. She was the daughter of a thatcher, so of low social rank, and she was a woman. However, we have to take Thomas' words with a huge fistful of salt, because he was a known misogynist, a vehement critic of the courts of Edward III and his successor, Richard II, and, his abbey near Oxney was one Alice worked hard to accumulate in her rapacious land-grab. So, make that a shovelful of salt.

Just who was this woman who rose from such humble beginnings to become the adored darling of an aging and increasingly senile king? There have been over the centuries plenty of theories. That she was the niece of William Wykeham, Bishop of Winchester, who became Edward's chancellor and was also very much disliked, leading to stories that he, too, was of low birth. That she was the daughter of a Devon weaver, or the daughter of John Perrers of Holt in Norfolk, or the illegitimate daughter of the Earl of Warenne.[22] She was born around 1348 and although her ancestry has been a hot topic of debate, it may be that Perrers was the surname of her first husband.

She entered Queen Philippa's household as a child of about 10 as a *damsel*. But she did not catch Edward's eye until she was around the age of 18, when he would have been in his mid-fifties.[23] The queen seems to have turned a blind eye to the relationship. Slowly becoming bedridden, with a broken collar bone that never healed properly and suffering from dropsy or possibly gout, Philippa could no longer travel around the country to be at her husband's side.[24]

Queen Philippa died in 1369, three years after Alice became Edward's mistress. Edward was distraught at his queen's death. She had been his strength and stay since their first meeting when his father was still king, all through the furore with Roger Mortimer, and had looked after England when he was fighting in France. However, Edward gave Alice jewellery that had not just belonged to Philippa but overrode the queen's will, which stated the jewels had been left to another woman.[25]

After Philippa's death, he leaned very much on Alice to help him through his grief, but this, not unnaturally, made her even more unpopular at court. At a tournament at Smithfield Alice was presented as 'The Lady of the Sun', taking pride of place next to the king. This was a shocking break in etiquette, since that place should have been taken by Joan of Kent, Edward's daughter-in-law, or one of his own daughters, but definitely not his mistress. She was also accused of sitting at the court of the king's Bench to ensure her friends and those who had bribed her were given preferential treatment.[26]

It didn't help that she was ambitious and rapacious regarding money and lands, especially when Edward showered her with gifts and made her not just a very wealthy and powerful woman, worth over £6 million in today's money, but one who it was not wise to cross. Her power after 1370 made her a person to fear, for she was seen to manipulate Edward to the point where he was said to be afraid of her.

In 1375, when it was clear his health was failing, Alice married Sir William de Windsor to ensure she would be fine after the king died. De Windsor was Edward's lieutenant in Ireland and spent long periods of time away from England. It was easy, therefore, to keep the marriage secret. De Windsor was 53. Alice was 27. They had no children, although she had three children with Edward, a son and two daughters.

Alice was at court during the tenure of the poet, Geoffrey Chaucer, brother-in-law to John of Gaunt's long-time mistress and later duchess, Katherine Swynford. It is thought that the poet based the character of the Wife of Bath in the *Canterbury Tales* on Alice.[27]

In 1376, Alice was tried for corruption and dismissed from court. Edward was furious but powerless. However, she soon returned by permission of John of Gaunt. When Edward died, she was accused of stripping the rings from his fingers and fleeing but other accounts say Edward's sons were at his bedside when he died.

In 1377, under Richard II, she was again accused of interfering in estate business and exiled, but she didn't leave, since her husband, William de Windsor, made an open statement that she was his wife.[28]

In 1379, the royal treasurer confiscated 21,868 pearls from her and returned them to the royal wardrobe. However, she was later able to return to England and regain some of her lands. At the height of her power, she possessed 56 manors, castles, and houses spread over 25 counties. When, in 1374, a property dispute arose with the abbot of St Albans, Edward intimidated the judges. The abbot, unsurprisingly, abandoned his claim.

Alice died in late 1400 or early 1401 at the age of around 52 and is buried in St Laurence's graveyard in Upminster, but there is no marker to show where her grave lies.

Richard II

RICHARD II, OR Richard of Bordeaux, was born in 1367 in the archbishop's palace at Bordeaux in Aquitaine, to Joan, Fair Maid of Kent and Edward of Woodstock – the Black Prince. He was the grandson of Edward III and is one of the most controversial monarchs England ever had, sometimes paired with Edward II when describing 'bad kings'. Richard's reputation, in common with that of Richard III, has been very much manipulated by Shakespeare's play.[1]

As Edward III descended into senility, his heir, the Black Prince contracted what many medical experts now believe was probably amoebic dysentery, but might also have been malaria or inflammatory bowel disease. All were recurring diseases very common in medieval times. When we consider that Edward had been more or less continuously fighting wars since the age of 16, when his diet would be prone to unpasteurised dairy food and raw meat, it is not surprising that for the final nine years of his life, his illness was chronic. He finally succumbed in 1476 at the age of 45.[2]

When Edward III died a year later, he left the throne to a 10-year-old child. Ecclesiastes 10:16 states: 'Woe to thee, O land, when thy king is a child, and thy princes eat in the morning!,' which basically means that the land is led by an irresponsible child and is therefore at the mercy of those who really govern, not the monarch. Edward, Richard's elder brother, died when the young Richard was 3. There was considerable disquiet at the prospect of a boy-king. The Black Prince, Richard's father, apparently, did not presume Richard would inherit after him. It was John of Gaunt who swore an oath that Richard should inherit, and that he, as Richard's uncle, would protect him and uphold his inheritance. Furthermore, it appears that Edward III, after the death of his eldest son, settled the order of succession, drawing up a document that stated Gaunt was now his heir apparent and after him, Gaunt's son, Henry of Bolingbroke. The document disappeared some time during Richard's reign although the witnesses to it knew what it said.[3]

For Richard's first years on the throne, he had regency councils, who, for political reasons were not led by his uncles, John of Gaunt, Duke of Lancaster, who was much hated, or Thomas of Woodstock, Earl of Buckingham. In fact, when the Black Prince died, parliament was so fearful John of Gaunt would usurp the crown, they quickly invested the young Richard as Prince of Wales, along with his dead father's other titles. He was crowned less than a month after Edward III's death.[4]

Despite this, fears over John of Gaunt's ambitions remained and a series of councils, from which Gaunt was excluded, helped Richard rule. Gaunt and Buckingham still held some influence, but Richard's friends and councillors gained increasing power as the years went on. However, parliament was not happy with their influence over the king and these councils were discontinued in 1380.

The unhappiness with the favourites was, in the main, due to a heavy rates of taxation in succeeding poll tax collections spent on futile military European expeditions. Life for the lower social orders had become increasingly difficult since the Black Death of 1348, and tension between landowners and those working for them grew. This lit a spark of rebellion, culminating in the Peasants' Revolt of 1381.[5] An army of peasants gathered at Blackheath and marched on London. They razed the hated Gaunt's Savoy Palace to the ground, marched on the Tower of London, dragged out the Archbishop of Canterbury, Simon Sudbury, and Robert Hales, the Lord High Treasurer, and executed them.

Richard, sheltering in the Tower, agreed that the crown did not have the forces necessary to disperse the mob and agreed to negotiate on their demands to abolish serfdom. What happened next fed Richard's view of kingship and his role as king. He rode out the next day but the crush of people made him turn back. However, on the following day, 14 June, he met the rebels, with Wat Tyler at their head, at Mile End, where he agreed to their demands. However, they didn't believe him, and why would they? They continued rioting. Richard met Tyler at Smithfield the next day and reiterated his promise, but this meeting ended when the Mayor of London pulled Tyler from his horse and killed him.[6]

Richard, aged only 14, acted with incredible composure, shouting to the rebels that he was their captain and leading them away. He agreed that they were pardoned, should disperse and return to their homes. They did. As soon as Richard was safe, he revoked all charters of freedom, personally subdued the rebels in Essex, and then ruthlessly hunted down the leaders and executed them. The fact of his personal courage, plus awareness of the dangers of civil disobedience, can only have bolstered his view of kingship as absolute.

He married Anne of Bohemia in 1382, a marriage that was not popular in the country. The marriage was childless, although very happy until Anne died in 1394, whereupon Richard married again, to the 8-year-old Isabella of Valois. Michael de la Pole – more of him later – had been instrumental in the marriage negotiations, as had Sir Simon Burley. Since de la Pole had come from the merchant class, Richard creating him Earl of Suffolk in 1383 made the king even more unpopular. Richard's close friendship with Robert de Vere, Earl of Oxford, was equally unpopular, especially when de Vere was made Duke of Ireland in 1386.

Things came to a head after various European military failures, led by John of Gaunt, which soured the relationship between uncle and nephew. Gaunt left England, married Constance of Castile and tried to have himself declared King of Castile. That failed, too.

Meanwhile back in England, tensions had deteriorated further. Richard had an elevated sense of his royal prerogative and formed a court party. The greatest lords in England placed the government of England into the hands of a parliamentary commission, which Richard only assented to when he was threatened he would share the fate of Edward II, his great-grandfather if he didn't agree.

Michael de la Pole had demanded an extraordinary level of tax for the defence of the realm. Parliament refused to even consider it until de la Pole was removed from office. Richard, now on his high horse of absolutism, replied that he would not dismiss so much as a scullion at the request of parliament. Bad move. Parliament threatened to depose him. Richard backed down.[7] But he was furious and immediately began to create a loyal military power base. Another bad move.

When Richard returned to London, he was confronted by Gloucester (formerly Earl of Buckingham), Warwick, and Arundel, all demanding that de la Pole, de Vere, the mayor of London, Sir Simon Burley, and the Archbishop of York should be attainted for treason. The peers were joined by Gaunt's son, Henry of Bolingbroke, Earl of Derby, and Thomas Mowbray, Earl of Nottingham. These five lords became known as the Lords Appellant. In the Merciless Parliament of 1388, Alexander Neville, Archbishop of York, was imprisoned for the rest of his life. De la Pole and de Vere fled England never to return. The others were executed. A delicate peace reigned and Richard bided his time. For almost ten years.

In 1397, Richard decided he was strong enough to enact his revenge. The following two years are known as the 'tyranny of Richard II'. He had Gloucester, Arundel, and Warwick arrested. Arundel was condemned and executed. Gloucester died awaiting trial, but whether Richard ordered him to be killed so as not to have to execute a prince of royal blood is only conjecture.

Warwick was condemned, but then exiled for life. Richard then visited his wrath on those who had been loyal to the Lords Appellant, although Henry Bolingbroke, Earl of Derby, and Thomas Mowbray, Earl of Nottingham, were given new titles, presumably because their executions would be too risky for the king. Derby, John of Gaunt's eldest son, was perceived by Richard as the biggest threat to his throne. The House of Lancaster was the wealthiest in the realm, and of royal descent. Then Bolingbroke played directly into Richard's hands by having a very public quarrel with Thomas Mowbray. He exiled both of them.[8]

With his most pressing opponents no longer in England, Richard voided all the acts of the Merciless Parliament and declared that no restraint could be put on the king, thus making him an absolute monarch. In 1399, Gaunt died. Richard seized the moment. He extended Henry Bolingbroke's exile to life and appropriated all the Lancastrian holdings. Further, he demanded he must now be called 'Highness', 'Royal Majesty', or 'High Majesty'. He would sit on his throne for hours without speaking but if he looked at anyone, they had to fall on their knees. He tried to develop an environment where the monarch was a distant but adored figure embracing art and culture instead of war. Well, I suppose it made a pleasant change from his father and grandfather! Not to mention his great and great-great grandfathers.

He rebuilt Westminster Hall, had statues of himself erected, and generally laid down the foundations of English as a literary language. Chaucer served him as a diplomat.[9]

Henry Bolingbroke spent most of his exile in Paris. Louis, Duc d'Orléans, not at all interested in entente with England, decided it was time Henry left France and said so. This coincided with Richard taking a force to Ireland to punish the Irish nobility who had broken their submissions to him. It was Henry's turn to seize the moment.

With a small band of followers, he arrived at Ravenspur on the Yorkshire coast, declaring he only returned to claim his inheritance. Percy of Northumberland believed him and let him pass. Richard had taken most of the nobility with him so there was very little resistance to Bolingbroke, especially when Richard extended his stay in Ireland. When the king finally returned, he was forced to surrender to Bolingbroke at Flint Castle with the promise that, if he abdicated, his life would be spared. Richard, the absolute monarch, was forced to ride behind Bolingbroke all the way back to London, where he was imprisoned in the Tower of London.

However, this put Bolingbroke in something of a tangle. He was determined to be king but needed to present a rational argument for taking the throne. He argued that Richard's tyranny rendered him unworthy to reign. But, there was a problem. Just one I hear you ask? The real heir was Edmund Mortimer, great-grandson of Gaunt's elder brother, Lionel. Bolingbroke solved that one by stating that Mortimer's claim was through his grandmother, Philippa of Clarence, whereas his own was through the direct male line from Edward III. Parliament, being pragmatic, agreed with him. Good move.

In October 1399, Richard was officially deposed and Bolingbroke became Henry IV. And what of Richard? Henry had agreed that Richard's life would be spared. Until several earls decided they would sooner have Richard back on the throne, expressing their feelings in the Epiphany Rising in 1400.

That really signed Richard's death warrant. The general opinion in Henry IV's court was that Richard could not be permitted to live. Nobody knows exactly how and when he died in Pontefract Castle, but it is thought he was starved to death, succumbing around 14 February 1400. His body was displayed in St Paul's Cathedral to show his body had suffered no violence, and he was buried in the priory at Kings Langley. In an act of atonement, in 1413, Henry V had his body reinterred in Westminster Abbey next to that of his wife, Anne.

Fun Fact

There is ample evidence that angels played a huge part in Richard's iconography. During his coronation procession, the Great Conduit in Cheapside was transformed into a tableau of the Heavenly City. A mechanical angel bowed and offered Richard a golden crown. Later, in 1392 when Richard was reconciled with the City of London, he processed through Cheapside again. An eyewitness account states, 'At his entry into Cheapside...came two angels down from a cloud, the one bearing a crown for the king...and the other another crown, which was presented to the queen...the conduits of the city...ran with wine...and angels made great melody and minstrelsy.'[10]

Robert de Vere

Robert de Vere was the son of the 8th Earl of Oxford and succeeded to the title in 1371 at the age of nine. He married Philippa de Coucy, cousin to King Richard, but began an affair with one of Queen Anne's ladies in waiting, Agnes Lancecrona. De Vere and Philippa separated, the marriage was annulled, and he married his mistress. Richard made him Duke of Ireland.[11] Agnes was described by chroniclers as 'low born and ugly'. In fact, the same thing that had been said of Edward III's mistress, Alice Perrers.

De Vere was hugely unpopular with the magnates – the high nobles of the land – because of his close friendship with King Richard and the fact that a year after making him marquess of Ireland, Richard conferred the dukedom of Ireland on him. This title was usually given to a royal, which de Vere was not.[12]

When the magnates organised opposition to the king's high-handed rule, calling themselves the Lords Appellant, de Vere led Richard's forces against them at the Battle of Radcot Bridge. Henry of Bolingbroke led the army for the Lords Appellant. He broke the central arch of the bridge over the Thames, impeding de Vere's progress and making him suffer a humiliating defeat. De Vere fled the field and headed for the Netherlands.[13]

He was found guilty of treason in his absence and sentenced to death. By 1392, he was living in Louvain in Belgium and, during a boar hunt, suffered injuries from which he died. Three years later, Richard had his body returned to England for re-burial, after he had had the coffin opened and kissed his friend's hand in farewell.[14]

De Vere's mother, who was descended from Henry III, supported his first wife, and in 1399, the annulment of the marriage was reversed. Philippa was granted her dower rights and an annuity.[15]

Simon Burley

Sir Simon Burley was born in 1336. Although his parentage is uncertain, he may have been a younger brother of Sir John Burley who received the Garter at the accession of Richard II. He first served in the fleet which destroyed the Spanish corsairs in 1350. In 1355 he took part in one of the expeditions of Edward, Prince of Wales (the Black Prince). By 1364 he was in attendance on the Prince in Aquitaine. Burley was attacked near Lusignan in 1369 and taken prisoner by the French. The Black Prince exchanged him for the Duchess of Bourbon in 1370, and Burley rejoined the Prince at Limoges.[16]

Edward seems to have rated Burley highly, because he made him responsible for the education of his son, Richard. This was such a successful collaboration that when Richard became king at the age of 10, Burley immediately became one of the most powerful people at court. He was granted lands and made Constable of Windsor Castle for life, the master of the king's falcons, and Constable of Guildford and Wigmore. When Richard was 14, Burley became his tutor and was one of the negotiators for his marriage to Anne of Bohemia, travelling with the bride to England. He was out of the country during the Peasants' Revolt, although rumours circulated that he had encouraged it, mostly because he was blamed for imprisoning an escaped villein in Rochester. At that time, should a villein escape and live as a free man for a year, he became a free man. Although Burley was blamed for his imprisonment, it must have been one of his household who ordered it, since Burley was, at that time on the Continent.[17] As a reward for the successful marriage negotiations, he was made a Knight of the Garter.[18]

Upon his succession, Richard made him his vice-chamberlain. This, along with some legal irregularities that gave him manors to which he was not entitled, made him very unpopular. He wielded immense power, controlling access to Richard and advising him. In 1386, the bubbling resentments within the court factions flared up, although for the moment, Burley was not in the sights of the Lords Appellants. Their first target was Robert de Vere. When de Vere's forces were defeated, the Lords confronted Richard and demanded the removal of more courtiers, Burley among them. Richard refused.

It all boiled up in the Merciless Parliament. Burley was put on trial and sentenced to death. This caused an enormous adverse reaction because Burley was respected by many lords. The Duke of York threatened his brother the Duke of Gloucester with a duel and both Henry of Bolingbroke and Thomas Mowbray objected to Burley's sentence. Even Queen Anne went on her knees to Gloucester begging him – allegedly for three hours – to show mercy. It was Gloucester who was more determined than anyone that Burley must die 'if Richard wished to be King'. Furthermore, Gloucester insulted the queen when she knelt to him, something Richard reminded him about in 1397 when he took his revenge.[19]

What really turned the tide was the residue of feeling left over from the imprisonment of the villein issue. The people of Burley's Kent estates marched on London threatening another Peasants' Revolt if Burley were not executed. With extreme reluctance, Richard signed the death warrant, but insisted Burley was merely – merely – beheaded and not hanged, drawn, and quartered.

The Lords Appellant didn't care, so long as Burley was executed, which he was in May 1388. Richard never forgave them. Burley had been his friend and mentor from a very early age and it is more than likely his forced execution that hardened Richard's resolve to have his revenge on the people who had compelled him to kill Burley. His sentence was formally reversed in March 1399 when Richard had his day of reckoning.[20]

Michael de la Pole

Michael, the eldest son of William de la Pole, was born around 1330. His father, a Hull wool merchant frequently financed Edward III's needs for money. Thus, the de la Poles had become rich and influential.[21] By 1352 he had decided on a military career and was knighted. His marriage to Catherine in 1358 brought him several estates in East Anglia, and in 1385, the title 1st Earl of Suffolk was bestowed upon him.

Michael fought alongside Edward, the Black Prince, and John of Gaunt during the Hundred Years' War with France. Possibly, because of his military service, he was appointed admiral north of the Thames. He rose to prominence under Richard II, and his association with John of Gaunt, Duke of Lancaster and Richard's father, the Black Prince may well have accelerated his rise.

Under Richard II, he took a role as an ambassador to negotiate the marriage of Richard in 1379, alongside Robert de Vere and Sir Simon Burley. He became advisor to Richard II in 1381, and in 1383 he was appointed chancellor. However, being what some would term a jumped-up son of a merchant, he had powerful enemies. The writer Froissart believed that de la Pole gave bad advice to the king and made him suspicious of Gaunt. However, it is believed that de la Pole warned Gaunt of a plot to arrest him at a council meeting, so the jury is still out as to whether or not he retained his loyalty to the house of Lancaster.

In 1385, de la Pole went on expedition to Scotland and in that same year he was given the title 1st Earl of Suffolk. He was one of the main negotiators representing Richard in the peace discussions with France, but these did not go well and many people felt England had come out of the negotiations as the underdog. John of Gaunt was totally against making peace.[22]

To make matters worse, England was in a parlous financial state and de la Pole was one of the main targets of resentment.

Parliament demanded he be removed from office and impeached. Richard refused, but the pressure from the Lords Appellant was relentless and eventually, Richard caved in. De la Pole was removed from office and impeached on his deficiencies while chancellor. Despite his cogent arguments, he was found guilty of embezzlement and misusing his position. His lands were forfeit, but he retained his title as Earl of Suffolk. He was the first official in English history to be removed from office by the process of impeachment.[23] He was also fined 20,000 marks – roughly £13,200 in 2023 – and spent a short time in prison. Richard later had the fine voided.

As tensions between Richard and the Lords Appellant grew, Michael realised how vulnerable he was. He fled to Calais to his brother, Edmund, who, possibly because Michael disguised himself, refused him entry. He was detained, returned to England, and permitted to travel to Hull. Whatever the power of his permission to be in England, he knew his days would be numbered if he remained in the country, so he fled to the Netherlands and then to Paris. When a royal sergeant arrived in Hull to arrest him, the bird had flown.

Just as in the case of Robert de Vere, de la Pole was sentenced to death in absentia. He was stripped of all his lands and the earldom. He died in Paris in 1389. His son, also called Michael, successfully petitioned Henry IV to have his father's judgement reversed. The Suffolk title was restored together with some estates, but not all his father's previous holdings were forthcoming.[24]

Henry IV

HENRY OF BOLINGBROKE was born at, yes, Bolingbroke Castle, a small castle near Spilsby in Lincolnshire. His father, John of Gaunt had, since the early death of his eldest brother, Edward, the Black Prince, become the prime influence in the court of the young Richard II, the Black Prince's son. He also held lands in almost every county of England and accumulated enormous wealth. This led to rumours that Gaunt wanted to unseat the new boy-king and make himself monarch, although there is ample evidence that he acted honourably as mediator between the king and opposing court factions, which included his own son, Henry. Bolingbroke and Richard II, being first cousins, had been childhood playmates, but that did not stop him from usurping Richard's throne – or freeing England from Richard's tyranny, whichever camp you happen to be in.

On 30 June 1399, Bolingbroke returned from exile, landing at Ravenspur, one of 30 Yorkshire towns that has been lost due to coastal erosion. It is interesting to note that 72 years later, Edward, Duke of York, also landed there, echoing the actions of Bolingbroke almost exactly. However, back to the plot. Henry had been banished by Richard II in the summer of 1398 as part of the latter's revenge against the Lords Appellant. When John of Gaunt died in February 1399. Richard lost no time in seizing the whole of the duchy of Lancaster; all lands that were the inheritance of Gaunt's son, Henry. Believing that all was hunky-dory in Richard II-land, the king then sailed to Ireland, allegedly to punish the Irish lords who had broken their commitments to him and possibly to avenge the death of Roger Mortimer, the lord lieutenant of Ireland, who had been killed in 1398.

And Bolingbroke pounced.

He landed on the Yorkshire coast with a handful of servants and fellow exiles, claiming that he was only here to claim his rightful inheritance. Most people believed he meant his father's titles and lands. As Henry progressed across England, disaffected elements, fed up with Richard's despotism and sheer arrogance, flocked to his banner. Support for Richard dwindled. He returned post haste and was captured at Flint Castle in North Wales. The two cousins met on 16 August 1399. One of Richard's valets recorded their conversation: 'My lord,' Henry said, 'I have come sooner than you sent for me and I shall tell you why: it is commonly said among your people that you have, for the last 22 years, governed them very badly and far too harshly. If it please Our Lord, however, I shall now help you to govern them better.' This is probably medieval king-speak for 'Get out of that, you slimy toad!'

Of course, Henry knew better than anyone, should Richard retain his crown, he would, sooner or later, take his revenge. Leopards and spots and all that. So, the reality was that Richard was escorted to London, not as King of England, but as Bolingbroke's prisoner. On 30 September, Richard signed the warrant of abdication, and on 13 October 1399, Henry was crowned Henry IV of England. It was the pinnacle of his ambition and the beginning of his sea of troubles.[1]

Henry himself, following the Lords Appellants' rebellion against Richard in 1387, was not punished by Richard but spent time abroad taking part in the siege of Vilnius in 1390, and again in 1392, although both campaigns were failures. He also went to Jerusalem on pilgrimage and vowed to lead a crusade to free that city from the infidels.[2]

Although his relationship with Richard was precarious at the best of times, things came to a head in 1398 when Thomas de Mowbray made a remark about the king that Henry believed to be treason. The two agreed to a duel of honour but Richard, with John of Gaunt's approval, banished Henry from England for six years, and exiled Mowbray for life. I imagine Gaunt felt it safer to have his beloved son abroad safe and living to fight another day, rather than in England living in constant peril. When Gaunt died, Richard decided to make Henry's banishment permanent. He repealed all the legal documents that allowed Bolingbroke to inherit his father's lands. I think the modern term for what Richard did was something along the lines of a 'reign-limiting' move.

What happened next was inevitable. Two things of note happened at the time of Henry IV's accession. The first was he founded the House of Lancaster, and the second that he passed an act through parliament that the duchy of Lancaster would always remain in the personal possession of the reigning monarch. That is still true some 600-odd years later. When Queen Elizabeth II came to the throne, among her titles was Duke – not Duchess – of Lancaster. Richard was sent to Pontefract Castle, where Thomas Swynford, Henry's half-brother, son of Gaunt's long-time mistress and later duchess, Katherine Swynford, was the constable.

Henry had his kingdom, but his reign was full of woes. Within three months of becoming king, in the Epiphany Rising, the earls of Kent,

Huntingdon and Salisbury plotted to ambush the new king and his sons at Windsor. Although the plot was uncovered and the plotters executed, it highlighted that while Richard was alive, Henry's throne could never be secure. It is believed that by February 1400, Richard was dead, allegedly by starving himself to death. Henry put his body on display in St Paul's Cathedral to prove that, not only was the ex-king dead, but that death had been natural and not violent. Needless to say, rumour circulated for years that Richard was still alive. He was buried at the Priory at Kings Langley until Henry V brought his body back to London, interring the remains in the tomb Richard himself had commissioned in Westminster Abbey.[3]

The dust began to settle, until the Welsh under Owain Glyndŵr rose in revolt. Glyndŵr declared himself prince of Wales in 1400. From 1403–06, he controlled most of Wales. He proposed reintroducing Welsh laws, establishing a separate church of Wales and the establishment of two universities. He also made an alliance with Charles VI of France and in 1405, a French army landed in Wales to support Glyndŵr. Although suffering several defeats, Owain was never captured. In 1415, he is recorded as having died. His son, Maredudd ab Owain accepted a formal pardon from Henry V in 1421, thus ending a nearly 20-year simmering rebellion.[4]

In 1403, a much more serious revolt against Henry was spearheaded by Henry Percy, Earl of Northumberland, his brother, Thomas, Earl of Worcester, and Northumberland's son, known as Hotspur. They raised an army and met Henry at the Battle of Shrewsbury on 21st July 1403.[5] It was a hard-fought, bloody affair that resulted in Hotspur's death. Henry's son, Henry of Monmouth – I'll save my breath about his birthplace – later Henry V, received an arrow wound on the left side of his face that would have killed most people. The Earl of Worcester was executed, but Northumberland who wasn't at the battle claimed ignorance of it. Henry had no option but to give him the benefit of the doubt, although he stripped him of the lands and offices he had bestowed on the earl since 1399. The Percy family had, until the beginning of the fourteenth century held lands mainly in Yorkshire, but by the end of the century, they owned most of Northumberland and Cumberland, spreading north as far as the Scottish border.[6]

Henry never trusted Northumberland again. And with reason, because the earl, in cahoots with Richard Scrope, Archbishop of York, rebelled again. From his pulpit, the latter had fulminated against Henry's heavy taxation and 'evil counsellors'. Such was his oratory, Scrope soon found himself the leader of an army. He was arrested, brought before King Henry, convicted of treason, and beheaded outside York's city walls. That a high-ranking prelate was beheaded was akin to murdering the Pope. The Pope excommunicated everyone involved in Scrope's death, although they were all pardoned in 1407.[7]

Henry was also in trouble with the French. Richard's second queen, Isabella of Valois, was the daughter of Charles VI of France, although due to her age and Richard's deposition and death, the marriage was never consummated. After Richard's death, she and the French king demanded her return to France, but Henry wanted her to marry his son, Henry of Monmouth. Isabella refused point blank. She was eventually allowed back to France but Henry IV kept her dowry. Isabella died in 1409 at the age of 19 in childbirth. Until 1407 when Louis of Orléans, Isabella's brother, was assassinated, he preyed on English shipping and raided English ports. In French eyes, Henry was dirt, something that Louis of Orléans voiced frequently. It was only after Louis' death that Henry was referred to as 'Henry, King of England', instead of 'Henry of Lancaster, despoiler and wrongfully ruler of the Kingdom of England'.[8]

After 1406, Henry's health broke down, a punishment some believed for beheading Archbishop Scrope. It is certainly true that when he took the throne at the age of 33, he was energetic and athletic. His illness was a recurring one, flaring up in 1405, 1406, 1408–09, 1412 and 1413, when he died. Thomas Gascoigne writes that after Henry had ordered the execution of Archbishop Scrope, he was 'suddenly stricken with horrible leprosy of the worst sort'. For over a century after his death, it was believed he had been suffering from leprosy.

Some researchers have claimed that he suffered from Hansen's Disease, which directly contradicts Gascoigne's description of Henry having 'pustules'. But Hansen's Disease is a gradual one, and Henry's bouts of illness were sudden. J.D. Griffith Davies believed that Henry suffered from congenital syphilis, contracted from his father, but Gaunt was not promiscuous and this theory has insufficient evidence to support it. Edward Hall, the Tudor chronicler dismissed the 'leprosy sent by God as retribution' theory as 'superstitious nonsense'.

Henry is described as dying with his face and extremities eaten away, but in 1832 when his tomb was opened, his skin was intact, not at all disfigured and, the nasal cartilage which would have supported the leprosy theory, was undamaged. Peter McNiven posits that the sheer stress of all Henry's troubles might have led to the skin complaint psoriasis, which is exacerbated by stress. It is certainly true that at moments of high tension, Henry was taken ill. Most historians claim that he suffered the guilt of the usurper and that his actions in deposing Richard II weighed heavily on his conscience. Later historians have put forward theories that he had a stroke and, possibly a thrombosis of the leg leading to circulatory issues.[9]

His Lancaster counsellors took advantage of his recurrent bouts of illness. Parliament became full of Lancastrians; treason and rebellion were dealt with in the most vicious manner possible. In some ways, Henry became a prisoner of his house instead of its master. Shakespeare never wrote a truer word than in *Henry IV, Part* 2 when he said: 'uneasy lies the head that wears the crown'. There were numerous uprisings from those excluded from power in the north and the Midlands. It was left to Henry of Monmouth to sort these out. The future Henry V shouldered more responsibility as his father's health deteriorated still further. Henry IV died on 20 March 1413 and was buried, as was his wish, in Canterbury Cathedral.[10]

Today, we see the reigns of the late fourteenth and fifteenth centuries mainly through the eyes of William Shakespeare, who had to tread a fine political line in the reign of Elizabeth I. Henry IV does not come off well in the two plays about him. It must be remembered, however, that he did stop Richard II's tyrannical rampage. He also saw off all his enemies and, had he not been beset with illness, he may well have become one of England's greatest kings, for he had all the attributes necessary for a strong monarch.

It was mentioned earlier that Edward IV, the first king of the House of York, also landed at Ravenspur when he came to regain his kingdom. He also declared he had only returned to claim his just inheritance. And one other thing Henry IV and Edward IV had in common was neither of them ever lost a battle they led.

Fun Fact

Henry IV was not the first English king to speak English, but he *was* the first who spoke it as his primary language. This is possibly due to the fact he was not brought up to reign but usurped the throne from Richard II.

Thomas Swynford

Thomas was born in 1367, to Katherine Swynford and Sir Hugh Swynford of Lincolnshire and, upon his father's death in 1371, he inherited his father's lands at Kettlethorpe in that county. There have been assertions that Thomas could have been an illegitimate son of John of Gaunt by his mistress, later duchess, Kathrine Swynford.[11]

It would appear that there is some doubt as to the year of his birth. Weir puts this down to inaccurate records However, in an Inquisition between 1394/5, taken to establish Thomas' age, 12 witnesses came forward to declare that Thomas was born in 1373, 15 months after the death of Hugh Swynford. By 1394, most of those witnesses were between 50 and 70 years old, very old in fact for that era. They may have confused Thomas' baptism with that of John Beaufort, the eldest of the children of John of Gaunt and Katherine Swynford.[12] In 1411, Thomas requested the letters patent attesting to his birth. In these letters, Henry IV acknowledges that some people are doubtful of his parentage, but this is the first time any serious doubts were raised and it appears that, through Henry's efforts in 1411, Thomas was declared legitimate and able to claim his Swynford inheritance in Hainault.

What is known is that Thomas joined Gaunt's retinue around 1382, taking his father's place, which was the normal procedure. He bore the Swynford arms, and by 1390, he had joined the household of Henry of Bolingbroke, by then the Earl of Derby. Thomas became his liege man and stayed loyal to Henry when the latter became Henry IV. He also accompanied him on his expedition to Prussia. When John of Gaunt died in February 1399, he left Thomas 100 marks – roughly the equivalent of £66 in 2024. Henry IV made him one of the guardians of Richard II in Pontefract castle and it has long been believed that it was Thomas who killed the former king.[13]

Henry IV granted him the custodianship of the castle of Somerton, and by 1402, he was sheriff of Lincoln. He worked with his cousin, Thomas Chaucer – Katherine Swynford was the sister-in-law of the poet, Geoffrey Chaucer – and also Thomas' half-brother, John Beaufort – son of John of Gaunt and Katherine. They accompanied Henry's daughter, Blanche to Cologne for her wedding to the Count Palatine.

By 1404, Thomas was Captain of Calais on behalf of John Beaufort and helped negotiate a treaty with France and Flanders. However, he didn't speak French at all well, and, in common with his father, Hugh, he was definitely not the epitome of a diplomat. Whilst sheriff of Lincoln, he was fined for allowing a prisoner to escape, and it seems he suffered financial problems for most of his life. In 1409, he is listed as owing a London draper money, and is listed as 'late sheriff of Lincoln'. This probably explains why he was so anxious to satisfy the Hainault authorities that he was Hugh's son, and therefore, entitled to Swynford lands in Hainault, especially as Katherine and her sister Philippa were co-heiresses in land their father owned in Hainault.

Thomas' first wife died between 1416 and 1421 and in 1421, he married again, to Margaret Grey, Lady Darcy, described as, 'a young and well-endowed widow'. Margaret had rights to rents from land in Ireland, and it is possible that with these he was able to reclaim the Swynford manor at Kettlethorpe, which had been lost due to his financial situation. Records indicate he had a son, William Swynford, with Margaret, but his money worries never relented and by the time of his death in 1432, he had very little to leave. He appears to have lost Kettlethorpe and Coleby and held no lands at all in Lincoln. [14]

John Beaufort

This particular John Beaufort became the first Earl of Somerset and must not be confused with the John Beaufort who later became the first Duke of Somerset. Glad we've sorted that out.

John Beaufort was the eldest of the four children of John of Gaunt and Katherine Swynford, being born around 1371/1373. The surname Beaufort is believed to have come from his birthplace in Champagne, the manor of Beaufort. Historians believe Gaunt considered Beaufort a safe name to give his illegitimate children by Katherine Swynford.

When Gaunt married his 'scandalous duchess' (Alison Weir) in 1396, he asked Pope Boniface IX to legitimise them, which the Pope duly did. This caused so many problems later when the then Henry, Duke of Richmond, descended from the Beaufort and Tudor lines – both considered illegitimate – became Henry VII. It didn't help that Richard III declared his brother's sons ineligible to reign because their father, Edward IV had a precontract of marriage with Eleanor Butler, before marrying Elizabeth Woodville. That meant *all* Edward IV's children were illegitimate, including his eldest daughter, Elizabeth, who married Henry VII. You can see why it all became so confused and messy, can't you? Notwithstanding, one must remember that Edward III was the paternal grandfather of the Beaufort brood.[15]

They were declared legitimate twice by parliament, firstly during the reign of Richard II and again by Henry IV, but the latter barred them and their descendants from succeeding to the throne by inserting the phrase *excepta regali dignitate* (except royal status) in the documents.

It is probable that John spent his first years at his mother's manor of Kettlethorpe in Lincolnshire. Not only was it the house of Katherine's first husband, Hugh Swynford, it was about 150 miles from London, and therefore easier for Gaunt to visit unobtrusively. Although it is clear Gaunt cherished his Beaufort children, he was always careful to ensure they could have no claim on his legitimate heirs' Lancastrian inheritance. The four Beaufort children were also held in high regard by their legitimate half-siblings.[16] And, as we shall see, throughout the reigns of Henry V and Henry VI, the Beauforts were ubiquitous. Sorry, I have gone off on a tangent again. Let's get back to John Beaufort.

In common with other young men of his age and standing, John saw military service in Europe. He was the Lord Warden of the cinque ports and Lieutenant of Aquitaine among other appointments. In 1397, shortly after his confirmation of legitimacy, he was created Earl of Somerset, and supported Richard in his battle with the Lords Appellant, at which point he was created Marquess of Somerset and Marquess of Dorset.[17] Later that year, he was made a Knight of the Garter and married Richard's niece, Margaret Holland. Her father, Thomas Holland was the son of Joan, nicknamed the Fair Maid of Kent from her first marriage to Thomas Holland, 2nd Earl of Kent. She then became the wife of the Black Prince.[18] Thomas remained in Richard's favour even though his half-brother Henry of Bolingbroke was banished.

When Henry IV deposed Richard, he rescinded all titles that had been given to the late king's supporters, but John Beaufort retained his earldom. He quickly became a trusted supporter of the new king and was sent on diplomatic missions as well as military ones. In 1404, he was made Constable of England.

He and Margaret had six children. His grand-daughter was Margaret Beaufort, who married Edmund Tudor, the son of Henry V's widowed queen and Owen Tudor, her servant. John died in 1410, at the approximate age of 37 at the Royal Hospital of St Katharine by the Tower and is buried in Canterbury Cathedral close to the tombs of his uncle Edward of Woodstock and the Black Prince. It is probable that Henry IV chose his last resting place.[19]

It is worthy to note that all British monarchs since Henry IV are descended from John of Gaunt and most European monarchies feature him in their ancestry.

Ralph Neville

The Nevilles were one of the greatest families in late medieval England. Ralph Neville had 22 children by his two wives, but it was only the offspring by his second wife who became predominant in the fifteenth century. His grandson, Richard Neville became Earl of Warwick; his daughter Cicely married Richard, Duke of York and their children included the future Edward IV and Richard III. They were prominent in national affairs. However, they were not always a united family, ending up on opposite sides during the Wars of the Roses. They were divided by disputes over property and influence.[20]

Ralph Neville was born around 1364. I shall call him Ralph, since there were so many Nevilles in court circles, it is easier to identify him thus. By 1380, he was fighting in Brittany under the banner of Thomas of Woodstock, who knighted him. His cousin, Henry Percy, aka Hotspur, joined Ralph to preside over a duel between an Englishman and a Scot and both Ralph and his father were deputed to receive 24,000 marks – about £16,000 in 2024 – for the ransom of King David.

In 1385, jointly with Sir Thomas Clifford, he was appointed governor of Carlisle and a year later, again with Clifford, Warden of the West March. He inherited the title on the death of his father in 1388 and was made responsible for ensuring the security of the Scottish border fortifications. In 1397, he was negotiating peace with Scotland. So, it is clear from this that he was highly regarded by Richard II, while not being part of the court faction since he spent most of his time in the north of England. Middleham Castle was his base.

In 1397, he supported Richard against the Lords Appellant and was created Earl of Westmorland. So far, all was clear water. However, in June 1396 his first wife, Margaret Stafford died and before November of that year, he had married Joan Beaufort, daughter of John of Gaunt, Duke of Lancaster, and Katherine Swynford. This, of course, made Gaunt his father-in-law and split his loyalties. When Richard banished Henry of Bolingbroke, it put Ralph in a cleft stick. He kept faith with Richard until the latter confiscated the Lancaster estates after Gaunt's death in 1399 and changed Bolingbroke's banishment from six years to life.

Ralph decided to support Bolingbroke and joined him when the latter landed at Ravenspur. When Richard was brought to the Tower of London later that year, Ralph, along with the Earl of Northumberland were in the party of people who witnessed the king's abdication. For this show of fealty, the new king, now Henry IV, appointed Ralph as Earl Marshal for life, although in 1412, he resigned. Two of his brothers – Lord Furnival, who for a time was war treasurer, and Lord Latimer – were peers, and towards the close of the reign Ralph began to make those fortunate marriages for his numerous family members by his second wife. This enabled the younger branch of Nevilles to play so decisive a political role in England in later years.

One of the earliest of these marriages was that of his daughter Catherine in 1412 to the young John Mowbray, brother and heir of the unfortunate earl marshal who had been entrusted to his guardianship by the king. Shortly after Henry V's accession Westmorland must have resigned the office of Marshal of England into the hands of his son-in-law, in whose family it was hereditary. He also became one of the king's council, carried the sceptre at Henry IV's coronation, and was granted the lordship of Richmond for life.[21]

When Edmund of Langley, first Duke of York, died in 1403, Ralph was made a Knight of the Garter. However, although he retained responsibility for the security of the border with Scotland, it became clear that the Percy family of Northumberland were taking over all the wardenships in the Marches – the border between England and Scotland. The rivalry between the Nevilles and the Percies became intense, so much so that when the Percies rebelled in 1403, leading to the death of Hotspur and the execution of Thomas of Worcester, Henry IV ordered Ralph to raise troops and stop the Northumberland army who were at that time marching south. Ralph's forces drove the Northumberland troops back to Warkworth.[22]

In 1403, he was made Warden of Berwick and the East March and shortly thereafter, Warden of Carlisle and the West March.[23] Two years later, in 1405, Northumberland rebelled again, and marched towards Ralph's castle at Witton-le-Wear hoping to capture him, but Ralph had already escaped. He, along with Henry's son John of Lancaster marched to confront the forces of Archbishop Scrope and Thomas Mowbray of Norfolk, at Shipton Moor.

The archbishop's troops outnumbered those of Ralph and Lancaster, so Ralph led the enemy to believe that their demands would be met and their personal safety guaranteed. The opposing forces disbanded, at which point Scrope and Mowbray were arrested and taken to Henry at Pontefract. They were condemned without trial and executed, but by that time, Henry had already sent Ralph north to seize Northumberland's castles, so he played no part in their fate. Northumberland fled to Scotland, his estates were forfeit and Henry gave Ralph many of the Percy lands in Cumberland and Westmorland.[24]

After Henry's death in 1413, Ralph's main responsibilities were keeping the northern border safe, which he did, defeating a Scottish force in 1415 at the Battle of Yeavering. He was not involved with Henry V's campaign in France, despite what Shakespeare says, but was one of the regency council with special responsibilities for the Scottish Marches.[25]

He was not as close to the new king, partly because his son-in-law was involved in the Southampton plot, organised to depose Henry V just as he was about to sail to France.

Ralph was a great builder. He rebuilt Sheriff Hutton castle and probably Penrith castle. In addition, he undertook extensive works on Raby Castle. It is also possible that he built the 'tall and striking tower' of Richmond Parish Church.

Ralph died in October 1425 at Raby Castle and was buried in the choir of the Collegiate church at Staindrop, where he had founded a college in 1410. His tomb has effigies of himself and his two wives and has been called the finest tomb in the north of England. However, his second wife, Joan Beaufort, is buried in Lincoln Cathedral, her tomb being situated at the foot of her mother, Katherine Swynford's tomb.[26]

Henry V

THE FUTURE HENRY V, known as Henry of Monmouth, was born in – guess where – in 1386. His birth was not officially documented and became the subject of some debate among future chroniclers. It was later established that his parents had been in Monmouth in 1386, but not the following year, which some historians had asserted was his birth year. His reign lasted for nine years but he did achieve a lot during it and before as Prince of Wales. Mostly on a battlefield somewhere in France.

The eldest son of Henry IV, the younger Henry was also cousin to Richard II, his paternal grandfather being John of Gaunt. When his father, then Henry of Bolingbroke, was exiled in 1398, the young Henry was taken in charge by his cousin, King Richard and accompanied him to Ireland. When Gaunt died and Bolingbroke usurped the throne, Prince Henry was recalled from Ireland and created Prince of Wales at his father's coronation.[1]

However, strictly speaking, his father's cousin, Roger Mortimer, great-grandson of the Roger Mortimer who had been Queen Isabella's lover while she was the wife of Edward II, had a better claim. Mortimer's sister married Henry Hotspur. When the Northumberland uprising that ended in the Battle of Shrewsbury occurred in 1403, Prince Henry was more than aware he was not just fighting off a possible rival to his father's throne, but also to his own claim.

For the rest of his life as Prince of Wales, and later king, Henry did everything he could to prove his claim was the one God promoted. He was, by his mid-teens, a formidable battle commander, suffering a serious facial wound at Shrewsbury. For those interested in such things, there is a YouTube video demonstrating how the arrow that pierced Henry's cheek on the battlefield was removed.[2]

Henry was frequently called on to substitute for his ailing father and this led to several serious clashes between the two. Nicholas Vincent also points out that the only portrait we have of Henry V is the one that looks as if his mother stuck a basin on his head and cut round it. The wood panel on which this portrait was painted has dated the painting to between 1504 and 1520, almost 100 years after his death.[3] So, in reality, we have no idea what

Henry actually looked like. But the haircut could be a shout back to the first Norman kings when showing the ears and necks trumpeted their austere qualities, as shown on the Bayeux Tapestry.[4]

Most people associate Henry V with a glorious victory at Agincourt, but this is far from the more complicated reality of the man. Peter McNiven states that few historians realise how powerful Prince Henry was in the political arena in the latter years of Henry IV's reign. His behaviour was not always chivalrous and perhaps for this reason those years are sometimes glossed over. Be that as it may, by 1410, the prince ended up at the head of a council full of his supporters. It was not long before Henry IV struck back, believing his heir to be overstepping his boundaries and, possibly, aiming to unseat his father. By 1412, there was an open breach between the two – shown brilliantly in *Henry IV Part 2: Act 4: Scene 3* where Prince Hal, sitting by his fathers' bedside and believing he is dead, tries on the crown, at which point King Henry wakes up.

Their main bone of contention was France; King Henry was determined on conciliation, Prince Henry on war. The prince found himself removed from the council. Despite his declaration of, 'unwavering affection, love, loyalty and submissiveness' to his father, some were convinced he was bent on an insurrection. From this distance in time, it is impossible to know the facts, but McNiven believes the prince was aiming to be reinstated on his father's council with the intention of diminishing the power of those people who supported his younger brother, Thomas, the king's favourite son. In short, Prince Henry believed he might be replaced in the succession by his brother on the orders of his father.[5]

However, this did not happen and upon his father's death in 1413, Prince Henry became Henry V. And this is where Shakespeare comes into the picture, which is, to be honest, distorted. The new king was a far more complicated and devious man than Shakespeare paints him and a lot less chivalrous.

Henry IV had left the royal treasury virtually empty, so much so, his nominated executors refused to accept the job. There were religious issues regarding the Lollards and heresy so, in the best traditions of Edward I and Edward III, not to mention Richard the Lionheart, Henry decided to make his crusade against the French a matter of good Englishmen against the evil French.[6]

Before he could descend on the French, he had to deal with the Oldcastle Revolt. Sir John Oldcastle was a very popular man and a friend of Henry when the latter was Prince of Wales. Many people have posited that he was reincarnated as Sir John Falstaff in Shakespeare's plays. And, had he not been a devoted follower of John Wycliffe and the Lollards, he might well have been a significant figure at the court of Henry V.

In 1413, Sir John was brought to trial accused of heresy, but he refused to recant and was sentenced to death. Henry V hoped to persuade him to change his mind, but he refused and was sent to the Tower of London. He escaped – some believe with the connivance of the king. If so, Sir John proved to be a false friend, for he immediately began to foment a revolt with the aim of overthrowing his erstwhile friend and forcing Lollard dogmas on the country.

The revolt was poorly planned and even more poorly executed. Oldcastle had deluded himself that he would have the support of the nobles. In the best traditions of such plots, he and his followers were betrayed and what was supposed to be an armed confrontation was more like a mild skirmish, which Henry's adherents won with ease.

Again, Oldcastle escaped and, despite being pardoned – a tribute to the strength of Henry's memories of past friendship – he went into hiding. Whilst Henry was fighting in France, in 1417, Oldcastle was recaptured and this time, there was no escape. He was sentenced to death for heresy and burned alive over a slow fire. Yes, I winced, too! What was worse, or would have been in Oldcastle's view had he still be alive, the Lollards were from then on regarded as opponents of the government determined to overthrow law and order. They were suppressed, their numbers diminished, and they are now regarded as a short-lived event in history. What is interesting, is that Paul Strohm posits the revolt was nothing to do with Oldcastle at all, but fomented by the monarchy to deflect any attention from the still-rumbling issue of Henry IV's usurpation of Richard II, thus making the nobility close ranks behind Henry V.[7]

In 1415, one of the most significant events in English history occurred. Agincourt. And Henry decided he would allow God to decide the validity of his cause, and his claim to the French throne. He landed at Harfleur and then, after subduing the locals, marched in the direction of Calais. His army was depleted by dysentery, but that didn't stop him. The statistics of the two armies has never been solidly agreed, but it is clear that the French, under the command of the Duc d'Orleans, outnumbered the English by at least two to one.

Rain had hindered progress, which gives it a lot in common with an English cricket match. The fields were quagmires, but Henry ensured his archers were within easy reach of the opposition and attacked before the French had organised themselves. It will not be a surprise to learn that the battle was nothing like the Shakespeare version of it. The dukes of York and Suffolk were both killed and the English soldiers paddled and splashed their way across the fields, pole-axing any French soldiers they encountered.

Nobody gave a thought to prisoners or ransoms. When Henry heard a rumour that the French were going to mount a charge, he ordered the massacre of those French prisoners – all unarmed – who were in English hands. He has been branded as a war criminal for this action, but, as Nicholas Vincent points out, these detractors weren't there making decisions on the ground.

The battle lasted for a few hours. And then it began to rain. Again. And, sorry to burst the Shakespeare bubble once more, but there was no arranged marriage with Katherine of Valois at this time, though we must thank the film version of *Henry V* for William Walton's glorious music. What actually happened was that, on the back of Agincourt, in 1417, Henry decided to retake Normandy from the French. To raise enough money to fund the campaign, he had to pawn the crown jewels. For the next two years, he won battle after battle in Normandy. In what was described as a 'Biblical precedent', when his cannon destroyed the walls of Caen, Henry ordered the entire population of that city to be massacred.[8] A thoroughly nice chap!

The French came to the negotiating table in 1420 for the Treaty of Troyes. Curry firmly declares this to be Henry's greatest victory. The French king, Charles VI, accepted that Henry had a claim to the throne, and to cement that, Henry married Charles' daughter, Katherine, in Troyes cathedral. She was crowned in Westminster Abbey in February 1421.[9]

Not content to sit on his laurels, Henry determined to claim more of France. Leaving his pregnant queen in England, he once more sailed across the Channel and laid siege to Meaux. His son and heir, the future Henry VI was born in December 1421 while Henry V was away fighting, but his progress to Paris was impeded by the hardships of the winter and dysentery. Henry died in August 1422 at Vincennes near Paris. Ironically, had he lived another 50 days, he would have achieved his ambition to be king of France, because his father-in-law died in October. That questionable honour was, instead, visited on his baby son, along with all the other problems that were to lead to the Wars of the Roses, and most of it the fault of Henry V and his last instructions, which majored on the Lancastrian family with little regard to the governance of England.[10]

Fun Fact

Henry V, although considered by most to be a warrior king, was very fond of music and reading. Well, I suppose it made a change from killing the French. He became the first English king who could read *and* write in the English language.

Thomas Beaufort

Thomas was the third son of John of Gaunt and Katherine Swynford and therefore, half-brother to Henry IV and uncle to Henry V. He was born around 1377 and, like his siblings, spent much of his childhood at Kettlethorpe in Lincolnshire. He married Margaret Neville, who bore him a son, Henry, but the child died in infancy.[11]

Thomas was a loyal supporter of Richard II. When Mowbray and Henry of Bolingbroke, Thomas' nephew, were exiled, he was given a share of Mowbray's estate. However, when Bolingbroke returned and usurped the throne, Thomas changed camps and became a supporter of his half-brother – it must be remembered that Henry's father, John of Gaunt, also supported his son's banishment, possibly to keep him safe abroad.[12]

When his half-brother became king, Thomas was made a Knight of the Garter, but Henry was not over-keen to promote new names to the aristocracy and it was not until 1411/12 that he was made Duke of Dorset. In the interim, he was, like most of his family, a military man, holding the posts of constable of Ludlow and Admiral of the North. In 1407, he became the Captain of Calais and held the post of Admiral of the North and West until his death in 1426.[13]

Thomas spent much of his time on military affairs, including repressing rebellions in Wales. It is likely he fought at the Battle of Shrewsbury, and his appointment as admiral gave him responsibility to repel any invasions, France being considered the greatest threat. In subsequent years, he became close to Henry, Prince of Wales, and was a member of the council when Henry IV was incapacitated through illness. He also shared in the prince's dismissal by the king in late 1410, although it appears that he did not fall out of favour with Henry IV.

He became one of Henry V's most trusted advisors, especially in the plan to renew the Hundred Years' War. The plan contained such preposterous terms, the new king knew the French would never accept them. When Henry V left for what would culminate in the Battle of Agincourt, Thomas was heavily involved in the siege of Harfleur.[14]

As with his father, Henry V was close to his Beaufort relations, and under him, Thomas gained more honours, including being made Duke of Exeter in 1416. He was one of the negotiators in the Treaty of Troyes, when Henry won the right to be recognised as having a claim on the throne of France. It is likely Thomas attended Henry's marriage to Katherine of Valois, so sweetly but so inaccurately portrayed by Shakespeare. Katherine's father was called Charles the Mad. He had delusions that he was made of glass. Mental instability was something about which little was known, and almost certainly nobody realised that it was genetic, since it skipped some people. Sadly, that malady was bequeathed through Katherine to their son, who became Henry VI, exacerbating the unrest that led to the Wars of the Roses. Katherine herself suffered from mental illness and was only in her mid-thirties when she died.[15]

Although Henry V returned briefly to England in 1417 to help deal with problems in Scotland, he returned to Normandy the following year, taking part in Henry's sieges of Evreux, Ivry and Rouen. In 1419, he overcame the Chateau Gaillard after a six-month siege. However, he was captured at the Battle of Baugé in 1421, and his nephew, Thomas of Lancaster was killed.

After Henry V's death near Paris, Thomas, being one of his executors, accompanied his former king's body back to England. He served on the governing council set up to look after the infant Henry VI and England.[16] Thomas' time in France was very successful and he proved so loyal to Henry V that he was made one of baby Henry VI's legal guardians. He fell out with Henry VI's youngest uncle, Humphrey, Duke of Gloucester, because of their differing political approaches.[17]

It is thought he died at the end of December 1426, or possibly early January 1427. All his titles became extinct on his death, although later, the duchy of Exeter was given to the Holland family and the earldom of Dorset to Thomas' nephew, Edmund.[18] His estate was split between various charities. He is regarded as a noble man as well as a nobleman, but he left no heirs.[19] No surprise there. He hardly ever had time to take his shoes off, let alone anything else.

In February 1772, some workmen, digging in the ruins of the abbey at Bury St Edmunds found a lead coffin allegedly belonging to Thomas Beaufort, Duke of Exeter. The physician who examined the remains determined that it must have lain there since before the Reformation, possibly for about 300 years. The cere cloth covering the face of the corpse had been applied so precisely that it left the mark of the eyes and nose.[20]

Henry Beaufort

Henry, Bishop of Winchester and also a cardinal, was another Beaufort son of John of Gaunt and Katherine Swynford. I did warn you there were a lot of them!

Historians long believed he was born at Gaunt's manor of Beaufort in France, but since Gaunt had lost the manor some time before, this is untrue. It may be that he was born at Kettlethorpe in Lincolnshire around 1374.[21]

From an early age, Henry was destined for the church. When he was about 15, he was given the wealthy prebend of Thame, a diocese of Lincoln. Prebends were administrative roles, rather than clerical ones. Later that year, he was given the prebend of Riccall in the York diocese. He studied law at Queens College, Oxford and canon law in Aachen and was later chancellor of Oxford University. When he was made Bishop of Lincoln in 1398, by Richard II, many people were astounded that such a post should be put in the hands of a 21-year-old man. However, at this point, he resigned his chancellorship of Oxford University, presumably to give time to his new responsibilities. As Bishop of Lincoln, he would have been responsible for the funeral rites and the placing of his mother's tomb in Lincoln Cathedral.[22] He fathered an illegitimate daughter while bishop.[23]

As a Beaufort, when his half-brother became Henry IV, Henry became a political heavyweight. He was chancellor of England in 1403 and chancellor to the king. He was then awarded the bishopric of Winchester, one of the richest sees in England. Although Henry IV made him chancellor, he sided with the young Prince Henry and was forced to resign his chancellorship, although when Prince Henry became Henry V, Henry the bishop was made chancellor again. At this point, he began the fulfilment of his ambition for a cardinal's hat, something he won in 1417 along with the title of papal legate, which is when he fell foul of Henry V who believed he might become too effective a power on the side of the papacy. He was forced to resign his ecclesiastical posts.[24]

When the baby Henry VI acceded to the throne, Beaufort re-entered royal circles again. He was still ambitious and proceeded to enrich himself by lending money to the crown at eye-watering rates of interest and, because the government needed to be solvent, there was little anyone could do about it. His power was assured, even though he continually clashed with Humphrey, Duke of Gloucester. He was made Cardinal of St Eusebius and papal legate in 1426, fending off attacks by Gloucester, but being forced to resign as chancellor. Again.

However, by the mid-1430s, he was, to all intents and purposes, governing England. He failed in his attempts to negotiate an end to the Hundred Years' War, admitted defeat, and retired from public life in 1443. His self-serving ambition and rapacious greed cannot be disputed, but neither can the fact that his political and financial judgement ensured England's stability.[25]

There is an unfounded rumour that he interrogated Joan of Arc at her trial. She was burned as a heretic, but Beaufort's name does not appear in any of the lists of those who took part in her trial and neither was he at her execution. Notwithstanding, despite the legend, when she was later made a saint, a statue of her was placed near the Lady Chapel in Winchester Cathedral.[26]

Henry Beaufort was buried in Winchester Cathedral. His tomb still shows his effigy, wearing his red cardinal's robes and hat.[27]

Sir John Oldcastle

Sir John was born circa 1378 in Herefordshire and is often attributed as being the pattern for the Shakespeare character of Sir John Falstaff in the history plays. Be that as it may, he is better known as a leader of the Lollards and part of the Lollard uprising during the reign of Henry V.

He was sent to Wales in 1401 to take charge of Builth Castle, but as Herefordshire's MP, he soon returned to Hay-on-Wye – now famous for its many bookshops – as a commissioner to prevent arms and provisions from reaching Welsh rebels. It was at this time he met Henry, Prince of Wales and became a close personal friend.[28] In 1406, he married Joan, daughter of the 3rd Lord Cobham, and was later made Lord Cobham. It was his third marriage and her fourth.[29]

During all this time, he had grown close to the Lollard community, a sect that began life in Antwerp but were persecuted in both Holland and Germany. They came by their name because of their dirge-like crooning, the German word for which is *Lollen*. Despite the unease in royal circles about Sir John's adherence to the Lollards, he was very popular in Herefordshire. He had become very unpopular with Catholics when he helped enact a law that said heretics should be imprisoned by the state not the Catholic church. He exacerbated his unpopularity by establishing a school for preachers in Kent.

In 1411, Sir John accompanied Prince Henry to assist the Duke of Burgundy, at that time being attacked by the French. The English forces won the day and this deepened Sir John's friendship with Prince Henry. However, in 1413, books supporting the Lollards and the writings of John Wycliffe were found in Sir John's belongings.[30] One of his books was found in a shop in Paternoster Row, London.[31]

Allegedly, the new king, Henry V was disgusted, and Thomas Arundel, Archbishop of Canterbury and other bishops attacked Sir John. Henry was divided. He was a pious, if warlike man, but Oldcastle was his friend. When confronted, Sir John lost his temper, stormed from the royal presence, and went to ground at Cowling Castle in Kent.

He refused to acknowledge a summons, which had been nailed to the door of Rochester Cathedral, declaring he must appear at a tribunal at Leeds

Castle. In the meantime, he was excommunicated. Despite pleas for him to change his views, Sir John refused, and Henry V granted him a 40-day stay of execution, before sending him to the Tower. He escaped and although a Lollard bookseller along with other Lollards, was accused of helping in Oldcastle's escape, it has long been believed Henry V himself was complicit. That didn't help the bookseller, who was executed for treason.[32]

Allegedly – and this has never been proved – Oldcastle was then accused of plotting to overthrow Henry and become regent while the king was in France. The plotters' intentions were to imprison the king and his brothers, dissolve religious orders and dismantle the Catholic Church in England to create a new ruling class consisting of Lollards. He is also believed to have been involved in the Southampton Plot immediately before Henry embarked for France. The aim was to depose Henry and make Edmund Mortimer, 5th Earl of March the king.[33]

The plot was discovered but Oldcastle again escaped. He stayed in hiding and on the run until he was discovered in 1417 being badly injured during his capture. He was taken to London on a horse litter and this time, there was no Henry to help him because the king was in France. He was hung in chains and burned, possibly alive, although nobody knows whether he was alive when the flames were lit.[34]

As a footnote, Shakespeare sought to refute the legend that Falstaff was Sir John Oldcastle. In *Henry IV Part 2*, the epilogue says: 'Falstaff shall die of a sweat, unless already a' be killed with your hard opinions; for Oldcastle died a martyr, and this is not the man.'[35]

Henry VI

YET ANOTHER CHILD king, but a very different kettle of fish from Richard II. David Grummitt points out that his enemies thought him an idiot and his friends a saint. Even as late as the 1970s, some factions of the church were attempting to get Henry canonised. Grummitt also claims that there was no full-length biography of Henry VI until Mabel Christie's biography published in 1922, intimating her book to be the first proper examination of Henry's life.[1]

The first paragraphs of Christie's book set the scene very appositely. She says: 'The infant was named Henry after his illustrious father, whom he was destined to resemble neither in character nor fortune.' She goes on to recount the rumour that Henry V expressly ordered his son should not be born in Windsor Castle, 'believing it to be unpropitious and that he was much distressed when he heard that it had been so as having an authenticity far from being well established.'[2]

Whatever the truth of the rumour, Henry VI *was* born at Windsor Castle on 6 December – St Nicholas' Day 1421. His father was, unsurprisingly, in France still fighting to ensure his being named the next heir, as agreed in the Treaty of Troyes the year before. Ironically, Henry never lived to fulfil his dream, dying shortly before the king of France. Instead, his son was crowned in London in 1429 and in Notre-Dame, Paris in 1431. The fact he was not crowned in Rheims, the traditional coronation church, says much for the feelings of the French.[3]

From the young Henry's early childhood, his mother, Katherine of Valois, was held in such suspicion by the English nobility, she was allowed very little part in his upbringing.[4] Anne Crawford, however, declares Katherine 'virtually abandoned him' for her second family with Owen Tudor, when Henry was eight.[5] In truth, Humphrey of Gloucester took charge of the child and I do not expect that Katherine had any choice in the matter.

Life was problematical for Henry almost from the moment of his birth. Henry V had, like his own father, concentrated the government of England in the hands of his Lancastrian family, but on his death, he left no written instructions for the government of either England or France, probably assuming his brothers John of Bedford and Humphrey of Gloucester would, assisted by their legitimised Beaufort relations, run England in his son's minority. And we all know what happens to assumptions, don't we?

What happened is that Bedford took responsibility for the French side of things, leaving Henry of Winchester and Humphrey of Gloucester to squabble about the English side of things. Which they did. A lot. So much so that the stability of England was well on the way to being compromised and the two constantly at daggers drawn.

It took until Bedford returned in 1424 to act as arbitrator. There were also anxieties that the young, widowed queen might remarry, have children thereby giving *them* a claim on the throne.[6] In fact, she married Owen Tudor, a junior member of her household. Although nobody knows exactly what his position in the household was, some think he may have been one of Katherine's bodyguards. Sixty years later, one of their descendants did claim the throne. Katherine and Owen's son, Edmund Tudor married Margaret Beaufort and their son was Henry Tudor, aka Henry VII. Margaret was legitimate in that she was the daughter of the legitimised Joan Beaufort, one of the Gaunt/Swynford children who, though also legitimised, were not considered of royal blood and precluded from any claim to the throne.

These squabbles lasted until well into Henry VI's teenage years. His tutor, John Somerset was still in his household until parliament insisted on his removal as being a dangerous influence on the king and against those who were attempting to rule through Henry.

By nature, Henry was shy, very pious and hated bloodshed or deception. This was fine until he took over the reins of kingship, whereupon the faction which wanted to carry on the French war led by Richard, Duke of York, and Humphrey, Duke of Gloucester, was at odds with the faction led by Henry Beaufort, Bishop of Winchester – yes, him again – and William de la Pole, Earl of Suffolk who wanted peace. There was also war with the Scots and it was suggested Henry marry a daughter of James I of Scotland, but this foundered. Meanwhile, Henry's 'coronation' for the French throne had been declared void by Charles VII and the House of Valois, which had become popular after Joan of Arc's victories. Nicholas Vincent calls Joan of Arc's career, beginning with her certainty that she had been called by God to reinstate the dauphin in his rightful position as King, as the House of Lancaster's Stalingrad.[7]

The dauphin chose to proclaim Joan was fulfilling a prophecy of 1390. Or maybe he was just using her. Whichever, he was crowned Charles VII in 1429. This led the English to insist on a coronation in Paris for the 'true' king, Henry, as per the Treaty of Troyes. Confused yet? The tide of opinion in France was certainly against the English, which can hardly be a surprise for anyone.

A week after John, Duke of Bedford died, the Anglo-Burgundian alliance collapsed. Richard, Duke of York did not help matters by watching everything disintegrate while he haggled over whether his title should be regent and governor or lieutenant-general.

Just to complicate things, Humphrey's wife consulted astrologers who stated the king would become ill in 1441. In the hothouse atmosphere of court, her 'prophecy' became public knowledge, as these things do. Humphrey was disgraced, his wife imprisoned for the rest of her life and the astrologers were hanged, drawn, and quartered. Humphrey himself clashed with William de la Pole, Earl of Suffolk, was arrested and somehow died in custody, an event that was passed off as a stroke, but most people did not believe that.

Through all this, Henry, the king, sailed oblivious and passive. By the then standards of kingship, he was, let's say, sadly lacking. Not warlike; in fact, he hated taking the life of an animal let alone a human being. He was too generous and too prone to pardon people; he was fastidious to the point of insisting the local bishop end the practise of naked men bathing in hot water pools in Bath. His 'virtues', perfect in a man of the cloth, were seen as shortcomings in a monarch.[8]

Henry of Winchester and the Earl of Suffolk decided the king should marry Margaret of Anjou, who was the niece of Charles VII of France. She was everything her husband was not, especially when it came to making war on people; in fact, she brooked no disloyalty to her royal husband. However, by being so different from her weak husband, she gained her own supporters, such as the Duke of Somerset, who was close to her. So much so, many people thought her son, when she eventually became pregnant, was his and not the king's.

Richard, Duke of York considered himself on a par with the king regarding royalty, and he was the heir to the throne since Henry remained childless for so long. Richard was side-lined and sent to Ireland. In his absence The earls of Somerset and Suffolk were promoted to dukes. The stability and financial state of England were perilous, there was a breakdown in law and order, and troops returning home from France were not paid.

In 1447, Suffolk, was impeached by parliament as a traitor and although Henry sent him into exile to ensure his safety, his ship was intercepted and he was murdered. Meanwhile things went from bad to worse in England. Private militia and rival bands fought with each other. Margaret of Anjou consolidated her position, while Henry was side-lined.

Law and order was breaking down so badly, Henry was publicly accused of mismanagement and misconduct in government by Richard, Duke of York. Friction between factions in the English court, plus France seizing what had been English territory, were major factions in the breakdown of Henry's mental health.[9]

In 1450, Jack Cade led a rebellion in Kent, seemingly in sympathy with Richard, Duke of York. Briefly, Cade took London, but that was quickly reversed. It did, however, show the level of disgruntlement in the country, especially the lawlessness of the southern counties. Discontented, unpaid, soldiers murdered the Bishop of Chichester. A few months later the Bishop of Salisbury was also attacked, probably because of the slump in the Wiltshire cloth trade. Nobody dared blame the king, but in the minds of most people, he was 'incapable of managing his own let alone the nation's affairs'.[10] In 1453, the king suffered his second complete mental breakdown. Since his maternal grandfather had suffered periods of mental instability, this may have been inherited. It has been suggested his illness was schizophrenia.

With the order of law collapsing, people were looking for a credible alternative and there was Richard, Duke of York, not now the heir, since Margaret had given birth to Edward of Lancaster. Despite this, York regarded himself as the only *real* heir, probably choosing to believe the new prince had not been fathered by the king. What tipped the scales was that Richard now had a powerful ally, Richard Neville, Earl of Warwick. In short order, York was named regent. It was the turn of Margaret – and her son – to be excluded. Or so York and Warwick believed.

Thus, in 1455, began the Wars of the Roses only a few years after the Hundred Years' War had finally finished. This is not the place for a detailed exposition of the progress of the next thirty years until the Battle of Stoke in 1487, but the fortunes of the Lancastrian and Yorkist camps ebbed and flowed.[11] In 1460, Henry was captured although Margaret and her son escaped, but it cemented the utter hatred between the House of York and the House of Lancaster.

For the next thirty years, arguments were settled with battles, not negotiations. In 1460, Henry was taken prisoner and Richard, Duke of York was made Lord Protector. In December of that year, York and his son Edmund were killed at the Battle of Wakefield. Edward of March was declared heir to the throne.[12] He took his revenge for his father and brother's deaths a few months later at the Battle of Towton, still known as the bloodiest battle ever fought on English soil, with some estimates of the dead being put as high as 28,000. Then he marched to London and claimed the crown.

For the next ten years, Edward, Earl of March reigned as Edward IV. Then he fell out in a big heap with Richard, Earl of Warwick, who went over to Margaret's side. Edward and his younger brother, Richard, fled to Burgundy. Warwick put Henry back on the throne, for a whole six months, until Edward IV landed, as had his ancestor, Henry of Bolingbroke, at Ravenspur, claiming all he wanted was his rights as Duke of York.

Warwick and his brother, John were killed at the second Battle of Barnet. Intelligence came to King Edward that Margaret had landed in the west with her son and they were heading for Wales and the protection of Jasper Tudor. Edward and his army marched to Tewkesbury where he was again victorious but this time, Edward of Lancaster, Margaret's son, was killed on the battlefield.[13]

When it became clear that all Lancastrian opposition had been wiped out, Edward marched back to London. Richard, Duke of Gloucester was left to mop up the remainder of the traitors, give them a fair trial and execute them. He then joined Edward in London and somehow, that same night, Henry VI died, allegedly of 'displeasure'. When his body was exhumed in 1910, it was clear from his blood-stained hair and damaged skull, that he had died by violence. It has long been believed that Gloucester, known to be his brother's fixer, was involved in the death.

Henry was buried in Chertsey Abbey, but in 1484, Richard had his body moved to St George's chapel at Windsor Castle. Thus, he ended where he had begun. It is clear he was not fit to be king at that point in history. He was far more esoteric than was considered healthy in a monarch. He built King's College, Cambridge and founded Eton College. The provosts of both institutions lay white lilies and roses, the respective emblems of King's and Eton, on the spot in the Wakefield Tower at the Tower of London, where it is believed Henry was killed whilst he knelt in prayer. There is a similar ceremony at St George's Chapel.[14]

Fun Fact

If we look at Henry VI and Alexander the Great's successor, they have a lot in common. Philip Arrhidaeus III, the man who was crowned king in the aftermath of Alexander the Great's death, and Henry VI suffered from mental illnesses that meant they were not regarded as *proper* kings, neither were they effective monarchs. They were both controlled by powerful and ambitious factions to the detriment of their realms.

John Somerset

Not to be confused with the Beaufort Dukes of Somerset. John Somerset was born in London and fled Oxford University when the plague hit, going instead to Cambridge where he graduated in 1418. Thomas Beaufort appointed him initially as a master at the grammar school in Bury St Edmunds, but a few years later, Somerset was the governor of a proposed school of medicine and surgery, which never came to fruition.

He joined Henry VI's household in 1427 as physician to the young king and also as his tutor. He quickly gained his pupil's confidence, rising to the post of chancellor of the Exchequer and warden of the Royal Mint, and was appointed to parliament for Middlesex, the first physician to sit in those hallowed walls. However, his tenure was not a happy one.[15]

Somerset was thought to hold too much influence over Henry, especially as he was not a member of the ruling council. The enduring feud between Gloucester and Beaufort probably led to Henry retaining most of the council members who had been there from the beginning of his reign. That said, records from his reign are patchy, mostly because the king failed to rule his council as would be expected. Somerset was an irregular member of it, something that highlighted the fact the majority of council members were from the royal household, rather than the nobility, as had always been the custom. It all fell apart in 1449–50 when Suffolk was murdered and the nature of the king's council changed.[16]

In fact, 1450 was very difficult for everyone. An economic recession had hit the country and the governmental finances were in flux, crown debt being almost £400,000. William de la Pole was considered to be corrupt, and Henry's keeper of the Privy Seal was murdered by a mob in Portsmouth. None of this made for stable government. Parliament declared the royal household, of which John Somerset was a member, was to blame for the crises. Because it was unthinkable that the king should be blamed, Somerset was made one of the scapegoats – obviously one of the penalties of greatness – and accused of giving Henry bad advice. There is a direct comparison here with the fate of Piers Gaveston and his influence over Edward II.

At this point, Somerset was still Henry's physician. He was accused of greed and taking advantage of a generous master. Since he had also been one of the commissioners to raise loans for the war in France in 1449, and that had failed, he was also blamed for England losing Normandy. In addition, he was thought to have encouraged Henry to 'waste money' on Eton and

King's College, Cambridge. He was barred from parliament, although he remained in post as Henry's physician.[17]

Somerset died intestate, in 1454.

William de la Pole

William was born in 1396, the second son of Michael de la Pole, a favourite of Richard II. He fought with Henry V in France, being wounded at the siege of Harfleur in 1415. His brother, Michael was killed at Agincourt. William was a commander at the Siege of Orléans, which ultimately failed, and captured by a French squire called Guillaume Renault, who knighted him before accepting his surrender, although he remained Charles VII's prisoner for two years. He married Alice Chaucer, grand-daughter of the poet, Geoffrey Chaucer in 1430.

On his return to England, William was appointed Constable of Wallingford Castle and became a close ally of Cardinal Beaufort, aka Henry, Bishop of Winchester. He quickly became one of Henry's intimate and most trusted allies. His nickname was 'Jackanapes', which was slang at that time for a monkey. This nickname led later to the definition of the word being 'a conceited and brazen person'. It is thought to be a snide reference to the fact William's great-grandfather had been a Hull wool merchant. Being 'in trade' remained a social slur up until the mid-twentieth century. Certainly, the composer, Elgar, was despised in some quarters because his father had owned a music shop in Worcester, which was a greater social sin apparently than being a Catholic, the faith in which the composer had been brought up.

William was at the vanguard of royal politics and the major force in arranging the marriage between Henry and Margaret of Anjou. He was made Marquess of Suffolk, but many believe part of the marriage negotiations included Maine and Anjou being returned to France, and that, true or not, would contribute to his downfall. Being close to the throne, he quickly gained more power and appointments, including Admiral of England. In 1447, he was created Earl of Pembroke and the following year Duke of Suffolk.

William favoured negotiation over war, especially when the situation in France deteriorated. This attitude, of course, chimed perfectly with the wishes of the pious Henry VI. Then it all began to go wrong for William. He was thought never to have paid his French ransom from the Siege of Orléans, and of passing council minutes detailing plans concerning a French invasion to the French authorities. Powerful enemies at court and in

East Anglia blamed him for corruption and the ongoing lawlessness in the region. He was also thought to have had a hand in the death of Humphrey, Duke of Gloucester. Eventually, William was arrested, accused of being a traitor.

Henry was reluctant to punish him, but finally agreed to banish him for five years. However, his ship was intercepted on the way to Calais. William was given a mock trial and beheaded, his body being left on Dover beach. He was eventually buried in the Carthusian Priory in Hull by his widow. No trace of the priory or his tomb exists following the Dissolution and the sieges in the seventeenth century civil war.[18]

Here, most biographies would end, but the effect of de la Pole's death was far reaching in a way few people could have imagined at the time. William's killers were never found, indeed one wonders if they were ever seriously sought. Why is this important? When we look at the rule – if one could call it that – of Henry VI, it is a story of mismanagement, English losses in France and the breakdown of law and order. In other words, chaos.

In medieval England, order was of supreme importance, which is why in *Henry IV: Part 2* when Shakespeare has Northumberland cry 'Let order die', upon hearing of the death of his son, Hotspur in battle, it is shorthand to the audience revealing the depth of his grief. Add to everything else that Henry's – foreign – queen also had around her a distinctly unpopular faction, and it is a recipe for disaster.

The years of Henry's reign were calamitous for England. They led to faction and strife between the houses of Lancaster and York, with York finally coming out on top until the illegitimate side of the Lancastrians, through Henry V's queen, brought Henry VII a throne, to which he had no right at all. If Richard III could declare his brother, Edward's children illegitimate and therefore ineligible to reign, how much more ineligible was Henry VII?

Roger Virgoe and Ronald Hall make the discovery of a new document regarding William de la Pole's death as central to the downfall of the House of Lancaster and the rise of the House of York. This document is a letter to John Paston the day after news of William's murder arrived in London. After William's impeachment in January 1450, he was brought before Henry, no doubt in a ceremony agreed between them beforehand. He submitted himself to the king's judgment. Henry declared him innocent of selling Anjou and Maine, but for the charge of interfering in affairs of justice and local government, he was banished for five years.

Despite him being secretly released from Westminster that night, William was pursued by a mob of angry Londoners. He escaped, although some of his servants were manhandled. William managed to reach Bury St Edmunds and waited for safe conduct documents from Henry and the court of the Duke of Burgundy, his proposed destination.

He was prohibited from going to France and the safe conduct from Burgundy proved his intention was to go to The Netherlands. However, one of his household, Henry Spenser, withheld letters from the king to the garrison at Calais, which is how William ended up in the Straits of Dover, at which point, his ship was stopped. The rest we know. His safe conduct was 'scorned and destroyed'.

Contemporaries did not know who was responsible, and neither do chroniclers offer anything except to say how hated William was. Some opine he was murdered by servants of the Duke of Somerset, others that he had fled with treasure. There is one theory that the ship was under the control of the son-in-law to the Duke of York. Indeed, three years later, a number of adherents to the dukes of York and Norfolk were indicted for raising the shires against King Henry and for Richard of York.[19]

Nobody really knows. In 1455, Richard of York began his bid for the throne; a bid that saw him cut down outside Sandal Castle but would eventually see his son, Edward create the royal House of York.

Edward IV

EDWARD IV, TALL, handsome, charismatic, charming, generous, but also cold, calculating, indolent, lascivious, and devious. The epitome of a doughty warrior, but then he had plenty of practise.

There is a lingering rumour that he was not the son of Richard of York, but of a Flemish archer called Blaybourne, who was also very tall. Richard's other sons were shorter, although George, Duke of Clarence was described as tall and fair. It was calculated from Richard III's femur that he stood at 5'8" (173 cms), of a similar height to his father but this only fed the rumour that the extremely tall Edward was illegitimate.

In fact, if one looks at the estimated heights of medieval monarchs, Richard the Lionheart topped 6' (182 cms), Edward I was about 6'2" (188 cms), Edward II about 6' (182 cms), Edward III was 5'10" (177 cms), Richard II 6' (182 cms), and Henry V was 6'3" (190 cms). So, Edward IV who stood at around 6'4" (193 cms) had a lineage of tall ancestors. The rumour that he was not the son of Richard of York has never entirely gone away even though Edward's mother, Cicely Neville was known to be pious and arrogant, her nickname being Proud Cis. In fact, the rumour fed down to the reign of Edward's grandson, Henry VIII – also tall at 6' 3" (190cms), and together with the mouldwarp accusation helped feed the momentum for the Pilgrimage of Grace in 1536. A mouldwarp is a 'proud, but contemptible coward with the skin of a goat'. Yes, that does just about sum Henry VIII up. A medieval prophecy was that the sixth king after King John would be a mouldwarp. The fact that the sixth king after John was Henry V was irrelevant to the rebels in 1536.[1]

But I digress and not for the first time. Let's get back to Edward. Of all our monarchs, he is the one I really would have liked to see in the flesh, just to see if his charisma and 'beauty' was real and not the usual royal propaganda. The most famous portrait we have of him was not painted until around 1540, almost 60 years after his death.

Edward was the eldest surviving son of Richard, Duke of York and Cecily Neville. Henry, his older brother, died shortly after birth. Edward was born in Rouen on 28 April 1442, although this has been disputed by John Ashdown-Hill because the original chronicler got the day of the week for 28 April 1442 wrong. This led to the foundation of the rumour that he was illegitimate, his father, Richard of York, not being with his mother on the supposed day of his conception.[2] Since projected dates of birth/conception are still not an exact science today, this theory does not really hold water.

Edward's childhood was spent amid the declining economy in England and defeats by the French abroad, all allegedly due to Henry VI's mismanagement in governing England as a king should, and being led by advisors who were more concerned with lining their own pockets rather than the wellbeing of the country. Some things never change.

Until the death of his father outside Sandal Castle at the Battle of Wakefield, Edward was known as the Earl of March. The life of Edward and his siblings was relatively quiet until 1453 when Henry VI went into what is described as a 'catatonic stupor' on hearing England had lost Gascony. Also in 1453, Henry's only child, Edward of Lancaster – sometimes called Edward of Westminster – was born, thus putting Richard Duke of York out of the succession. By 1455, the breach between York and the king, in the shape of his warlike queen, Margaret of Anjou, was complete and the thirty-year conflict, the Wars of the Roses, began.

By the age of 17, Edward of March was a seasoned fighter, but, after the Yorkists lost the Battle of Ludford in 1459, he, his father, and his brother, Edmund, fled to Ireland. Other Yorkist leaders, including Richard Neville, Earl of Warwick escaped to Calais. At this point, the Yorkist leaders, including Edward, made it publicly known that their only quarrel was with the king's 'evil advisors'.[3] This is a phrase we have heard more than once.

In 1460, Edward marched to London and claimed the throne, a declaration met with silence. This claim was then watered down so that Henry was still the king and the Duke of York his chosen successor. However, this caused serious opposition to the Yorkists. While Edward was sent later that year to suppress an uprising in Wales, Richard of York and his son, Edmund marched north to be killed at the Battle of Wakefield – a disaster for the Yorkists. Margaret of Anjou's army then marched south. In a seriously stupid, but typical move – let's just say she wasn't that nice a woman, but she was a good warrior – Margaret gave her troops leave to sack and pillage as they progressed. York, Grantham, and Stamford were all subject to the queen's ire, through the lawlessness of her soldiers. It was, as Charles Ross says, 'such a grave political blunder, for the threat to property and fear of the malice of the Northernmen, stiffened support for the rival cause'.[4]

So much so that support for Edward flourished, and it grew still more after the Battle of Mortimer's Cross in February 1461 when a parhelion, or three suns, appeared in the sky. This caused Edward to declare his emblem as the 'Sunne in Splendour', and the appearance as a sign from heaven that he was the rightful king.

On Palm Sunday 1461, the bloodiest battle ever fought on English soil took place at Towton in Yorkshire – estimates have ranged between a modest 9,000 to 28,000, although it is probably much closer to the second figure. The river Cock ran red with blood. Edward's forces were outnumbered, but he won the day, and in one fell swoop destroyed the strength of the lords of the north, such as the Percies, and Dacres, who had been loyal to Lancaster.[5]

In her fictional account of the lives of Edward IV and Richard III, Sharon Kay Penman describes Edward's reaction when he enters York after Towton, to be confronted by the heads of his father, adorned with a paper crown, and the Earl of Salisbury, father to Richard and John Neville. That this happened is incontrovertible.[6] Penman's story gives the reader the first intimation of how devasted the normally phlegmatic and calculating Edward was at the gruesome sight. What is also true is that John Neville, at that time imprisoned in York begged Edward to spare the citizens from his wrath.

Edward marched south and took the throne. Henry and Margaret fled to Scotland. Most of the northern lords remained loyal to Lancaster, even though their forces were very much reduced. This meant Edward had to rely on the Nevilles, although John Neville, later Earl of Northumberland, further depleted the opposition at the Battle of Hexham in 1464. In all this time, Richard, Earl of Warwick, John Neville's elder brother had been the power behind the throne. It was not long before Edward became restive under his cousin's autocratic, arrogant, control. Affairs came to a head when, although Edward knew Warwick was negotiating a French marriage for him, the king himself decided to marry Elizabeth Woodville, the widow of a Lancastrian. A secret he kept from everyone for around five months. Warwick was beyond livid at being deceived. In fact, the person most deceived, was Warwick himself, who in his hubris, believed he was the real power in the land, a belief he would not only come to regret, but that, ultimately, led to his death.

The Privy Council told Edward bluntly that Elizabeth was not a suitable wife for a king. Edward ignored them and did as he had, in truth, always done. Gone his own way in his own time. Although not a wise marriage, it was clear that Edward and Elizabeth never lost their affection for each other, despite Edward's staggering sexual appetite.

However, there was one huge and secret fly in the royal ointment and that was the alleged pre-contract of marriage Edward had, allegedly, made with Eleanor Talbot. That the two had a relationship is widely known and acknowledged. However, if there was a pre-contract, even though Eleanor later married someone else, it would mean Edward's marriage to Elizabeth Woodville was invalid and their children illegitimate. Ashdown-Hill argues this in some detail, and its later effect on Henry VII.[7]

But the marriage he had neither arranged, nor approved of, was the last straw for Warwick. Along with Edward's younger brother, George, Duke of Clarence, whose life was an endless round of being offended by something or someone, Warwick decided to raise a rebellion. Initially, he was successful, holding Edward for a few months at Warwick Castle before moving his prisoner to Middleham Castle. However, there was no support for Warwick in either environment, even though both castles were his bases. Edward waved him a chilly farewell and returned to London.

An uprising in Lincolnshire in April 1470, very likely fomented by Warwick, resulted in, not a battle as such, more of a skirmish at Empingham just north of Stamford straddling what is now the A1. It was the first battle in England in which cannons were used. Two volleys and the opposition fled, discarding their surcoats, with the arms of Warwick and Clarence emblazoned on them, on the battlefield. This led to the battle being given the nickname Losecote Field.

Warwick and Clarence fled to France to cosy up to Margaret of Anjou before returning in force to oust Edward. When it became clear that his life was in jeopardy from the resurgence of the Lancastrians, Edward and his younger brother, Richard, fled to Burgundy. Warwick rode in state to London, released the captive Henry VI, who, compared with the handsome, shining Edward, looked like a confused beggar dressed in a scruffy, stained, gown. But the important thing for Warwick was that he was once more in charge. Ever distrustful, Margaret of Anjou and her son, Edward of Lancaster, chose to remain abroad until Henry's throne was secure.

Which of course, it wasn't and was never going to be. Edward bided his time, brought a force to land at Ravenspur and in short order won the battles of Barnet and Tewkesbury. Warwick and his brother, John Neville, were killed at Barnet. Edward of Lancaster was killed at Tewkesbury. Edward of

York was once more king. And this time, apart from the 14-year-old Henry Tudor, Duke of Richmond, there was no real Lancastrian faction left. The young Henry and his uncle fled into exile.

However, uneasy lies the head that wears the crown, as Shakespeare tells us. Elizabeth Woodville, though beautiful, was a virago and haughty with it. She insisted on honours and titles for her relations and generally put everybody else's noses out of joint.

In 1476, Edward began a relationship with Jane Shore, also known as Elizabeth Lambert. She was an intelligent woman and, despite Edward's regular liaisons with other women, they remained close until Edward's death. She died in 1527, just as Edward's grandson, Henry VIII was trying to replace his wife with another 'concubine', Anne Boleyn.

George, Duke of Clarence continued to be a thorn in his elder brother's side, although everybody acknowledges that Richard, Duke of Gloucester, was totally loyal to Edward. It is thought an easily suppressed rebellion in 1474 had the petulant Clarence's fingerprints all over it. In 1477, Edward accused Clarence, 'of violating the laws of the realm and having threatened the security of judges and jurors'. He was sent to the Tower and in 1478, Clarence was charged with high treason. Edward made it publicly known that he would have happily forgiven the duke had he not 'continued in his evil ways'.[8]

In February 1478, Clarence was privately put to death in the Tower, probably to lessen the scandal of a public execution. However, the legend persists that George chose to be drowned in a butt of Malmsey wine, his favourite tipple. Rumours that Queen Elizabeth had pressured Edward to execute his brother because he was claiming their marriage was illegal have never been proved either. One theory to support the malmsey wine legend is that, since Clarence was interred in Tewkesbury Abbey alongside his wife, his body may have been transported from London to Tewkesbury in alcohol to stop it decaying.

What is true is that Edward's fratricide eroded his reputation and popularity. His health began to fail, mainly caused by his excessive intake of rich food and wine, followed by emetics to disgorge it, not to mention his numerous sexual relationships. Modern historians posit he developed diabetes, but everything from poison through pneumonia to malaria have been suggested. In April 1483, he fell seriously ill, only rallying to declare his loyal brother, Richard of Gloucester, as regent to the 10-year-old heir.

Edward IV died on 9 April 1483, leaving yet another child to be king of England.

> ## Fun Fact
>
> Edward IV knew his worth. At a heart-stopping 6'4 and incredibly handsome to boot, he must have looked like someone from a miraculous fable to the ordinary people of England.
>
> He knew full well, he had to be as different from Henry VI as possible. His height and good looks helped that, as did his passion for luxurious clothes made from wonderful fabrics and adorned with fabulous jewels. Edward really was the first king of bling and he knew how to make the most of his looks and bearing! Add to that he was unbelievably charismatic – a trait, along with his height, he bequeathed to his grandson, Henry VIII.

John Neville, Earl of Northumberland, and Marquess of Montagu

The brother of Richard Neville, Earl of Warwick, was born sometime between 1428 and 1435. He was a leader of the northern magnate quarrel between the Percies of Northumberland and the Nevilles, which came to a head in 1453 and led directly to the Wars of the Roses. John Neville was dominated, initially, by his desire to control the Scottish marches and, despite a close tie to Henry VI, being knighted by him in 1449, he supported his cousin Edward, Earl of March, the two having been friends from an early age. John led the victorious Yorkist forces at the battles of Hedgeley Moor and Hexham in 1464, for which he was created Earl of Northumberland, a title that had hitherto been held by the Percy family, the last holder being Henry Percy who had died at Towton.[9]

John was very active maintaining the Yorkist claim to the throne against the Lancastrians. In 1457, he helped defeat the opposition at Castleton, near Guisborough in Cleveland, capturing the enemy leaders and taking them to Middleham Castle. In 1457, he married Isabel, the daughter of Sir Edmund Ingoldesthorpe, and with her, sired two sons and five daughters. But he was never far away from a battlefield or military conflict.

Again in 1459, he was active at the Battle of Blore Heath, this time pursuing the fleeing Lancastrians so precipitately, he was captured and taken to Chester Castle. John was given the title Baron Montagu and made lord chamberlain to Edward IV, a post that gave him a place on the king's privy council.

His next foray into battle was at the second Battle of St Albans and this time, John was on the losing side. However, Margaret of Anjou spared his life, possibly because of his closeness to her husband. He was imprisoned in York and after the Battle of Towton, when Edward, who was at that point Duke of York, rode into the city, John interceded with Edward to spare the citizens from the king's wrath.

In the early 1460s, he was given more honours, including the Garter. He also laid siege to Bambrough Castle which surrendered to him on Christmas Eve 1462. But things were about to become less than rosy. At the bidding of his queen, Edward arranged. for the designated wife of John's son, the heiress of the Duke of Exeter, to be married to Thomas Grey, the queen's son by her previous husband.

In a typical move, when relations began to sour between the king and the Nevilles, Edward betrothed John's son, George to his eldest daughter, Elizabeth of York, an attractive match since Edward had at that point, no son. This would have the double-whammy effect of making John's loyalty greater while at the same time *really* giving George, Duke of Clarence something about which to be offended.

John Neville is generally portrayed as having a heartfelt loyalty to Edward. In his turn, Edward is portrayed as gambling that John would have serious doubts about being disloyal. However, Edward then made what could in hindsight be seen as a rare error of judgement. Ever mindful of the delicacy of the balance of power, the king released and pardoned Henry Percy, son of the Percy who had died at Towton. He then took the Northumberland title, and its monies, away from John and gave them back to Percy. It was a risk, but one Edward considered worth taking.

Historians have posited that Edward always felt uncomfortable at having given the Northumberland title to John Neville, especially after Warwick's defection. Henry Percy did not, as one might have expected, immediately join Warwick and Clarence after they fled to France, so Edward possibly thought it had been a sound move. John Neville didn't think so and complained. He was left with the title Marquess of Montagu, that brought with it neither lands nor money.

It cannot be a surprise then, that when he heard his brother, Richard, Earl of Warwick had landed, Neville immediately assembled an army at Pontefract, declared his allegiance to Henry VI, and marched on Doncaster to capture Edward. The latter escaped, with Richard of Gloucester, to Burgundy in the autumn of 1470. However, Edward had not been totally mistaken in his assessment of John. When Edward landed with Richard at Ravenspur six months later, John's forces did not move from Pontefract to intercept him. This has been taken by some as disloyalty to Henry VI, but John Neville was prone to the mantra of 'wait and see'. Instead, he joined his brother, Warwick at Coventry. It is interesting that Percy of Northumberland also kept his army on readiness but made no move to recapture the man who now declared his only ambition to be given his rightful title of Duke of York.

The two Neville brothers joined forces and met Edward's army at the second Battle of Barnet. Both were killed. Whether or not John really was wearing the murray and blue of the Yorkist livery under the Lancastrian colours, as some have suggested has never been proved, but it has long been the legend that he did so, and that he never truly lost his loyalty to the House of York, or possibly, his affection for Edward.

The bodies of both Neville brothers were taken to St Paul's in London and put on display to prove that they were really dead. They were then taken to Bisham Abbey, where they were interred.[10]

Sir John Tiptoft

Sir John Tiptoft, first Earl of Worcester, comes across as being two people. He was a learned scholar, studying in Oxford and Italy, and at the same time, Edward IV's enforcer, who carried out his duties with ferocity and cruelty. So much so, he became known as 'The Butcher of England'. Born in 1427/8, Tiptoft was, through his father, descended from Charlemagne, and to Llewellyn the Great and Henry III through his mother.[11]

In 1449, he married Cecily Neville, aunt of the Cecily Neville who married Richard, Duke of York. He was also made Earl of Worcester by Henry VI in the same year, but his wife died in 1450, by which time Tiptoft had transferred his loyalty to Richard, Duke of York. He was made lord high treasurer in 1452 and lord deputy of Ireland in 1456, both appointments being the vanguard of a general shift towards the Yorkists and away from the Lancastrian Henry VI.

Henry Pancoast tells us that when sent to Ireland, he brought about the execution of his predecessor, Lord Desmond on a charge of treason and, it was rumoured that, at the same time, he killed Desmond's young sons. Desmond's death has sometimes been attributed to Elizabeth Woodville, who apparently had a grudge against him. This has never been substantiated. He was dismissed from his post as Lord High Treasurer in 1455.[12]

Tiptoft spent three years travelling abroad on embassies to the Pope, and then travelled to the Holy Land.[13] Some historians believe his jaunt abroad was to ensure he was out of the initial turmoil during the late 1450s and the strife between the houses of Lancaster and York. He would have been in fear of his life, being seen as straddling both sides. He returned from Jerusalem via Venice and Padua, winning distinction by a much-acclaimed oration before Pope Pius II, after which he spent time studying 'new learning' at Ferrara.[14]

It is because of this time studying Greek, Latin, and law in Italy that Tiptoft has also been called 'England's First Renaissance Prince.' That said, it is also considered his time in Italy may have exacerbated his predilection for cruelty because of his proximity to the machinations of Italian politics and the classical texts he studied.

By 1460, he was back in England, probably because Edward IV was now king. Edward appointed him as Constable of England and whilst in office, Tiptoft tried Sir John de Vere and Sir Charles Grey for treason and had them executed. He was awarded the Order of the Garter by Edward. As time passed, his brutality accelerated. In 1469, during the Warwick/Clarence uprising, his treatment of Lancastrian prisoners reached a depth few have plumbed. Warkworth's chronicle details his executions of 20 Warwick adherents: 'persones of gentylmen and yomenne were hangede, drawne, and quartered, and hedede; and after that thei hanged uppe by the leggys, and a stake made scharpe at bothe endes, whereof one ende was putt in att bottokys, and the other ende ther heddes were putt uppe one'.[15] This was seen as excessive, even in those times, but it stopped the rebellion in its tracks. It was this act that earned him the 'Butcher of England' title, although this did not appear until the Tudors were in power and anyone who had been a Yorkist was vilified.

When Henry VI was briefly reinstated the following year, Tiptoft did not manage to flee the country. He was caught after trying to take money from the treasury for Edward's campaign to regain his throne. According to some sources, he was found disguised as a shepherd and taken prisoner.[16] However, Pancoast states he was found hiding at the top of a high tree. Taken to Westminster, he was tried before the Earl of Oxford, whose father and brother Tiptoft had executed eight years before on Tower Hill. His execution was delayed by the number of people who wanted to see him put to death. The mob was so numerous, Tiptoft is believed to have feared they would 'eat him alive'.[17]

He was beheaded at the Tower of London in October 1470. His execution scaffold was decked out with garlands and expensive cloth. He instructed the executioner to make sure his death took three blows of the axe to represent the Holy Trinity.

History, it is said, is written by the victors. I would amend that to written by those with an agenda. Although Tiptoft's cruelty appals us now, it is important to remember the late fifteenth century as a very bloody time in history, when families' loyalties were frequently divided, power changed hands alarmingly frequently, and in truth, nobody could really know if those in their families, or social circles were friend or foe. Peter Moore and John Horgan who write the *Worcesterhousehold* blog, argue convincingly that Tudor propaganda, not to mention Shakespeare, blackened Richard III's name so effectively, it has taken centuries to accept that he was, in truth, a fair and honest king, and that the same could be said of John Tiptoft.

Tiptoft's body was taken to Blackfriars in Ludgate. He had donated money for a chapel there and was buried in it, despite the fact a tomb in Ely Cathedral had also been intended to be his last resting place. That tomb shows an effigy of Tiptoft with two of his three wives. The occupant, however, is believed to be that of his son, Edward, 2nd Earl of Worcester, who died in August 1485, the same month as the last Yorkist king, Richard III.[18]

We will leave the last word to Pancoast. Tiptoft represents the best and worst of that era. Civil strife brought forth incredible cruelty, brutality and vindictiveness and he personified that. At the same time, he is regarded as an intellectual new light in the world. As Pancoast terms it, 'he is the butcher and the first fruits of the Italian Renaissance'.[19]

Richard III

I ALWAYS FEEL sorry for Richard III. He appears, even to some historians, as a Marmite man, but I look upon him with sympathy. He was Edward IV's enforcer, quite as much as John Tiptoft was, except Richard was not so wantonly cruel. In modern times, some would say Edward emotionally abused Richard, knowing his loyalty was absolute, so not bothering to be assiduous about keeping him on side. And perhaps that is one reason Edward kept Richard in the north. Not just because he was a doughty soldier but possibly so that Richard never saw the truth of Edward's louche existence, and the scales of loyalty never had an opportunity to fall from his eyes. Edward knew his younger brother would always be totally steadfast, mop up after him and excuse his faults. Which is what I believe happened at the end of Edward's life when Richard blamed the Woodvilles for his brother's dissolute lifestyle. Richard was, in temperament very different from Edward. He was far from lazy, very pious, a family man, and a book lover.

Richard III, these days known almost affectionately as 'the King in the Car Park' has been, possibly, the monarch about which there is most division of opinion. Blackened by Shakespeare and Sir Thomas More, both of whom were writing in Tudor England and dared not give him the least praise, and whose texts were believed by historians up until the last hundred years or so, Richard has been one of history's prime sufferers from a bad press. In his defence arose the mighty Richard III Society whose mission statement is, 'working since 1924 to secure a more balanced assessment of the king and to support research into his life and times'.

Richard was born on 2 October 1452 at Fotheringhay Castle in Northamptonshire, to Richard, Duke of York and Cecily Neville. He was the eleventh child of 12 and their youngest to survive infancy.[1] His birth heralded the beginnings of the War of the Roses, a conflict that would last 30 years, the final battle being at Stoke, fought near the village of East Stoke in Nottinghamshire close to the River Trent in 1487, two years after Richard's death on Bosworth Field.

Richard's childhood was probably quite a happy one. Being young, he would not, as were his elder brothers, Edward and Edmund, be involved in the fighting against the Lancastrian Henry VI and his warlike spouse, Margaret of Anjou. When Richard of York rode off in 1459 to the Battle of Ludford Bridge, he left his duchess and three youngest children, George, Richard, and Margaret, at Ludlow Castle. After the defeat of the Yorkists, the Lancastrian army sacked Ludlow. Although their lives would be sacrosanct, it must have been a frightening experience for the York family, which resulted in Cecily and the three young children being put into the custody of her sister who was married to the Duke of Buckingham, a Lancastrian supporter.[2]

A year after Ludford Bridge, Richard of York and his son, Edmund, were killed at the Battle of Wakefield and Edward, Earl of March became the head of the family. Cecily sent George and Richard to the Netherlands for their own safety. On their return, Richard was sent to Middleham Castle to learn to become a squire, the normal career path for the male children of nobility. Middleham was in the control of Cecily's nephew, Richard, Earl of Warwick, a title he inherited through his wife, Anne Beauchamp. Warwick would later style himself Warwick the Kingmaker. Richard became very fond of his cousin, although Warwick's later disloyalty to Edward IV made them implacable enemies.

Whilst at Middleham, Richard met Anne Neville, Warwick's younger daughter, Francis Lovell, and Robert Percy. Anne would become Richard's wife in 1472; Lovell and Percy would become Richard's lifelong friends and staunch supporters. His time at Middleham was, arguably, the happiest of his life. And it is worth noting that, although all the charismatic plaudits are given to his elder brother, Edward, Richard must have had some qualities that made people give him their unwavering loyalty, unlike the middle brother, George, the petulant Duke of Clarence, who few trusted and even fewer seem to have liked.

Edward gave Warwick £1000 (£950,968,49 in December 2023) to be a tutor to Richard. Warwick did an excellent job because from an early age, Richard proved to be an accomplished warrior.

The big weed that floated into Richard's sunny garden came in the shape of Edward's choice of queen, Elizabeth Woodville. Seen as an arrogant, disrespectful, haughty, and vengeful commoner, she brooked no dissent from anybody. So, when Edward blithely declared to Warwick that, not only was he already married, but named Elizabeth, the two were instant enemies. Probably because Warwick was also haughty, arrogant etc., but whilst it was becoming in a man and a soldier, it was certainly not how women, and particularly queens, were supposed to behave. Elizabeth, distrustful and probably jealous of Richard's influence over Edward, disliked her husband's younger brother. The feeling was mutual. Warwick declared Elizabeth had bewitched Edward, and although this is errant nonsense, her mother, Jacquetta of Luxembourg, was believed to be a witch. Notwithstanding, Edward continued, despite his numerous adulteries, to be fascinated by his wife.

Soon the breach at court was an open one. Warwick took advantage of George, Duke of Clarence's petulant discontent to inveigle him into a rebellion that never really took off. For a brief few months, Warwick held Edward prisoner at Middleham, but his supposed support never materialised and Edward was soon back in London. The Battle of Losecote Field/Empingham in April 1470 was so short as to not be recognised by some as a battle. That said, the fact Edward ordered Lord Richard Welles to be marched out between his army and the forces led by Welles' son, Robert, and summarily beheaded, showed that the usual easy-going, indolent king was rapidly changing.

Edward's march north to the Lancastrian heartlands, together with his demand that Warwick and Clarence appear before him, stifled opposition before it got its act together. The rebel leaders fled to the Continent and Margaret of Anjou. Her hatred of Warwick made her keep him on his knees in front of her for over 15 minutes. That must have stung! But her need of him was greater and although she made no secret of her hatred, she was happy to use him if it meant regaining her husband's throne.

Warwick marched back to England and, now reconciled with his brother, John an erstwhile Yorkist supporter, released Henry VI from the Tower and paraded him through London. John Neville, whose defection had been caused by Edward taking the earldom of Northumberland away from him and giving it back to Henry Percy, almost caught Edward and Richard napping at Doncaster. Their escape to Kings Lynn and subsequent flight to the Continent was so hurried that Edward is said to have paid for his passage with his fur cloak and Richard had to borrow money from the Zeeland Town Bailiff to pay for his crossing. In their absence, both were attainted in a parliament led by Warwick.

The brothers were not welcomed particularly by the Duke of Burgundy, whose wife was their sister, but he was finally persuaded to help them when France declared war on him. The Hanseatic merchants also chipped in and Edward's fleet sailed for England. Warwick supporters prevented them from landing in East Anglia and Hull refused Edward entry. Notwithstanding, he landed at Ravenspur and headed for York. But now he was not king, not even, officially, Duke of York, but come merely to claim his inheritance as Duke of York. And it is at this point that the 18-year-old Richard came into his own as a military leader.

Edward's forces marched to Coventry to confront Warwick in his castle. Warwick refused to come out, but George, Duke of Clarence did with protestations that he had been misled, had always been secretly loyal to Edward, blah, blah. It was convenient for Edward to believe George although he never trusted him again. Richard was possibly given charge of the vanguard at the second Battle of Barnet and acquitted himself well. The battle was fought in dense fog, and he lost several of his personal household, which tends to confirm he was in the thick of the fighting. It was at this battle that Warwick and John Neville were killed and one must wonder what Richard's reaction was at losing two men who had until recently been close friends for almost the whole of his life.[3]

But there was no time to sit on laurels. Edward learned that Margaret had landed in Weymouth with her son, Edward of Lancaster – sometimes styled Westminster, but never Prince of Wales – to regain the kingdom and defeat the Yorkists for ever. Her objective was to cross the River Severn and meet up with Jasper Tudor in Wales. Edward was caught unaware and had to scramble his troops and march west.

Richard was certainly leading the vanguard at the Battle of Tewkesbury in May 1471 and it was of prime importance that the Yorkists won it. Margaret of Anjou had finally agreed to come to England but, not only did the Lancastrians lose the battle, her son was killed on the field. After that, Margaret was really a broken woman. She took refuge, possibly in Little Malvern Priory, but was captured and lodged in the Tower of London until ransomed four years later and sent back to France.

Edward, and by definition, Richard, was triumphant. The king left Richard to exercise his authority as Constable of England, put the remaining Lancastrians who had taken refuge in Tewkesbury Abbey on trial and execute them in the marketplace. Which he did. The full story of the battle is not relevant here, but it is interesting in that it was only by a whisker Tewkesbury was a Yorkist victory. The Lancastrian Duke of Somerset is alleged to have galloped up to Lord Wenlock, accused him of failing to come to his aid, and dashed out his brains with a battleaxe.[4]

The House of York once more reigned over England, but peaceful it wasn't. Edward asked parliament for money to support the Duke of Burgundy. Richard is known to have contributed a large number of soldiers although he was against the treaty signed eventually with Louis XI, mostly because it had gained England nothing, but cost much. He also refused pensions offered as sweeteners.[5]

For the last few years of Edward's reign, Richard stayed as much as he could in the North. He had finally married Anne Neville in 1472 after a protracted dispute with his brother, George, Duke of Clarence, by that time heir to the Warwick lands through his wife, the Kingmaker's elder daughter. George was, to use Dickens' description of Scrooge, 'squeezing, wrenching, grasping, scraping, clutching, and covetous', not to mention being a drunkard and never doing anything unless it was absolutely convenient and entirely to his own advantage.

That said, Richard did hurry south when he heard that Edward had charged their brother with treason, and he pleaded with the king to spare George's life, but the Woodville clan were in no mood to see Clarence pardoned, possibly because Clarence had come across the pre-contract to Eleanor Butler rumour which would threaten the royal children's inheritance. Elizabeth persuaded Edward not to yield to Richard's pleas.[6]

Richard and Anne had a son, also called Edward, and, from all accounts, their marriage was a happy one. It seems clear from all sources that Richard preferred being at Middleham, looking after the northern lands and, especially, the Scottish border, and enjoying life as High Sheriff of Cumberland. He was particularly revered in the city of York. He still is.

In 1480, Richard was made lieutenant-general of the North and, together with the Earl of Northumberland, launched counter-raids by the Scots who were attempting to negotiate an alliance with France. This situation continued until 1482 when Richard took Berwick-on-Tweed, the last time it changed hands, although it was not officially annexed to England until 1746.

When Edward suddenly became seriously ill in April 1483, he made a codicil to his will naming Richard as regent to his 10-year-old son, Edward, who, on 9 April became Edward V. At the urging of Lord Hastings, Richard hurried south, removed the young king from the custody of Elizabeth Woodville's brother, Earl Rivers, and travelled to London. But not before he had Rivers, Richard Grey, and their associate, Thomas Grey taken to Pontefract where they were executed by the Earl of Northumberland, for high treason against the Lord Protector, i.e Richard.[7]

The last time Richard saw his elder brother, in February 1483, he was shocked at the change in him. Edward was now immensely fat, very lazy, and his only desire was the pursuit of pleasure. Richard, by contrast, was pious, not to say puritanical, and probably blamed the Woodvilles and Lord Hastings for Edward's decline. On Edward's death, the Woodvilles planned to crown the young Edward V immediately he arrived in London, but Richard prevented that. He did, however, swear allegiance to the young king.

Richard feared that, with a child once more on the throne, family in-fighting would result in a re-hash of the recent civil war. He declared, however valid or invalid, that his brother's marriage to Elizabeth Woodville was bigamous and her children illegitimate. The two sons, Edward, then aged ten and his younger brother, Richard were last seen playing in the Tower of London in July 1483, beginning one of the greatest mysteries in history.

His justification for seizing the throne was detailed in the *Croyland Chronicle*:

> It was set forth…that the sons of King Edward were bastards, on the ground that he had contracted a marriage with one Lady Eleanor Butler before his marriage to Queen Elizabeth; add to which, the blood of his other brother, George, Duke of Clarence, had been attained; so that, at the present time, no certain and uncorrupted lineal blood could be found of Richard, Duke of York, except in the person of…Richard, Duke of Gloucester.[8]

What this means in effect is that George of Clarence, Richard's elder brother and his heirs, would have superseded any claim by Richard. However, Clarence had been executed for high treason in 1478, thus barring those heirs from the succession. George left a son with what would now be called learning difficulties, and a daughter. Both had tragic lives. George's son, Edward, Earl of Warwick, was executed by Henry VII on a trumped-up charge of treason. This was solely to satisfy Ferdinand of Aragon and Isabella of Castile so they would send Katherine of Aragon to England to marry his own heir, Prince Arthur. George's daughter would become Margaret Pole, Countess of Salisbury, executed in 1542 by Henry VIII for nothing other than being of Yorkist descent and because he was a paranoid tyrant – but then I freely admit my bias.

Going back to Richard, Mortimer Levine points out that the only point really to have ever been at issue was the truth or otherwise of the precontract with Eleanor Butler née Talbot. She had died in 1468 before all this furore arose. And, before either of Edward's sons were born, so, in truth, even if there had been a precontract, by 1473 when Edward, Prince of Wales was born, Eleanor had been dead for five years. Some made an argument that since the precontract died with Eleanor, the boys must be legitimate. Levine goes on to point out that the true loser in all this is Elizabeth of York, who was born in 1465 and would, therefore, be affected by any precontract.

Which is quite amusing when one considers Henry Tudor married Elizabeth not just to join the red and white rose emblems of York and Lancaster, but to bolster his regime, since his forebears *did* come from illegitimate stock. Furthermore, Henry would be aware of this, which is probably one reason he simply ignored the issue, repealed Richard's *Titulus Regulus* and carried on. It was also more than his throne was worth to open up the death of the two young princes and allow fresh speculation, which, only being a year or so after their supposed deaths, might shine a light where he didn't want it shone.

In June 1483, Richard moved against Lord Hastings, one of the young king's most ardent supporters. He accused Hastings of plotting with Margaret Beaufort to put her son, Henry Tudor on the throne. Hastings was executed without trial.[9] Richard declared himself king, backed by an army from the northern shires who were camping at Finsbury Fields.[10] Richard was crowned on 6 July 1483. Four months into his reign, Henry Stafford, Duke of Buckingham, raised a rebellion in another attempt to put Henry Tudor, the last surviving Lancastrian, then in exile in France, on the throne. This attempt failed, too.[11]

What might have been his motivation for seizing the throne? His own safety or fear of what the Woodvilles would do, because it was an open secret that Elizabeth Woodville neither liked nor trusted her husband's younger brother? The Woodville family was known to be quite as rapacious as Isabella of France had been, only there were more of them. Or did Richard consider it his duty to keep England stable when history had proved that child-monarchs made for instability and conflict?

He presented himself as a pious, reforming force for good. He put his own northern supporters into positions of influence in southern England, which was regarded as tyranny. He was also used to the plain-speaking habit of northerners which, when they exercised their new powers, did not go down well with the less blunt – or more refined, depending on your view – southerners.

After Buckingham's failed rebellion, he and other Woodville supporters fled to France, where, on Christmas Day, they proclaimed Henry Tudor as king of England. Elizabeth Woodville also agreed with Margaret Beaufort that Edward IV's eldest daughter, Elizabeth, would marry Henry Tudor when he became king.[12]

Richard suffered two enormous setbacks in 1484 and early 1485. In 1484, his son, Edward of Middleham died before his tenth birthday, perhaps unluckily, on the first anniversary of Edward IV's death, 9 April. The Croyland Chronicle states: 'this only son of his, in whom all the hopes of the royal succession, fortified with so many oaths, were centred, was seized with an illness of but short duration, and died at Middleham Castle'.[13] Then in March 1485, Richard's queen, Anne Neville died, possibly of tuberculosis, at Westminster. There was an eclipse on the day she died, which some took as an omen of her husband's doom.[14] The loss of his son and wife within the space of a year must have devastated Richard. He must have wondered what would happen to him next.

What happened, of course, was the Battle of Bosworth on 22 August 1485, where – forgive me for being partisan – he rode to his death like a hero, betrayed by one of the Stanley clan, who always had a foothold in both camps and changed sides so often, they needed revolving doors in their houses. This particular Stanley, Lord William, sat on top of a hill waiting to see who was likely to win before coming down and attacking the Yorkist forces. Richard, probably realising all was lost, made one last courageous charge through the men surrounding and hiding Henry Tudor, who made no move to come and meet his foe in combat. Richard was unhorsed, cut down, stripped naked, his body defiled and slung over a horse to take to Leicester. For centuries, it was believed his body had been discarded in the River Soar, but, as we now know, he was entombed in the priory in Leicester, later to be covered by a council car park.

Thomas Stanley, William's elder brother and stepfather to Henry Tudor, then retrieved the crown from a thorn bush and crowned the new king of England. However, ten years later, karma came hunting. William Stanley was convicted of treason for supporting the pretender, Perkin Warbeck, and executed. Oh dear, how sad. Never mind!

Henry started as he meant to go on. He backdated his reign to the day before Bosworth, 21 August 1485, thus at one stroke making everyone who had fought for Richard traitors to the crown and enabling him to go on a huge land grab.

The Tudor era – one that would change the face of England forever – had begun.

Fun Fact

Not so much fun as interesting. Contemporary accounts of Richard claim he was a hunchback. His nickname was 'Crookback' and Tudor accounts, anxious to pour opprobrium on anyone of the Yorkist persuasion, made much of this. As, of course, did Shakespeare. However, when Richard's skeleton, discovered in the remains of Greyfriars, was examined, it was discovered he suffered from scoliosis, which meant one shoulder was higher than the other. This did not mean he could not fight and he was, indeed, a seasoned warrior by the time he was 19 years old, leading the vanguard at the Battle of Tewkesbury in 1471. When the furore over his discovery led to several documentaries, one of them featured a young man called Dominic Smee, who had the same kind of scoliosis as Richard. The producers had a set of medieval armour made for Dominic and he amply demonstrated that his scoliosis in no way affected his ability to fight.[15]

The Cat, the Rat, and the Dog

In July 1484, a year into Richard III's short reign, William Collingbourne posted a lampoon on the door of St Paul's Cathedral: 'The Cat, the Rat and Lovell our dog, Rule all England under a Hog.'

This referred to Richard's counsellors and close friends. William Catesby, Sir Richard Ratcliffe, and Francis Lovell – whose badge was a wolf. The hog refers to Richard, whose heraldic badge was a white boar. These men were Richard's most trusted friends. All of them suffered for their utter loyalty to him.[16]

William Catesby

Catesby was born in Northamptonshire, trained to be a lawyer and was such a good one, he won positions as a legal advisor to various noble families, including that of the Duke of Buckingham and Lord Hastings. The latter so trusted Catesby, he recommended him to the new Richard III as a nominee for the royal council. When the failed Buckingham rebellion occurred in the last months of 1483, Sir Thomas More believed that Catesby knew of the plot and warned Richard. More wrote this in his account of the accession of Richard III. Furthermore, he described Catesby as, 'a man of dignified bearing, handsomely featured, and of excellent appearance, not only suitable for carrying out assignments but capable also of handling matters of grave consequence'.[17]

In the resulting fallout, he gained lands and annuities. After this, Richard placed his total trust in Catesby, and not without reason. The *Croyland Chronicle* states that Catesby and Ratcliffe's opinions were such that Richard did not oppose them. In fact, it would seem the two advisors always acted as one. Catesby became Richard's Esquire of the king's body and in 1484, speaker in parliament.[18]

In 1485, rumour had it that Richard, now a widower, planned to marry his niece, Elizabeth of York; when this rumour reached the exiled Henry Tudor, it was said he was 'pinched to the very stomach'.[19] However, Catesby and Ratcliffe both opposed this idea, Catesby telling Richard the whole of the north of England would rise against him if he went forward with the plan, and even bringing doctors of Divinity to point out to Richard that the Pope would never grant such a dispensation.

In mid-1485, it became clear that the Stanley clan were planning something. Catesby and Richard's other councillors advised him to refuse Lord William Stanley leave to go to his estates. However, although Catesby was at Richard's side at Bosworth, he begged the king to retreat – 'a single battle need not decide all'. Richard refused, but Catesby did not follow him in his final charge towards Henry Tudor. He was captured and executed at Leicester, despite begging for mercy and claiming in his will he had always 'loved Henry Tudor'.[20]

Sir Richard Ratcliffe

Richard III spent his first few months in power, degrading some holders of the Order of the Garter. These included Anthony Woodville, Earl Rivers, brother of Elizabeth Woodville, who Richard had intercepted taking the young Edward V to London. Earl Rivers was taken to Pontefract and executed in front of Ratcliffe, together with Richard Grey, Elizabeth Woodville's son by her first husband.[21] William, Lord Hastings, summarily executed for the Buckingham plot was another holder of the garter, as was Buckingham himself, also executed. By the end of 1483, Sir William Parr, grandfather of Katherine Parr, sixth wife of Henry VIII, had also died. This left empty places in the Order.

One of the winners was Sir Richard Ratcliffe, who helped hold the canopy over Richard's head when he was anointed at his coronation. Ratcliffe was in Richard of Gloucester's retinue by 1475. He was Constable of Barnard Castle and joined Gloucester's campaigns on the Scottish border, when the French king was attempting a Franco-Scottish alliance. Gloucester knighted Ratcliffe during the successful siege of Berwick-on-Tweed and was very close to all the preparations between Edward IV's death and Richard III's accession. Ratcliffe was made a companion of the Order of the Garter in 1484 and granted lands and offices producing an annual income of around £1,000 (around £832,781.07 in 2023).[22]

Many of the lands Richard III dished out to his Northern adherents when he came to power, lay in the south of England and Ratcliffe's share lay in the south-west. This was possibly a huge mistake on Richard's part because the discontent it engendered solidified support for Henry Tudor, Duke of Richmond. The *Croyland Chronicle* describes it as a lament, 'among his northern adherents, whom he planted…throughout his dominions, to the disgrace and loudly expressed sorrow of all the people of the south, who daily longed…for the…return of their ancient rulers, rather than the present tyranny of these people'.[23]

He became one of Richard's most trusted lieutenants and died on the battlefield at Bosworth.

Francis, Viscount Lovell

I have purposely left Francis Lovell to be the last person in this book purely for the selfish reason he, along with John Neville, who we met earlier, has always fascinated me, simply because he disappeared from history. We have no idea what happened to him after the Battle of Stoke in 1487, and precious little of his life before that.

Lovell was born in 1454, son of John Lovell, 8th Baron of Tichmarsh. Francis was a seasoned military man, knighted by Richard of Gloucester on the 1480 Scottish campaign.

He carried the sword of state at Richard's coronation and also provided the coronation ring, slipped onto Queen Anne Neville's finger.[24]

We know he was Richard's chamberlain, and that he fought at Bosworth before escaping and going into sanctuary at Colchester. In 1486, he led a doomed rebellion against Henry VII, before travelling to the Netherlands and Ireland with Richard's designated successor, John de la Pole, Earl of Lincoln. He, with de la Pole and a troop of German mercenaries came to England and were defeated at the Battle of Stoke, at which de la Pole was killed.[25] After that, we know nothing for certain. So, who was Francis Lovell? It is a question so many people, historians, novelists etc., have tried to answer in the past 500-odd years.

He is probably best known from the Collingbourne lampoon referred to at the beginning of this section. Collingbourne was executed after pinning his doggerel to the door of St Paul's, but Nicola Cornick believes he hated Lovell. Collingbourne had been the steward of lands held by Cecily Neville in Wiltshire, but this post was then given to Lovell.

Richard of Gloucester and Francis Lovell were childhood friends, having both been wards of Richard Neville, Earl of Warwick at his castle in Middleham. Francis was married at a young age to Anne FitzHugh, niece of Richard Neville, Earl of Warwick and cousin to Anne Neville, Warwick's younger daughter and future queen of Richard III. But whether the marriage was successful is open to question. Michele Schlindler posits that the couple were friendly and that Anne helped Francis after Bosworth.[26] He was mistakenly listed as having been killed in the battle, but it is certain that he was a thorn in Henry VII's flesh until the Battle of Stoke.

The chronicler Polydore Vergil believed that Lovell died at Stoke, but the Tudor chroniclers, Edward Hall and Ralph Holinshed, both believed he fled the field and died later. There are a number of theories, one of which is that he fled to his home at Minster Lovell and went into hiding This gained some credibility in 1708 when a skeleton was allegedly found in a secret chamber there, only to crumble the instant air entered the room. However, beguiling though this theory is, Minster Lovell was given to Jasper Tudor, Henry VII's uncle, in 1486, so it is hardly likely Francis would go there.

Alternative theories say he fled the battlefield at Stoke and headed for his mother's castle at Stoke Bardolph, where he died shortly afterwards. This theory gained some impetus in the nineteenth-century when a tomb with an effigy from the fifteenth-century was discovered and declared to be that of a knight who died at the Battle of Stoke. This is possible but Henry VII, still in the early years of his reign would have had an effective spy network. That said, it might be that even if he were informed of the tomb and who might be its occupant, he would not want to stir the whole thing up again and so let it lie.

And yet, Francis' mother, Anne Lovell was writing to John Paston in 1488 actively searching for news of her son, possibly in Scotland or on the Continent. What is certain is that James IV of Scotland issued a safe conduct to Francis Lovell in June 1488, but there is no record he was ever in Scotland or anywhere else.[27]

Another factor that makes this whole situation fascinating is that Lovell was a prominent figurehead of the Yorkist cause; the only one perhaps who could awaken memories of the Yorkist monarchy. It is surprising if he were still alive after that last mention of the Scottish safe conduct that he never attempted to get in touch with anyone, let alone his fellow Yorkist sympathisers. He was only 31 years old, still strong, physically and mentally. Not someone who would settle for obscurity and safety, one would imagine.

Sir Francis Bacon writing in 1622 suggests that he might have swum across the river Trent on his horse, been unable to get his mount up the steep bank on the other side and drowned. Or that he perhaps lived in a cave – one assumes as a hermit![28] But the intriguing truth is we shall in all likelihood never know. So, for a crime writer who is fascinated by history, the wealth of what-ifs make Francis Lovell an irresistible subject for speculation.

Endnotes

Introduction

1. https://tvtropes.org/pmwiki/pmwiki.php/Funny/BeyondTheFringe.

Preamble

1. David Starkey, *The Monarchy of England*, vol. 1 (Chatto and Windus, 2004), p. 99.

THE NORMANS – 1066–1154

William I – *The Conqueror*

1. Ibid., p. 127.
2. David Crouch, *The Normans: The History of a Dynasty* (Hambledon and London, 2002), p. 87.
3. Ibid.
4. Ibid., p. 94.
5. Ibid., p. 101.
6. Hugh M. Thomas, 'The Significance and Fate of the Native English Landholders of 1086', *The English Historical Review* 118, no. 476 (2003): 303-33. http://www.jstor.org/stable/3490123.
7. Ibid., p. 107.
8. D. C. Douglas, 'Companions of the Conqueror', *History* 28, no. 108 (1943): 129-47. http://www.jstor.org/stable/24401893.
9. https://en.wikipedia.org/wiki/William_the_Conqueror.
10. Crouch, *The Normans*, pp. 117-18.
11. Ibid., pp. 132-34.
12. Ibid., pp. 161-62.
13. https://en.wikisource.org/wiki/Dictionary_of_National_Biography,_1885-1900/FitzOsbern,_William.

14. https://spartacus-educational.com/NORosbern.htm.
15. https://biography.wales/article/s-FITZ-WIL-1071.

William II (Rufus)

1. Crouch, *The Normans*, pp. 129-166.
2. David Starkey, *Crown and Country: A History of England through the Monarchy* (Harper, 2010), p. 122.
3. Ibid., p. 137.
4. Ibid p. 123.
5. Crouch, *The Normans*, p. 139.
6. Ibid., p. 151.
7. C. Warren Hollister, 'The Strange Death of William Rufus', *Speculum* 48, no. 4 (1973): 637-53. https://doi.org/10.2307/2856221.
8. Crouch, *The Normans*, pp. 154-55.
9. Starkey, *Crown and Country*, p. 129.
10. Hollister, 'The Strange Death of William Rufus'.
11. Ibid.
12. Starkey, *Crown and Country*, p. 126.
13. https://en.wikipedia.org/wiki/Ranulf_Flambard.
14. R. W. Southern, 'Ranulf Flambard and Early Anglo-Norman Administration', The Alexander Prize Essay, *Transactions of the Royal Historical Society* 16 (1933): 95-128. https://doi.org/10.2307/3678666.

Henry I

1. https://www.englishmonarchs.co.uk/normans_3.htm.
2. https://www.berkshirehistory.com/bios/henry1.html.
3. David Hume, *The History of England, vol. 1: From the Invasion of Julius Caesar to the Revolution in 1688*, chap. 6.
4. Charles Spencer, *The White Ship* (William Collins, 2020), p. 77.
5. Ibid., p. 78.
6. Hume, *The History of England*, chap. 6.
7. Spencer, *The White Ship*, p. 102.
8. Hume, *The History of England*, chap. 6.
9. Spencer, *The White Ship*, p. 2.
10. Ibid., p. 175.
11. Ibid., p. 178.

12. Ibid., p. 184.
13. Hume, *The History of England*, chap. 6.
14. https://www.bbc.co.uk/news/av/uk-england-gloucestershire-65475642.
15. Barbara MacDonald Walker, 'King Henry I's "Old Men"', *Journal of British Studies* 8, no. 1 (1968): 1-21. http://www.jstor.org/stable/175259.
16. Ibid.
17. https://en.wikipedia.org/wiki/Investiture_Controversy.
18. Ibid.
19. Norman F. Cantor, *The Civilization of the Middle Ages* (HarperCollins, 1993), p. 286.
20. MacDonald Walker, 'King Henry I's "Old Men"'.
21. Sally N. Vaughn, 'Robert of Meulan and Raison d'État in the Anglo-Norman State, 1093–1118', *Albion: A Quarterly Journal Concerned with British Studies* 10, no. 4 (1978): 352-73. https://doi.org/10.2307/4048166.
22. Paul Dalton, 'Eustace Fitz John and the Politics of Anglo-Norman England: The Rise and Survival of a Twelfth-Century Royal Servant', *Speculum* 71, no. 2 (1996): 358-83. https://doi.org/10.2307/2865417.
23. https://en.wikipedia.org/wiki/Eustace_fitz_John.

Stephen, Matilda, and the Anarchy 1135–1154

1. W.C. Sellar and R.J. Yeatman, *1066 and All That* (Methuen, 1930).
2. https://www.worldhistory.org/King_Stephen_of_England/.
3. Crouch, *The Normans*, p. 239.
4. Ibid., p. 246.
5. Ibid.
6. https://en.wikipedia.org/wiki/Stephen,_King_of_England.
7. Edmund King, 'Stephen of Blois, Count of Mortain and Boulogne', *The English Historical Review* 115, no. 461 (2000): 271-96. http://www.jstor.org/stable/579081.
8. http://www.historicalnovels.info/When-Christ-and-His-Saints-Slept.html#:~:text=by%20Sharon%20Kay%20Penman&text=%22And%20they%20said%20openly%20that,daughter%20Maude%20as%20his%20heir.
9. Edward J. Kealey, 'King Stephen: Government and Anarchy', *Albion: A Quarterly Journal Concerned with British Studies* 6, no. 3 (1974): 201-17. https://doi.org/10.2307/4048242.
10. Ibid.

11. https://museumofoxford.org/empress-matilda-lady-of-the-english#:~:text=Matilda%20is%20said%20to%20have,nearby%20Abingdon%2DUpon%2DThames.

12. Kealey, 'King Stephen'.

13. Jean-François Nieus, 'The Early Career of William of Ypres in England: A New Charter of King Stephen', *The English Historical Review* 130, no. 544 (2015): 527-45. http://www.jstor.org/stable/24474332.

14. Ibid.

15. https://en.wikipedia.org/wiki/William_of_Ypres.

16. https://en.wikisource.org/wiki/Dictionary_of_National_Biography,_1885-1900/William_of_Ypres.

17. Nieus, 'The Early Career of William of Ypres in England'.

18. https://en.wikisource.org/wiki/Dictionary_of_National_Biography,_1885-1900/William_of_Ypres.

19. https://en.wikipedia.org/wiki/William_d%27Aubigny,_1st_Earl_of_Arundel.

20. Crouch, *The Normans*, p. 257.

21. https://thesignsofthetimes.com.au/30/57062.htm.

22. https://en.wikipedia.org/wiki/Robert,_1st_Earl_of_Gloucester.

23. Crouch, *The Normans*, pp. 198-202.

24. Ibid.

25. Joe W. Leedom, 'William of Malmesbury and Robert of Gloucester Reconsidered', *Albion: A Quarterly Journal Concerned with British Studies* 6, no. 3 (1974): 251-65. https://doi.org/10.2307/4048246.

26. Ibid.

27. Ibid.

28. https://en.wikipedia.org/wiki/Robert,_1st_Earl_of_Gloucester.

29. https://en.wikipedia.org/wiki/Rout_of_Winchester.

The House of Plantagenet 1154–1485

1. Desmond Seward, *The Demon's Brood: The Plantagenet Dynasty that Forged the English Nation* (Constable, 2014), Introduction.

Henry II

1. C. Warren Hollister and Thomas K. Keefe, 'The Making of the Angevin Empire', *Journal of British Studies* 12, no. 2 (1973): 1–25. http://www.jstor.org/stable/175272.

2. Ralph V. Turner, 'The Problem of Survival for the Angevin "Empire": Henry II's and His Sons' Vision versus Late Twelfth-Century Realities', *The American Historical Review* 100, no. 1 (1995): 78-96. https://doi.org/10.2307/2167984.
3. https://en.wikipedia.org/wiki/The_Lion_in_Winter_(1968_film).
4. https://ianstone.london/2020/04/05/who-was-henry-ii/.
5. W. L. Warren, *Henry II* (Methuen, 1991), p. 30.
6. Dan Jones, *The Plantagenets: The Kings Who Made England* (Harper Collins, 2013), p. 31.
7. Warren, *Henry II*, pp. 48-50.
8. Warren, *Henry II*, chap. 9.
9. Ibid.
10. https://ianstone/2020/04/05/who-was-henry-ii/.
11. L.F. Salzman, *Henry II* (Houghton, 1914), p. 13.
12. Warren, *Henry II*, pp. 560-61.
13. Bernard S. Bachrach, 'Henry II and the Angevin Tradition of Family Hostility', *Albion: A Quarterly Journal Concerned with British Studies* 16, no. 2 (1984): 111–30. https://doi.org/10.2307/4049284.
14. Sharon Bennett Connolly, *King John's Right-Hand Lady: The Story of Nicholaa de la Haye* (Pen & Sword, 2023), chap. 4.
15. Warren, *Henry II*, p. 621.
16. Ibid., p. 626.
17. David Crouch, Anthony Holden, Stewart Gregory, eds., *History of William Marshal*, vol. 1 (Anglo-Norman Text Society, 2002–2006).
18. Sidney Painter, *William Marshal: Knight-Errant, Baron, and Regent of England* (Johns Hopkins University Press, 1933).
19. Peter Konieczny, 'The Marshal', *Medieval Warfare* 7, no. 2 (2017): 58–58. https://www.jstor.org/stable/48578168.
20. https://www.creativehistorian.co.uk/blog/read_134639/on-this-day-coronation-of-henry-iii.html.
21. T. F. Tout, 'The Fair of Lincoln and the "Histoire de Guillaume Le Maréchal"', *The English Historical Review* 18, no. 70 (1903): 240–65. http://www.jstor.org/stable/549462.
22. Bennett Connolly, *King John's Right-Hand Lady*, chap. 4.
23. https://en.wikipedia.org/wiki/Thomas_Becket.
24. https://parish.rcdow.org.uk/royston/patronsaint1/.
25. https://en.wikipedia.org/wiki/Thomas_Becket.
26. Nicholas Vincent, *A Brief History of England 1066–1485* (Constable and Robinson, 2011), p. 186.

27. Ibid., pp. 186-87.
28. https://constitution.org/1-History/eng/consclar.pdf.
29. M. D. Knowles, Anne J. Duggan, and C. N. L. Brooke. 'Henry II's Supplement to the Constitutions of Clarendon', *The English Historical Review* 87, no. 345 (1972): 757-71. http://www.jstor.org/stable/562200.
30. Warren, *Henry II*, p. 55
31. Ibid., p. 55.
32. Ibid., p. 56
33. Ibid., pp. 328-30.
34. https://en.wikipedia.org/wiki/Robert_de_Beaumont,_2nd_Earl_of_Leicester.
35. https://en.wikipedia.org/wiki/Richard_de_Luci.
36. Nicholas Vincent, 'New Charters of King Stephen with Some Reflections upon the Royal Forests during the Anarchy', *The English Historical Review* 114, no. 458 (Sept., 1999): 899-928.
37. Emilie M. Amt, 'Richard de Lucy, Henry II's Justiciar', *Medieval Prosopography* 9, no. 1 (Spring, 1988): 61-87.
38. https://www.lucey.net/webpage62.htm.
39. Ibid.

Richard I – The Lionheart

1. https://www.englishmonarchs.co.uk/plantagenet_2.htm).
2. Richard R. Heiser, 'Castles, Constables, and Politics in Late Twelfth-Century English Governance', *Albion: A Quarterly Journal Concerned with British Studies* 32, no. 1 (2000): 19-36. https://doi.org/10.2307/4053985.
3. https://en.wikipedia.org/wiki/Richard_I_of_England.
4. https://www.britannica.com/biography/Richard-I-king-of-England.
5. Vincent, *A Brief History of England 1066–1485*, pp. 177-79.
6. https://en.wikipedia.org/wiki/Richard_I_of_England.
7. Vincent, *A Brief History of England 1066–1485*, p. 178.
8. https://en.wikipedia.org/wiki/Richard_I_of_England.
9. Vincent, *A Brief History of England 1066–1485*, p. 221.
10. https://www.english-heritage.org.uk/visit/places/cliffords-tower-york/history-and-stories/massacre-of-the-jews/.
11. Vincent, *A Brief History of England 1066–1485*, p. 222.

12. Peter Raleigh, 'Narrative, History, and Kingship in Angevin England', PhD diss., University of North Carolina, 2019.
13. Ralph V. Turner and Richard Heiser, *The Reign of Richard Lionheart: Ruler of The Angevin Empire, 1189–1199* (Routledge, 2000), chap. 7.
14. https://en.wikipedia.org/wiki/William_de_Longchamp.
15. Heiser and Turner, *The Reign of Richard Lionheart*, chap. 7.
16. Ibid.
17. David Balfour, 'The Origins of the Longchamp Family', *Medieval Prosopography* 18 (1997): 73-92. http://www.jstor.org/stable/44946257.
18. Richard R. Heiser, 'Castles, Constables, and Politics in Late Twelfth-Century English Governance', *Albion: A Quarterly Journal Concerned with British Studies* 32, no. 1 (2000): 19-36. https://doi.org/10.2307/4053985.
19. Bennett Connolly, *King John's Right-Hand Lady*, chap. 6.
20. https://en-academic.com/dic.nsf/enwiki/560659.
21. https://en.wikipedia.org/wiki/Walter_de_Coutances.
22. Richard R. Heiser, 'The Royal "Familiares" of King Richard I', *Medieval Prosopography* 10, no. 2 (1989): 25-50. http://www.jstor.org/stable/44946111.
23. https://en.wikipedia.org/wiki/Walter_de_Coutances.
24. Heiser, 'The Royal "Familiares" of King Richard I'.
25. https://en.wikipedia.org/wiki/Walter_de_Coutances.
26. https://en-academic.com/dic.nsf/enwiki/560659.

King John

1. There is evidence to believe Robin Hood existed. However, the first literary reference to him is in 1377 and there is nothing in the records that makes a connection with King John. https://www.historic-uk.com/HistoryUK/HistoryofEngland/Robin-Hood/.
2. C. Warren Hollister, 'King John and the Historians'. *Journal of British Studies* 1, no. 1 (1961): 1-19. http://www.jstor.org/stable/175095.
3. https://en.wikipedia.org/wiki/John,_King_of_England.
4. https://en.wikipedia.org/wiki/Maud_de_Braose.
5. https://en.wikipedia.org/wiki/Maud_de_Braose.
6. https://www.englishmonarchs.co.uk/plantagenet_3.htm.
7. https://en.wikipedia.org/wiki/John,_King_of_England.
8. https://www.englishmonarchs.co.uk/plantagenet_3.htm.

9. Vincent, *A Brief History of England 1066–1485*, p. 230.
10. https://www.historyhit.com/facts-about-king-john/#:~:text=He%20 was%20also%20known%20as,to%20ever%20inherit%20substantial% 20lands.
11. https://hauntedpalaceblog.wordpress.com/2023/06/18/the-rat-in-the-skull-the-mystery-of-william-longespees-tomb/.
12. https://hauntedpalaceblog.wordpress.com/2023/06/18/the-rat-in-the-skull-the-mystery-of-william-longespees-tomb/.
13. https://en.wikipedia.org/wiki/William_Longespée,_3rd_Earl_of_ Salisbury.
14. Vincent, *A Brief History of England 1066–1485*. https://www.oxforddnb. com/display/10.1093/ref:odnb/9780198614128.001.0001/odnb-9780198614128-e-95591.
15. https://en.wikipedia.org/wiki/William_Longespée,_3rd_Earl_of_ Salisbury.
16. https://hauntedpalaceblog.wordpress.com/2023/06/18/the-rat-in-the-skull-the-mystery-of-william-longespees-tomb/.
17. The scope of this book does not allow a comprehensive study of Nicholaa, but for those wishing to know more, I recommend *King John's Right hand Lady: The Story of Nicholaa de la Haye* by Sharon Bennett-Connolly.
18. Bennett Connolly, *King John's Right-Hand Lady*, chap. 1.
19. https://catherinehanley.co.uk/historical-background/nicola-de-la-haye/.
20. https://historytheinterestingbits.com/2015/06/13/nichola-de-la-haye-englands-forgotten-heroine/.
21. Ibid.
22. Bennett Connolly, *King John's Right-Hand Lady*, chap. 12.
23. https://catherinehanley.co.uk/historical-background/nicola-de-la-haye/
24. https://historytheinterestingbits.com/2015/06/13/nichola-de-la-haye-englands-forgotten-heroine/.
25. Bennett Connolly, *King John's Right-Hand Lady*, chap. 12.

Henry III

1. https://youtu.be/9Q-UU8i23Tg?si=jqA-xXlK__vdLuCc.
2. https://www.historytoday.com/archive/king-henry-iii-born-winchester-castle.

3. https://en.wikipedia.org/wiki/Henry_III_of_England.
4. Vincent, *A Brief History of England 1066–1485*, p. 245.
5. https://britainsbestguides.org/blogs/a-coronation-anomaly-the-crowning-of-king-henry-iii/.
6. Vincent, *A Brief History of England 1066–1485*, p. 145.
7. David Hume, *The History of England, vol. 1, part B* (1688).
8. Vincent, *A Brief History of England 1066–1485*, p. 248.
9. https://en.wikipedia.org/wiki/Henry_III_of_England.
10. Darren Baker, *Henry III: The Great King England Never Knew It Had* (The History Press, 2017), Introduction.
11. https://en.wikipedia.org/wiki/Henry_III_of_England.
12. https://www.encyclopedia.com/women/encyclopedias-almanacs-transcripts-and-maps/eleanor-provence-c-1222-1291.
13. Jones, *The Plantagenets*, p. 263.
14. https://en.wikipedia.org/wiki/Simon_de_Montfort,_6th_Earl_of_Leicester.
15. https://en.wikipedia.org/wiki/Henry_III_of_England.
16. https://www.battleofevesham.co.uk/The_Battle/History.html.
17. Vincent, *A Brief History of England 1066–1485*, p. 262.
18. https://www.lrb.co.uk/the-paper/v45/n18/ferdinand-mount/frisking-the-bishops.
19. John Maddicott, 'Who Was Simon de Montfort, Earl of Leicester?', *Transactions of the Royal Historical Society* 26 (2016): 43-58. http://www.jstor.org/stable/26360512.
20. Vincent, *A Brief History of England 1066–1485*, pp. 262-64.
21. https://en.wikipedia.org/wiki/Second_Barons%27_War.
22. Baker, *Henry III*, chap. 15.
23. Ibid.
24. https://en.wikipedia.org/wiki/Simon_de_Montfort,_6th_Earl_of_Leicester.
25. Jones, *The Plantagenets*, pp. 280-81.
26. https://en.wikisource.org/wiki/Dictionary_of_National_Biography,_1885-1900/Grosseteste,_Robert.
27. https://en.wikipedia.org/wiki/Robert_Grosseteste.
28. https://en.wikisource.org/wiki/Dictionary_of_National_Biography,_1885-1900/Grosseteste,_Robert.
29. https://en.wikipedia.org/wiki/Robert_Grosseteste.
30. https://en.wikisource.org/wiki/Dictionary_of_National_Biography,_1885-1900/Grosseteste,_Robert.

31. John Flood, James R. Ginther, and Joesph G. Goering, eds., *Robert Grosseteste and his Intellectual Milieu: New Editions and Studies* (Pontifical Institute of Mediaeval Studies, 2013).

Edward I

1. Vincent, *A Brief History of England 1066–1485*, p. 270.
2. https://en.wikipedia.org/wiki/Edward_I_of_England.
3. Marc Morris, *A Great and Terrible King: Edward I and the Forging of Britain* (Cornerstone Digital, 2010), Preface.
4. Ibid., chap. 1.
5. Vincent, *A Brief History of England 1066–1485*, p. 277.
6. Morris, *A Great and Terrible King*, chap. 1
7. Vincent, *A Brief History of England 1066–1485*, p. 277.
8. https://www.britannica.com/biography/Edward-I-king-of-England.
9. https://www.historic-uk.com/HistoryUK/HistoryofEngland/Edward-I/.
10. Vincent, *A Brief History of England 1066–1485*, p. 269.
11. Vincent, *A Brief History of England 1066–1485*, p. 277.
12. Vincent, *A Brief History of England 1066–1485*, p. 278.
13. https://www.parliament.uk/about/living-heritage/evolutionof parliament/originsofparliament/birthofparliament/overview/edward/.
14. https://www.heritagedaily.com/2021/04/edward-longshanks-iron-ring-of-castles/138718.
15. https://en.wikipedia.org/wiki/Edward_I_of_England.
16. https:en/wikipedia.org/wiki/Battle_of_Stirling_Bridge.
17. https://www.britannica.com/biography/Edward-I-king-of-England.
18. Vincent, *A Brief History of England 1066–1485*, p. 297.
19. https://scottmanning.com/content/edward-longshanks-sent-his-heart-and-bones-to-war/.
20. Morris, *A Great and Terrible King*, chap. 12.
21. Deborah Seiler, "Medieval Bromance": Royal Friendship and Kingship in the Reigns of Edward I and Edward II', PhD diss., University of Western Australia, 2021.
22. Andrew M. Spencer, 'Royal Patronage and the earls in the Reign of Edward I', *History* 93, no. 1 (January, 2008): 20-46. https://www.jstor.org/stable/24428625.
23. Jones, *The Plantagenets*, p. 295.
24. Seiler, 'Medieval Bromance'.
25. Ibid.
26. https://www.catholic-hierarchy.org/bishop/bburnell.html.

27. Morris, *A Great and Terrible King*, chap. 4.
28. Seiler, 'Medieval Bromance'.
29. https://www.english-heritage.org.uk/visit/places/acton-burnell-castle/history/#:~:text=In%201284%20Robert%20Burnell%20obtained,instead%20perhaps%20designed%20to%20impress.
30. https://en.wikipedia.org/wiki/Robert_Burnell.
31. https://en.wikisource.org/wiki/1911_Encyclopædia_Britannica/Warenne,_Earls.
32. https://en.wikipedia.org/wiki/John_de_Warenne,_6th_Earl_of_Surrey.
33. G. Lapsley, 'John De Warenne and the *Quo Waranto* Proceedings in 1279', *The Cambridge Historical Journal* 2, no. 2 (1927): 110-32. http://www.jstor.org/stable/3020694.
34. https://www.battleofevesham.co.uk/royals/john-de-warenne.
35. https://www.wikiwand.com/en/John_de_Warenne,_6th_Earl_of_Surrey.
36. Morris, *A Great and Terrible King*, chap. 10.
37. https://en.wikipedia.org/wiki/John_de_Warenne,_6th_Earl_of_Surrey.
38. https://en.wikisource.org/wiki/1911_Encyclopædia_Britannica/Warenne,_Earls.
39. https://www.northeastwalestrails.com/ecdcf89c7ec6473185 10cf4240572105.html.
40. https://en.wikisource.org/wiki/Dictionary_of_National_Biography,_1885-1900/Lacy,_Henry_de.
41. https://en.wikipedia.org/wiki/Ralph_de_Hengham.
42. https://en.wikipedia.org/wiki/Henry_de_Lacy,_Earl_of_Lincoln.
43. https://en.wikisource.org/wiki/Dictionary_of_National_Biography,_1885-1900/Lacy,_Henry_de.
44. https://en.wikipedia.org/wiki/Henry_de_Lacy,_Earl_of_Lincoln.

Edward II

1. https://en.wikipedia.org/wiki/Edward_II_of_England.
2. https://www.discovermiddleages.co.uk/kings-and-queens/king-edward-ii-condemned-monarch.
3. https://en.wikipedia.org/wiki/Edward_II_of_England.
4. https://www.historyextra.com/period/medieval/kings-and-queens-in-profile-edward-ii/.

5. Helen Castor, *She Wolves: The Women Who Ruled England Before Elizabeth* (Faber and Faber, 2010), pp. 227-29.
6. Ian Mortimer, *The Perfect King: The Life of Edward III* (Jonathan Cape, 2006), p. 18.
7. Castor, *She Wolves*, p. 228.
8. Ibid.
9. Ibid., p. 230.
10. https://en.wikipedia.org/wiki/Piers_Gaveston,_1st_Earl_of_Cornwall.
11. Mortimer, *The Perfect King*, p. 18.
12. Castor, *She Wolves*, p. 232.
13. Ibid., pp. 235-36.
14. Ibid., pp. 238-40.
15. Kathryn Warner, *Long Live the King: The Mysterious Fate of Edward II* (The History Press, 2017), chap. 2.
16. Castor, *She Wolves*, p. 248.
17. Ibid., p. 250.
18. Mortimer, *The Perfect King*, p. 20.
19. Warner, *Long Live the King*, chap. 1.
20. https://en.wikipedia.org/wiki/Battle_of_Bannockburn.
21. http://edwardthesecond.blogspot.com/2014/09/our-very-sweet-heart-two-letters-of.html.
22. Warner, *Long Live the King*, chap. 2.
23. https://en.wikipedia.org/wiki/Edward_II_of_England.
24. Warner, *Long Live the King*, p. 12, 'Timeline'.
25. https://everything2.com/title/The+death+of+Edward+II.
26. Warner, *Long Live the King*, pp. 1-2.
27. Ibid., p. 13, 'Timeline'.
28. http://edwardthesecond.blogspot.com/2012/04/edward-iis-favourites-comparative-study.html.
29. https://en.wikipedia.org/wiki/Roger_d%27Amory.
30. http://ceirseach.blogspot.com/2011/03/judgement-and-death-of-roger-damory_14.html.
31. https://en.wikipedia.org/wiki/William_Montagu,_2nd_Baron_Montagu.
32. The author first came across them in Paul Doherty's *The Great Revolt*, one of that author's Brother Athelstan mysteries – see bibliography below.
33. Warner, *Long Live the King*, p. 58.

34. Frédéric J. Tanquerey, 'The Conspiracy of Thomas Dunheved, 1327', *The English Historical Review* 31, no. 121 (1916): 119-24. http://www.jstor.org/stable/550704.
35. Ibid.
36. Ibid.
37. Warner, *Long Live the King*, p. 58.
38. Ibid., p. 49.
39. Warner, *Long Live the King*, p. 71.

Edward III

1. Adam Rutherford, *A Brief History of Everyone Who Ever Lived* (W&N, 2017).
2. https://en.wikipedia.org/wiki/Edward_III_of_England.
3. Ian Mortimer, *The Perfect King: The Life of Edward III, Father of the English Nation* (Jonathan Cape, 2006), p. 80.
4. Mortimer, *The Perfect King*, pp. 1-4.
5. Tout, 'The Fair of Lincoln'.
6. Mortimer, *The Perfect King*, pp. 84-85.
7. Ibid.
8. Ibid., p. 85.
9. W. M. Ormrod, 'Edward III and His Family', *Journal of British Studies* 26, no. 4 (1987): 398-422. http://www.jstor.org/stable/175720.
10. https://www.historic-uk.com/HistoryUK/HistoryofEngland/Origins-Hundred-Years-War/.
11. https://www.britannica.com/event/Black-Death/Effects-and-significance.
12. https://en.wikipedia.org/wiki/Edward_III_of_England.
13. May McKisack, 'Edward III and the Historians', *History* 45, no. 153 (1960): 1-15. http://www.jstor.org/stable/24403881.
14. https://www.ianmortimer.com/EdwardII/death.htm.
15. Ibid.
16. https://en.wikipedia.org/wiki/Walter_Manny,_1st_Baron_Manny.
17. https://brill.com/display/book/9789004407671/BP000009.xml?language=en.
18. https://en.wikipedia.org/wiki/Walter_Manny,_1st_Baron_Manny.
19. https://www.luminarium.org/encyclopedia/waltermanny.htm.
20. https://www.bankofengland.co.uk/monetary-policy/inflation/inflation-calculator.

21. J. S. Bothwell, 'Brother of the More Famous Thomas: John Beauchamp of Warwick (d. 1360): A Network of Patronage, and the Pursuit of a Career in the King's Service', *Medieval Prosopography* 24 (2003): 247-66. http://www.jstor.org/stable/44946424.

22. W. M. Ormrod, 'Who Was Alice Perrers?', *The Chaucer Review* 40, no. 3 (2006): 219-29. http://www.jstor.org/stable/25094322.

23. https://en.wikipedia.org/wiki/Alice_Perrers.

24. https://www.creativehistorian.co.uk/blog/read_188156/royal-mistresses-alice-perrers.html.

25. Ibid.

26. Ibid.

27. https://en.wikipedia.org/wiki/Alice_Perrers.

28. https://www.creativehistorian.co.uk/blog/read_188156/royal-mistresses-alice-perrers.html.

Richard II

1. https://en.wikipedia.org/wiki/Richard_II_of_England.

2. https://www.bmj.com/company/newsroom/chronic-dysentery-unlikely-killer-of-edward-the-black-prince-as-is-commonly-believed/#:~:text=And%20most%20later%20accounts%20of,was%20common%20in%20medieval%20Europe.

3. Ian Mortimer, 'Richard II and the Succession to the Crown', *History* 91, no. 3 (2006): 320-36. http://www.jstor.org/stable/24427962.

4. https://en.wikipedia.org/wiki/Richard_II_of_England.

5. https://www.britannica.com/biography/Richard-II-king-of-England.

6. https://historicalbritainblog.com/category/richard-ii/.

7. James Tait, 'Knight-Service in Cheshire', *The English Historical Review* 57, no. 227 (July, 1942), pp. 379-83.

8. https://en.wikipedia.org/wiki/Richard_II_of_England.

9. https://en.wikipedia.org/wiki/Geoffrey_Chaucer.

10. https://www.angelroofs.co.uk/258855-why-angels-at-westminster.

11. https://en.wikipedia.org/wiki/Robert_de_Vere,_Duke_of_Ireland .

12. https://thehistoryjar.com/2021/06/29/robert-de-vere-his-ugly-mistress-and-the-kings-grand-daughter/.

13. https://meanderingthroughtime.weebly.com/history-blog/category/robert-de-vere.

14. https://en.wikipedia.org/wiki/Robert_de_Vere,_Duke_of_Ireland.

15. https://thehistoryjar.com/2021/06/29/robert-de-vere-his-ugly-mistress-and-the-kings-grand-daughter/.
16. https://en.wikisource.org/wiki/Dictionary_of_National_Biography,_1885-1900/Burley,_Simon.
17. https://historicalbritainblog.com/sir-simon-burley-richards-unfortunate-chamberlain/.
18. https://en.wikisource.org/wiki/Dictionary_of_National_Biography,_1885-1900/Burley,_Simon.
19. https://historicalbritainblog.com/sir-simon-burley-richards-unfortunate-chamberlain/.
20. Ibid.
21. https://thehistoryjar.com/2017/07/18/michael-de-la-pole-earl-of-suffolk-chancellor-traitor-and-retainer/.
22. http://hullhistorycentre.blogspot.com/2020/09/michael-de-la-pole-1st-earl-of-suffolk.html.
23. https://en.wikipedia.org/wiki/Michael_de_la_Pole,_1st_Earl_of_Suffolk.
24. http://hullhistorycentre.blogspot.com/2020/09/michael-de-la-pole-1st-earl-of-suffolk.html.

Henry IV

1. Chris Given-Wilson, 'Henry IV: The Usurper', *BBC History Magazine* (Feb., 2016): 22-27.
2. https://en.wikipedia.org/wiki/Henry_IV_of_England.
3. Ibid.
4. https://en.wikipedia.org/wiki/Glyndŵr_rebellion.
5. Given-Wilson, 'Henry IV'.
6. J. M. W. Bean, 'Henry IV and the Percies', *History* 44, no. 152 (1959): 212-27. http://www.jstor.org/stable/24403655.
7. https://en.wikipedia.org/wiki/Henry_IV_of_England.
8. Given-Wilson, 'Henry IV'.
9. Peter McNiven, 'The Problem of Henry IV's Health, 1405–1413', *The English Historical Review* 100, no. 397 (1985): 747-72. http://www.jstor.org/stable/572564.
10. Ibid.
11. https://fmg.ac/phocadownload/userupload/foundations1/issue3/164Swynfd2.pdf

12. Alision Weir, *Katherine Swynford: The Story of John of Gaunt and his Scandalous Duchess* (Jonathan Cape, 2007), pp. 80-81.
13. https://en.wikisource.org/wiki/Dictionary_of_National_Biography,_1885-1900/Swynford,_Catherine.
14. https://fmg.ac/phocadownload/userupload/foundations1/issue3/164Swynfd2.pdf.
15. https://en.wikipedia.org/wiki/John_Beaufort,_1st_Earl_of_Somerset.
16. https://www.unofficialroyalty.com/john-beaufort-1st-earl-of-somerset/.
17. https://en.wikipedia.org/wiki/John_Beaufort,_1st_Earl_of_Somerset.
18. https://www.englishmonarchs.co.uk/plantagenet_47.html.
19. https://en.wikipedia.org/wiki/John_Beaufort,_1st_Earl_of_Somerset.
20. Michael Hicks, 'Cement or Solvent? Kinship and Politics in Late Medieval England: The Case of the Nevilles', *History* 83, no. 269 (1998): 31-46. http://www.jstor.org/stable/24423694.
21. https://en.wikisource.org/wiki/Dictionary_of_National_Biography,_1885-1900/Neville,_Ralph_(1364-1425).
22. https://en.wikipedia.org/wiki/Ralph_Neville,_1st_Earl_of_Westmorland.
23. https://www.wikitree.com/wiki/Neville-53.
24. https://en.wikipedia.org/wiki/Ralph_Neville,_1st_Earl_of_Westmorland.
25. https://www.wikitree.com/wiki/Neville-53.
26. https://en.wikipedia.org/wiki/Ralph_Neville,_1st_Earl_of_Westmorland.

Henry V

1. https://en.wikipedia.org/wiki/Henry_V_of_England.
2. https://youtu.be/s982-bufjh8?si=_W85pn4V1JWUW15E.
3. https://www.rct.uk/collection/403443/henry-v-1387-1422.
4. Vincent, *A Brief History of England 1066–1485*, pp. 436-39.
5. Peter Mcniven, 'Prince Henry and the English Political Crisis Of 1412', *History* 65, no. 213 (1980): 1-16. http://www.jstor.org/stable/24419123.
6. Vincent, *A Brief History of England 1066–1485*, p. 238.
7. https://www.britainexpress.com/History/medieval/oldcastle-revolt.htm.
8. Vincent, *A Brief History of England 1066–1485*, pp. 440-47.
9. Anne Curry, 'Henry VI's Greatest Victory', *BBC History Magazine* (March 2020): 22-27.
10. Vincent, *A Brief History of England 1066–1485*, pp. 447-48.

11. https://en.wikipedia.org/wiki/Thomas_Beaufort,_Duke_of_Exeter.
12. https://www.shakespeareandhistory.com/thomas-beaufort-duke-of-exeter.php.
13. https://en.wikipedia.org/wiki/Thomas_Beaufort,_Duke_of_Exeter.
14. https://www.shakespeareandhistory.com/thomas-beaufort-duke-of-exeter.php.
15. https://tudorsdynasty.com/catherine-valois-family-history-with-mental-illness/.
16. https://en.wikipedia.org/wiki/Thomas_Beaufort,_Duke_of_Exeter.
17. https://www.shakespeareandhistory.com/thomas-beaufort-duke-of-exeter.php.
18. https://en.wikipedia.org/wiki/Thomas_Beaufort,_Duke_of_Exeter.
19. https://www.shakespeareandhistory.com/thomas-beaufort-duke-of-exeter.php.
20. Charles Collignon, 'Some Account of a Body Lately Found in Uncommon Preservation, under the Ruins of the Abbey, at St. Edmund's-Bury, Suffolk: With Some Reflections upon the Subject', *Philosophical Transactions (1683–1775)* 62 (1772): 465-68. http://www.jstor.org/stable/106064.
21. https://en.wikipedia.org/wiki/Henry_Beaufort.
22. https://www.unofficialroyalty.com/cardinal-henry-beaufort-bishop-of-winchester/.
23. https://en.wikipedia.org/wiki/Henry_Beaufort.
24. Ibid.
25. https://www.britannica.com/biography/Henry-Beaufort.
26. https://en.wikipedia.org/wiki/Henry_Beaufort.
27. https://www.unofficialroyalty.com/cardinal-henry-beaufort-bishop-of-winchester/.
28. https://herefordshirepast.co.uk/people/sir-john-oldcastle/.
29. https://en.wikipedia.org/wiki/John_Oldcastle.
30. https://herefordshirepast.co.uk/people/sir-john-oldcastle/.
31. https://en.wikipedia.org/wiki/John_Oldcastle.
32. https://herefordshirepast.co.uk/people/sir-john-oldcastle/.
33. https://en.wikipedia.org/wiki/John_Oldcastle.
34. https://herefordshirepast.co.uk/people/sir-john-oldcastle/.
35. https://en.wikipedia.org/wiki/John_Oldcastle.

Henry VI

1. David Grummitt, *Henry VI* (Routledge, 2015), Introduction.
2. Mabel Christie, *Henry VI: Constable* (1922), pp. 1-2.
3. Vincent, *A Brief History of England 1066–1485*, pp. 454-55.
4. https://en.wikipedia.org/wiki/Henry_VI_of_England.
5. Anne Crawford, *Letters of the Queens of England 1100–1547* (Sutton, 1997), p. 119.
6. Vincent, *A Brief History of England 1066–1485*, p. 449.
7. Ibid., p. 455.
8. Ibid., pp. 460-61.
9. https://www.historic-uk.com/HistoryUK/HistoryofEngland/King-Henry-VI/ -
10. Vincent, *A Brief History of England 1066–1485*, p. 464.
11. https://www.historic-uk.com/HistoryUK/HistoryofEngland/King-Henry-VI/.
12. https://www.timeref.com/people/edward_iv_earl_of_march_and_king_of_england_1461_1470_1471_1483.htm.
13. Vincent, *A Brief History of England 1066–1485*, pp. 469-73.
14. https://en.wikipedia.org/wiki/Henry_VI_of_England.
15. https://en.wikipedia.org/wiki/John_Somerset.
16. A. L. Brown, 'The King's Councillors in Fifteenth-Century England', *Transactions of the Royal Historical Society* 19 (1969): 95-118. https://doi.org/10.2307/3678741.
17. Compton Reeves, 'The 1450 Purge of the English Royal Circle', *Medieval Prosopography* 33 (2018): 103-22. https://www.jstor.org/stable/26630018.
18. https://en.wikipedia.org/wiki/William_de_la_Pole,_1st_Duke_of_Suffolk.
19. Roger Virgoe and Ronald Hall, eds., 'The Death of William de La Pole, Duke of Suffolk', *Bulletin of the John Rylands Library, Manchester* 47, no.2 (1965): 489-502. https://jstor.org/stable/community.28211836.

Edward IV

1. You can read more about the legend here: https://en.wikipedia.org/wiki/Mouldwarp.

2. John Ashdown-Hill, *The Private Life of Edward IV* (Amberley, 2016), pp.18-21.
3. https://en.wikipedia.org/wiki/Edward_IV_of_England.
4. Charles Ross, *Edward IV* (Yale University Press, 1973), p. 30.
5. Ibid., p. 38.
6. Ibid., p. 30.
7. Ashdown-Hill, *The Private Life of Edward IV*, pp. 50-51.
8. Ross, *Edward IV*, pp. 241-42.
9. https://www.britannica.com/biography/John-Neville-earl-of-Northumberland-Lord-Montagu.
10. https://www.luminarium.org/encyclopedia/montagu.htm.
11. https://en.wikipedia.org/wiki/John_Tiptoft,_1st_Earl_of_Worcester.
12. Henry S. Pancoast, 'Notes on John Tiptoft, Earl of Worcester,' *PMLA* 10 (1895): vii–xi. https://doi.org/10.2307/456102.
13. https://www.worcesterhousehold.co.uk/history.htm.
14. Pancoast, 'Notes on John Tiptoft'.
15. https://historycollection.com/here-is-how-the-most-infamous-man-during-the-war-of-roses-got-his-nickname-the-butcher-of-england/.
16. https://www.worcesterhousehold.co.uk/history.htm.
17. Pancoast, 'Notes on John Tiptoft'.
18. https://www.worcesterhousehold.co.uk/history.htm.
19. Pancoast, 'Notes on John Tiptoft'.

Richard III

1. https://en.wikipedia.org/wiki/Richard_III_of_England.
2. https://www.shropshirestar.com/news/2015/03/21/ludlows-part-in-the-life-of-a-rediscovered-king/.
3. https://en.wikipedia.org/wiki/Richard_III_of_England.
4. https://en.wikipedia.org/wiki/Battle_of_Tewkesbury.
5. https://en.wikipedia.org/wiki/Richard_III_of_England.
6. https://englishhistory.net/middle-ages/richard-iii/.
7. https://en.wikipedia.org/wiki/Richard_III_of_England.
8. Mortimer Levine, 'Richard III: Usurper or Lawful King?', *Speculum* 34, no. 3 (1959): 391-401. https://doi.org/10.2307/2850815.
9. Alison Hanham, 'Richard III, Lord Hastings and the Historians', *The English Historical Review* 87, no. 343 (1972): 233-48. http://www.jstor.org/stable/563284.
10. https://www.britannica.com/biography/Richard-III-king-of-England.

11. https://englishhistory.net/middle-ages/richard-iii/.
12. https://www.britannica.com/biography/Richard-III-king-of-England.
13. https://en.wikipedia.org/wiki/Edward_of_Middleham,_Prince_of_ Wales.
14. https://en.wikipedia.org/wiki/Anne_Neville.
15. You can see part of the documentary here: https://youtu. be/9BUn6iI1NhA?si=cblkEtXw5GU4MMl3.
16. https://www.historytoday.com/archive/feature/cat-rat-and-dog.
17. https://thehistoryofparliament.wordpress.com/2021/08/25/it-was-the-dissimulation-of-this-one-man-that-stirred-up-that-whole-plague-of-evils-which-followed-william-catesby-speaker-in-the-parliament-of-1-484-and-the-accession-of-richard-iii/.
18. https://www.warsoftheroses.com/people/sir-william-catesby/.
19. Tracy Borman, *The Private Lives of the Tudors* (Hodder & Stoughton, 2016).
20. https://www.warsoftheroses.com/people/sir-william-catesby/.
21. https://www.susanhigginbotham.com/posts/a-tragic-day-at-pontefract/.
22. http://www.thericardian.online/downloads/Ricardian/24/08.pdf.
23. https://war_of_roses.en-academic.com/297/Richard_III%2C_ Northern_Affinity_of.
24. http://www.thericardian.online/downloads/Ricardian/24/08.pdf.
25. https://www.britannica.com/biography/Francis-Lovell-Viscount-Lovell.
26. https://historytheinterestingbits.com/2019/11/16/guest-post-anne-fitzhugh-lovell-by-michele-schindler/.
27. https://aspectsofhistory.com/the-final-resting-place-of-francis-viscount-lovell/.
28. https://brumafriend.medium.com/francis-lovell-the-ricardian-rebel-who-disappeared-a8e4bf20b61a.

Select Bibliography

Ashdown-Hill, John. *The Private Life of Edward IV* (Amberley, 2016).

Baker, Darren. *Henry III: The Great King England Never Knew It Had* (The History Press, 2017).

Bennett Connolly, Sharon. *King John's Right-Hand Lady: The Story of Nicholaa de la Haye* (Pen & Sword History, 2023).

Borman, Tracy. *The Private Lives of the Tudors* (Hodder & Stoughton, 2016).

Cantor, Norman F. *The Civilization of the Middle Ages* (HarperCollins, 1993).

Castor, Helen. *She Wolves: The Women Who Ruled England Before Elizabeth* (Faber and Faber, 2010).

Chadwick, Elizabeth. *The Greatest Knight: The Story of William Marshal* (Sphere, 2009).

Christie, Mabel. *Henry VI.* (Constable, 1922).

Crawford, Anne. *Letters of the Queens of England 1100–1547* (Sutton, 1997).

Crouch, David: *The Normans: The History of a Dynasty* (Hambledon and London, 2003).

Dingle, Brian. *In the Footsteps of Longshanks: The Places and People of Edward I*: Vanguard Press; 2022

Doherty, Paul. *The Great Revolt: Book 16 in the Brother Athelstan Mysteries* (Canelo Severn House, 2022). Kindle edition.

Grummitt, David. *Henry VI* (Routledge, 2015).

Hume, David: *The History of England: Vol. 1* (1762).

Jones, Dan. *The Plantagenets: The Kings Who Made England* (Harper Collins, 2013).

Morris, Marc. *A Great and Terrible King: Edward I and the Forging of Britain* (Cornerstone Digital, 2010). Kindle edition.

Mortimer, Ian. *The Perfect King: The Life of Edward III, Father of the English Nation* (Jonathan Cape, 2006).

Niven, David. *The Moon's a Balloon* (1994).

Penman, Sharon. *The Sunne in Splendour* (Macmillan, 2012). Kindle edition.

Ross, Charles. Edward IV (Yale University Press, 1974).

Seward, Desmond. *The Demon's Brood: The Plantagenet Dynasty that Forged the English Nation* (Constable, 2024).

Spencer, Charles: *The White Ship* (William Collins, 2020).

Starkey, David. *The Monarchy of England, Vol 1* (Chatto & Windus, 2004).

Starkey, David. *Crown and Country: A History of England through the Monarchy* (Harper, 2010).

Tout, T. F. *The History of England From the Accession of Henry III to the Death of Edward III (1216–1377)*. Project Gutenberg.

Vincent, Nicholas. *A Brief History of Britain 1066–1485* (Robinson, 2011).

Warner, Kathryn. *Long Live The King: The Mysterious Fate of Edward II* (The History Press, 2017).

Warren, W. L. *Henry II* (Methuen, 1991).

Weir, Alison. *Katherine Swynford: The Story of John of Gaunt and his Scandalous Duchess* (Jonathan Cape, 2007).

Dear Reader,

We hope you have enjoyed this book, but why not share your views on social media? You can also follow our pages to see more about our other products: facebook.com/penandswordbooks or follow us on X @penswordbooks

You can also view our products at www.pen-and-sword.co.uk (UK and ROW) or www.penandswordbooks.com (North America).

To keep up to date with our latest releases and online catalogues, please sign up to our newsletter at: www.pen-and-sword.co.uk/newsletter

If you would like a printed catalogue with our latest books, then please email: enquiries@pen-and-sword.co.uk or telephone: 01226 734555 (UK and ROW) or email: uspen-and-sword@casematepublishers.com or telephone: (610) 853-9131 (North America).

We respect your privacy and we will only use personal information to send you information about our products.

Thank you!